GEDDES & GROSSET

CHRONOLOGY OF
WORLD HISTORY

Published by Geddes & Grosset, an imprint of
Children's Leisure Products Limited

© 1995 Children's Leisure Products Limited, David Dale House,
New Lanark, ML11 9DJ, Scotland

First published 1995
Second edition 1999, reprinted 1999

Cover image of Double Hemisphere Map by Petrus Plautinus,
*c.*1599, courtesy of DigitalVision

ISBN 1 85534 684 2

Printed and bound in the UK

CHRONOLOGY OF WORLD HISTORY

EARLY MIDDLE EASTERN CIVILIZATIONS

4000
- Meslim, King of Kish, becomes overlord of Sumeria (Southern Babylonia).

3000
- Ur-Nina founds a dynasty at Lagash in Sumeria; builds temples and canals.
- Fourth Egyptian Dynasty founded by Snefru; later kings of the dynasty, Cheops, Chephren and Mycerinus, build the Great Pyramids at Gizeh.

2900
- Eannatum, King of Lagash: conquers Umma, Kish Opis, Erech, Ur; repels the Elamites.

2850
- Fu-hi, first Emperor of China.

2800
- Urukagina, King of Lagash: a great reformer; Lagash defeated and destroyed by Lugai-Zaggisi, ruler of Umma and King of Erech, who becomes overlord of all Sumeria.

2650
- Sargon founds Akkadian Empire in Mesopotamia.

2600
- Naram-Sin, son of Sargon.
- Sixth Dynasty in Egypt ends the ancient Empire: Pepy I conquers Palestine; Pepy II reigns 94 years, longest reign in the world's history.

2500-2000
- Legendary period of the second city on the site of Troy; destroyed by fire.

2500
- Early Minoan Age of Cretan civilisation begins.

2450
- Gudea, ruler of Lagash.

2400
- Dynasty of Ur in Sumeria established by Ur-Engur; he reigns for 18 years; Dungi; his son, reigns for 58 years, extends Empire over all Babylonia and also conquers Elam.

2300
- Asshur, the oldest Assyrian city, founded not later than this date.
- Dynasty of Isin in Sumeria, established by Ishbi-Ura; overthrow of Ur because of Elamite invasion.

2100
- First Dynasty of Babylon established by Sumu-Abu after fall of Isin;

the Sumerians finally give way to the Semites.

2000
- Twelfth Egyptian Dynasty begins, with Thebes as capital.

2000-1850
- Middle Minoan Age in Crete.

2000-1800
- Twelfth Egyptian Dynasty: Amenemhet I, Usertesen I, Amenemhet II, Usertesen II, Usertesen III (conquered Nubia), Amenemhet III, Amenemhet IV and Queen Sebknofru; all great builders.

2000-1700
- Proto-Mycenean civilisation of the island of Thera (now Santorini) destroyed by volcanic upheaval.

2000
- Hammurabi, the greatest king of the first Babylon dynasty: noted for agricultural improvements and law reform.

1860
- Construction of Stonehenge begins in Britain.

1840
- Ismi-Dagan, oldest known ruler of Assyria.

1800-1600
- Late Minoan Age in Crete.

1800-1200
- Babylon ruled by Kassite invaders.

1800
- Hyksos rule in Egypt begins.

1700-1000
- Mycenaen Civilisation in Greece.

1700
- Assyria becomes independent of Babylonia around this time.

1600
- Amasis I finally drives the Hyksos from Egypt and founds the New Empire; conquers Palestine and Phoenicia.

1600-1100
- The Sixth City on the site of Troy (Homeric Troy).

1560
- Thutmosis I of Egypt completes conquest of Nubia.

1515
- Thutmosis III of Egypt: conquers Syria and penetrates to Assyria.

1450
- Amenophis III of Egypt: noted temple-builder.

1415
- Amenophis IV of Egypt: replaces the old religion by sun worship.

1410
- Conflict between Assyria and Babylonia begins.

1355
- Rameses I begins Nineteenth Dynasty in Egypt.

1350
- Sethos I of Egypt: wars against Libyans, Syrians and Hittites.

1340
- Rameses II, the most celebrated king of Egypt; wages long war with the Hittites, retains Palestine; greatest builder among the Egyptian kings.

1330
- Shalmaneser I, King of Assyria.

1300-1000
- Hellenic conquests in Greece.

1290
- Tukulti-ninib, King of Assyria: conquers Babylonia.

1273
- Meneptah, King of Egypt: wars against Libyans and Asiatic pirates.

1200
- Rameses III of Twentieth Egyptian Dynasty.

1120
- Tiglath-pileser I, King of Assyria.

1100
- Herihor, high priest of Ammon: seizes the throne of Egypt; deposed by a Tanite Dynasty.

1000
- David, King of Israel.
- Iron Age begins.
- *Rigveda* (India).

970
- Solomon, King of Israel.

950
- Sheshonk, Libyan King of Egypt: conquers Palestine.

930
- Hebrew kingdom is divided on death of Solomon: Jeroboam I becomes King of Israel in the north; Rehoboam King of Judah in the south.

900
- Homer's *Iliad* and *Odyssey* date from about this time.

884
- Asur-nasir-pal III, King of Assyria.

875
- Ahad, King of Israel.

860
- Shalmaneser II, King of Assyria: subdues Babylon and Syria.

854
- Battle of Karkar: Benhadad of Da-

mascus and Ahab of Israel defeated by Shalmaneser II.

850
- Carthage founded as a Phoenician colony (traditional).

842
- Jehu, King of Israel.

797
- Jehoash, King of Israel, successfully repels Syrian attacks.

782
- Jeroboam II, King of Israel: defeats Syria and increases prestige of Israel.

776
- The first Olympiad in Greece.

753
- Legendary date of the Foundation of Rome by Romulus.

745
- Tiglath-Pileser III raises Assyria to greatest power.

740
- Conquest of Messenia by Sparta (first Messenian War).

738
- Menahem, King of Israel.

734
- Ahaz, King of Judah.

729
- Tiglath-Pileser III subdues Babylon.

721
- Sargon, King of Assyria, takes Samaria and transports a large number of the Israelites to Mesopotamia and Media; the northern kingdom of Israel never revives.
- Merodach-baladan ends Assyrian power in Babylon and reigns as king for twelve years.

720
- Hezekiah becomes king of Judah: noted religious reformer and skilful leader.

705
- Sennacherib, King of Assyria.

701
- Sennacherib fails in his attack on Jerusalem.

700
- Deioces founds the Medean monarchy; Midas, King of Phrygia; Gyges, King of Lydia.

685
- Second Messenian War; Messenians again defeated by Sparta.

683
- End of monarchy in Athens.

680
- Esarhaddon, King of Assyria.

670
- Esarhaddon defeats Taharka, Ethiopian King of Egypt and captures Memphis.

668
- Asur-bani-pal, King of Assyria: Babylon again subdued; Elam overthrown.

660
- Psammetichus I, aided by Gyges of Lydia, makes Egypt independent again.

647
- Phraortes, King of Media.

637
- Josiah, King of Judah: noted religious and political reformer.

628
- Birth of Zoroaster around this time.

625
- Nabopolassar, King of Babylon.

624
- Cyaxares, King of Media.

621
- Legislation of Draco at Athens.

609
- Necho, King of Egypt.

608
- Battle of Megiddo; Josiah of Judah

defeated and killed by Necho of Egypt.

606
- Nineveh captured and destroyed by Nabopolassar of Babylon and Cyaxares of Media; end of the Assyrian Empire.

605
- Battle of Carchemish; Egyptian power in Syria overthrown by Babylon.

604
- Nebuchadnezzar, King of Babylon.

598
- Jerusalem taken by Nebuchadnezzar; Jehoiachin, the king, Esekiel, the prophet and others taken to Babylon; Sedekiah made King of Judah.

594
- Psammetichus II, King of Egypt.

594
- Legislation of Solon at Athens.

588
- Apries (Hophra), King of Egypt.

586
- Zedekiah's revolt against Babylonian rule; Jerusalem taken and destroyed by Nebuchadnezzar.

585
- Battle between Cyaxares of Media

and Alyattes of Lydia stopped by eclipse of sun.
• Tyre taken by Nebuchadnezzar.

584
• Astyages, King of Media.

570
• Athens conquers island of Salamis.

569
• Amasis, King of Egypt.

568
• Buddha born in India.

561
• Evil-Merodach, King of Babylon.

560
• Croesus, King of Lydia: subdues Greek cities in Asia Minor.
• Pisistratus becomes Tyrant of Athens (expelled 555 BC).

555
• Nabonidus, King of Babylon.

55 1
• Confucius born in China.

550
• Sparta becomes supreme in the Peloponnesus.
• Cyrus conquers Media and founds the Persian Empire.
• Second Tyranny of Pisistratus at Athens (expelled 549 BC).

546
• Cyrus conquers Lydia.
• Asiatic Greek cities conquered by Persia.

540
• Pisistratus again Tyrant of Athens until his death (528 BC).

538
• Cyrus conquers Babylon.

CLASSICAL GREECE AND PERSIA

529
• Cambyses, King of Persia.

528
• Hippias and Hipparchus in power at Athens.

525
• Persian conquest of Egypt.

521
• Darius I, King of Persia.

520
• Persian conquest of Babylon.

515
• Dedication of the New Temple at Jerusalem after the return from the Babylonian Captivity.

512
• Persian conquest of Thrace.

510

- Pisistratid Tyranny at Athens ends; Hippias expelled; Athens joins Peloponnesian League.

508

- Treaty between Rome and Carthage.

507

- Reforms of Cleisthenes at Athens.

500

- End of monarchy at Rome: Republic founded.

499

- Asiatic Greeks revolt from Persia.

497

- Athenians assist in the burning of Sardis.

493

- First Secession of Plebeians at Rome; Tribunes of the Plebs first appointed.

492

- Persians conquer Thrace and Macedonia.

490

- Battle of Marathon: Persians defeated by Greeks under Miltiades; Aeschylus flourishes at this time.

486

- First Agrarian Law (Land Reform) at Rome passed by Spurius Cassius.

485

- Xerxes, King of Persia.

480

- Battle of Thermopylae: Persians defeat Greeks (Leonidas).
- Battle of Salamis: Athenians under Themistocles defeat Persians in naval battle.
- Battle of Himera: Carthaginian attack on Sicily repelled by Sicilian Greeks.

DEATHS

Buddha

479

- Battle of Plataea: Persians defeated by Greeks under Pausanias.
- Battle of Mycale: Greek naval victory over the Persians.

477

- Confederacy of Delos founded by Athens for defence against Persia.

471

- Lex Publilia passed at Rome; Tribunes to be chosen by the Comitia Tributa (popular assembly).

465

- Battle of the Eurymedon: Persians defeated by Greeks under Cimon.

464

- Artaxerxes I, King of Persia.

463

- Democratic reform at Athens; powers

of the Areopagus limited by Ephial-
tes.

462
- Influence of Pericles begins at Athens; Sophocles and Euripides flourish around this time.

458
- Long Walls to Piraeus built by Athens.
- Ezra returns with many Jews from
  Babylon to Jerusalem.

456
- Athens conquers Aegina.
  DEATHS
  Aeschylus, Greek dramatist.

454
- Athenian expedition to Egypt fails
  after initial successes.

453
- Treasury of Confederacy of Delos
  removed to Athens; Athenian Empire at its height.

452
- Decemvirs drew up laws of the
  Twelve Tables at Rome.

448
- Second Secession of the Plebeians
  at Rome; great increase in powers
  of Comitia Tributa.

447
- Battle of Coronea, Athens loses Boeotia.

- Building of Parthenon begins.
  DEATHS
  Pindar, Greek musician and poet.

445
- Lex Canuleia at Rome legalised marriage between Patricians and Plebeians.
- Nehemiah begins rebuilding walls
  of Jerusalem.

431
- Peloponnesian War begin: Athens
  and allies against Sparta and allies;
  Thucydides its historian.
  DEATHS
  Herodotus, Greek historian.

424
- Darius II, King of Persia.

422
- Battle of Amphipolis: Athenian defeat.

421
- Peace of Nicias between Athens and
  Sparta.

418
- Battle of Mantinea: Athenians defeated by Spartans.

413
- Athenian defeat at Syracuse.

405
- Battle of Aegospotami: naval victory
  of Sparta under Lysander over Athens.

406
• Death of Euripides and Sophocles.

404
• Peloponnesian War ends; Spartans enter Athens and set up the Thirty Tyrants.
• Artaxerxes II, King of Persia.

403
• Thirty Tyrants overthrown at Athens.

401
• Battle of Cunaxa: a force of Greeks help Cyrus in his rebellion against Artaxerxes II, among them Xenophon.

400
• Etruscan city of Veii captured by Romans.

399
• Socrates executed.

398
• First Punic War of Dionysius of Syracuse.

394
• Battle of Coronea: Spartans under Agesilaus defeat confederacy against them.
• Battle of Cnidus: Spartan fleet destroyed by a combined Persian and Athenian fleet.

390
• Rome burned down by Gauls under Brennus.

387
• Peace of Antalcidas between Sparta and Persia.
DEATHS
Aristophanes, Greek dramatist.

371
• Battle of Leactra: Sparta defeated by Thebes under Epaminondas.

366
• Licinian Laws passed at Rome; first Plebeian consul.

362
• Battle of Mantinea: Sparta defeated by Thebes (Epaminondas killed).

359
• Artaxerxes III, King of Persia.
• Philip II becomes King of Macedonia.

347
• Death of Plato.

343-340
• First Saminite War waged by Rome.

340-338
• Rome conquers Latium.

339
• Publilian Laws at Rome; decrees of Comitia Tributa to bind whole people; one Censor to be a Plebeian.

338
• Battle of Chaeronea: Athens and

Thebes defeated by Philip of Macedon, who becomes supreme in Greece.
• Arses, King of Persia.

336

• Philip II assassinated and succeeded by his son Alexander the Great.

ALEXANDER THE GREAT

336

• Alexander the Great becomes King of Macedon.
• Praetorship at Rome thrown open to Plebeians.
• Alexander elected supreme general of the Greeks.

335

• Alexander's campaign in Thrace and Illyria.
• Alexander captures Thebes (in Boeotia) and destroys it except the house of Pindar.
• Darius III, King of Persia.
• Aristotle begins teaching at Athens.
• Memnon of Rhodes opposes Alexander's lieutenant Parmenio in Asia Minor.

334

• Alexander crosses the Hellespont into Asia.
• Battle of the Granicus: Alexander defeats the Persians.
• Alexander captures Sardis and conquers Lydia.
• Capture of Ephesus.
• Siege and capture of Miletus.
• Siege and capture of Halicarnassus.

333

• Alexander at Gordion; cuts the Gordian knot.
• Battle of Issus: Alexander defeats Darius.

332

• Siege and capture of Tyre.
• Capture of Gaza.
• Alexander enters Egypt.

331

• Alexander founds Alexandria.
• Alexander visits the temple of Zeus Ammon.
• Battle of Arbela (Gaugamela): Darius again defeated.
• Babylon submits to Alexander.
• Alexander at Susa.
• Battle of Megalopolis: Spartans under Agis defeated by Macedonian regent Antipater.

330

• Alexander at Persepolis.
• Alexander at Ecbatana.
• Death of Darius III: end of the Persian Empire.

330-327

• Alexander conquers Hyrcania, Gedrosia, Bactria, Sogdiana.

327

• Alexander enters India.
• Second Samnite War between Rome and the Samnites begins.

326

- Alexander crosses the Indus near Attock.
- Battle of the Hydaspes: the Punjab conquered.

323

- Alexander dies at Babylon.

RISE OF ROME

323

- Ptolemy I founds the dynasty of the Ptolemies in Egypt; makes Alexandria the intellectual centre of the Hellenic world; Euclid flourishes in his reign.

322

- Lamian War; Antipater of Macedonia defeats insurgent Greeks at Battle of Crannon.

DEATHS

Aristotle, Greek philosopher.

321

- The Samnites capture a Roman army at the Caudine Forks.

312

- The Seleucid Dynasty in Asia founded by Seleucus I (Nicator); capital at first Babylon.

304

- Second Samnite War ends.

301

- Battle of Ipsus determines distribu-

tion of Alexander's Empire among his generals.

300

- Antioch founded by Seleucus Nicator as capital of his Syrian kingdom.

300

- Lex Ogulnia at Rome provides for Plebeian Pontiffs and Augurs.

300

- Zeno, founder of Stoicism and Epicurus, founder of Epicureanism, flourish at this time.

298

- Third Samnite War begins.

295

- Battle of Sentinum: Romans defeat Samnites and allies.

295

- Pyrrhus becomes King of Epirus.

294

- Demetrius I becomes King of Macedonia.

290

- Third and Last Samnite War ends: Rome ruler of central Italy.

287

- Third Secession of the Plebs at Rome.

286

- Lex Hortensia at Rome makes the

popular assembly (Comitia Tributa) the supreme legislative power.

285
- Ptolemy II King of Egypt.

283
- Battle of the Vadimonian Lake: Romans defeat Gauls and Etruscans; Rome ruler of northern Italy.

280
- Pyrrhus invades Italy; Romans defeated in Battle of Heraclea.
- Achaen League revived in Greece.
- Gauls invade Greece.

279
- Battle of Asculum: Pyrrhus again defeats Romans.

275
- Battle of Beneventum: Romans defeat Pyrrhus and drive him from Italy.

266
- Rome ruler of all Italy.

264
- First Punic War (Rome v. Carthage) begins.

262
- Battle of Agrigentum: Roman victory.

260
- Battle of Myloe: Roman naval victory.

256
- Romans invade Africa.

255
- Romans under Regulus heavily defeated by Carthaginians in Africa.

251
- Battle of Panormus: Romans defeat Carthaginians.

247
- Ptolemy III King of Egypt.
- Hamiclar Barca assumes Carthaginian command in Sicily.

245
- Aratus becomes leader of the Achaean League.
- Agis IV attempts to reform Sparta.

241
- Battle of Aegates Islands: Roman naval victory over Carthage; First
- Punic War ends with cession of Sicily to Rome.
- Sicily becomes the first Roman province.

240
- Livius Andronicus, the first Roman poet.

239
- Rome seizes Sardinia and makes it a province.

237
- Carthage begins conquest of Spain.

236
- Cleomenes III, the last King of Sparta.

222
- Conquest of Cisalpine Gaul by Rome completed.
- Ptolemy IV, King of Egypt; beginning of Egypt's decline.
- Cleomenes III defeated by Achean League at Battle of Sellasia.

220
- Philip V, King of Macedon.

219
- Hannibal, the great Carthaginian leader, captures Saguntum in Spain.

218
- Second Punic War begins; Hannibal crosses the Alps into Italy.
- Battle of the Trebia: Hannibal victorious.

217
- Battle of Lake Trasimene: Hannibal victorious.

216
- Battle of Cannae: Hannibal victorious.

214
- First Macedonian War; Romans victorious over Philip V; war ends in 205.
- Great Wall of China constructed.

212
- Romans under Marcellus capture Syracuse.
  DEATHS
  Archimedes, Greek mathematician.

208
- Philopoemen becomes leader of the Achaean League.

207
- Hasdrubal, brother of Hannibal, crosses the Alps into Italy; defeated and killed in Battle of Metaurus.

206
- Conquest of Spain by Scipio.

205
- Ptolemy V, King of Egypt; period of anarchy.

204
- Scipio carries the war into Africa.

202
- Battle of Zama: Hannibal completely defeated near Carthage by the younger Scipio; end of Second Punic War.

200
- Roman poets Ennius and Plautus flourish at this time.
- Second Macedonian War begins.

197
- Battle of Cynoscephaloe: Roman victory ended Second Macedonian War.

196
• Romans proclaim freedom of Greece.

190
• Battle of Magnesia: Romans defeat Antiochus the Great of Syria.

181
• Ptolemy VI, King of Egypt.

175
• Antiochus IV becomes King of Syria.

171
• Third Macedonian War begins.
• Battle of Pelusium; Antiochus Epiphanes takes Memphis.

170
• Roman poet Terence flourishes at this time.

168
• Battle of Pydna; Perseus of Macedonia crushed; end of Third Macedonian War.

166
• Death of Mattathias, the Jewish priest who led revolt of Jews against Hellenizing policy of Antiochus Epiphanes; succeeded by his son, Judas Maccabaeus.

161
• Judas Maccabaeus killed at Elasa; succeeded by his brother Jonathan.

149
• Fourth Macedonian War.
• Third Punic War begins.

147
• Roman victory under Mummius at Corinth; Macedonia becomes a Roman province.

146
• Greece becomes a Roman province.
• Carthage destroyed; Roman province of Africa formed.
• Ptolemy IX, King of Egypt.

143
• Simon, a brother of Judas Maccabaeus, becomes leader of the Jews.

142
• Syrian garrison expelled from Jerusalem.

140
• Roman conquest of Lusitania (now Portugal).

135
• John Hyrcanus becomes leader of the Jews.

134
• Roman provinces in Spain are formed.
• Attalus III, King of Pergamom, bequeathes his dominions to Rome; province of Asia formed.

DECLINE OF THE ROMAN REPUBLIC

133
- Tiberius Gracchus becomes tribune of the Plebs at Rome; attempted to solve the land problem.

123
- Cais Gracchus, brother of Tiberius, becomes tribune of the Plebs; further land reform.

121
- Caius Gracchus killed in a riot.

120
- Roman province in Southern Gaul (hence Provence).

111
- War between Rome and Jugurtha, King of Numidia in Africa; Roman generals, Metellus and Marius.

106
- Jugurtha defeated and captured by Marius.

102
- Barbarian Teutones moving to invade Italy defeated by Marius at Aix.

101
- Barbarian Cimbri moving towards Rome defeated by Marius at Vercellae.

90
- Social War: revolt of the Italians Cities against Rome.

89
- Roman franchise granted to some Italians; soon afterwards to all.

88
- First Mithradatic War begins: Rome v. Mithradates VI (the Great), King of Pontus, in Asia Minor; Sulla the Roman general.

88
- Civil War in Rome: Marius v. Sulla; immediate occasion was rivalry for the command in Asia.

87
- Massacres in Rome by Marius and Cinna.

86
- Death of Marius.

84
- End of first Mithradatic War.

83-82
- Second Mithradatic War.

83
- Sulla returned to Rome; many citizens proscribed and executed.

82
- Sulla made Dictator of Rome; makes the constitution more aristocratic.

79
- Sula resigns (d.78).

76-71
- Pompey suppresses the rebellion of Sertorius, a follower of Marius, in Spain.

75
- Cicero, the orator, comes into prominence at Rome.

74
- Third Mithradatic War begins; Roman leaders Lucullus and Pompey.

73-71
- Revolt of gladiators and slaves under Spartacus.

64
- Pompey conquers Syria and makes it a Roman province.

63
- Pompey takes Jerusalem.
- The conspiracy of Catiline exposed and foiled by Cicero.

60
- First Triumvirate: Caesar, Pompey and Crassus.

58
- Caesar begins the conquest of Gaul; the Helvetii defeated at Bibracte; Ariovistus, the German leader, defeated.

55
- Caesar's first invasion of Britain.

54
- Caesar's second invasion of Britain.

53
- Battle of Carrhoe: Crassus defeated and killed by Parthians.

52
- Battle of Alesia: Vercingetorix, leader of the Gauls, defeated and captured by Cæsar.

50
- Conquest of Gaul complete.

49
- Caesar crosses the Rubicon and invades Italy.

48
- Battle of Pharsalia: Cæsar defeats Pompey (Pompey murdered soon afterwards in Egypt).

48-47
- Caesar in Egypt; under the influence of Cleopatra, Queen of Egypt.

47
- Battle of Zela: Caesar defeats Pharnaces, King of Pontus.

46
- Battle of Thapsus: the republicans defeated by Caesar in Africa; Cato commits suicide rather than survive the republic.
- Calendar reformed by Caesar.

45
- Battle of Munda: Pompey's sons defeated in Spain by Caesar.

44
- Caesar made Perpetual Dictator.
- Assassination of Caesar.

43
- The Second Triumvirate constituted: Octavius, Antony and Lepidus; Cicero executed.

42
- Battle of Philippi: Brutus and Cassius, the leaders of the revolt against Caesar, are defeated and they commit suicide.

40
- Virgil and Horace, the Roman poets, flourish about this time.

31
- Battle of Actium: Antony and Cleopatra defeated in naval battle by Octavius.

30
- Suicide of Antony and Cleopatra; Egypt becomes a Roman province.

29
- Temple of Janus closed, denoting a world at peace - the first time for 200 years; Livy, the great historian flourishes at this time.

27
- The Senate gives Octavius the title of Princeps of the Roman State; beginning of the Principate, an Empire under the forms of the old republic.

- Senate gives Octavius the title of Augustus.

ROMAN EMPIRE

27
- Beginning of Roman Empire with Augustus in the form of the Principate.

23
- Readjustment of the authority of Augustus.

20
- Restoration of Temple at Jerusalem begun by Herod the Great.

4
- Death of Herod the Great; Herod Antipas becomes tetrarch of Galilee and Perea; Herod Archelaus becomes ethnarch of Judaea, Samaria and Idumea.

AD

9
- Roman army under Varus defeated in Germany by Arminius: Teutonic Civilisation saved from absorption by Rome.

14
- Tiberius becomes Emperor.

17
- Death of Livy.

18

- Death of Ovid.

26

- Pontius Pilate becomes Roman procurator of Judaea.

30

- Probable date of crucifixion of Jesus Christ.

31

- Sejanus, minister of Tiberius, executed.

37

- Caligula becomes Emperor.

41

- Claudius becomes Emperor.
- Herod Agrippa I recognised as King of Judaea and Samaria.

43

- Roman conquest of Britain begins under Aulus Plautius.

44

- Death of Herod Agrippa I; Judea governed afterwards by Roman procurators.

50

- St Paul begins missionary work in Europe.

54

- Nero becomes Emperor; last of the Caesar family.

- The philosopher Senecca flourishes at this time.

61

- Revolt of Boadicea, Queen of the Iceni in Britain; defeated and killed by Suetonius Paulinus.

61

- St Paul arrives in Rome.

63

- Death of St Paul at Rome.

64

- Great fire in Rome.

65

- First persecution of Christians at Rome.

DEATHS

Senecca, Roman philosopher.

68

- Death of Nero.

68

- Galba usurps the Empire.

69

- Otho murdered and displaces Galba.
- Vitellius proclaimed Emperor at Cologne; defeats Otho and accepted as Emperor.

70

- Vespasian becomes Emperor by the defeat of Vitellius; first of the Flavian Emperors.

204
- Origen, a Greek Father of the Church, begins teaching at Alexandria.

210
- Severus strengthens Hadrian's Wall across Britain.

211
- Death of Severus at York; his sons Caracalla and Geta become joint Emperors; Geta murdered in 212.

212
- Roman citizenship conferred upon all free men.

217
- Caracalla murdered; Macrinus becomes Emperor.

218
- Heliogabalus becomes Emperor; tries to establish worship of Syrian sun-god.

222
- Alexander Severus becomes Emperor after murder of Heliogabalus.

229
- Sassanid Empire begins in Persia with Ardashir I, who overthrew the Parthians; he re-establishes the Zoroastrian religion.

231
- Alexander Severus at war with Persia.

235
- Alexander Severus murdered; Maximinus becomes Emperor.

238
- The elder and younger Gordians proclaimed joint Emperors in Africa, acknowledged by the Senate; defeated and killed after 36 days' reign; Balbinus and Maximus proclaimed joint Emperors by the Senate and associated with the third Gordian; Maximinus murdered by his own troops; Maximus and Balbinus murdered, leaving the third Gordian sole Emperor.

243
- Battle of Resaena: Gordian defeats the Persians under Sapor I.

244
- Gordian murdered by his mutinous soldiers; Philip (an Arabian) becomes Emperor.

249
- Decius becomes Emperor, after defeating and killing Philip.

250
- Cyprian, Bishop of Carthage, Latin Father of the Church.
- Persecution of the Christians.

251
- Battle of Forum Trebonii: Decius defeated and killed in Moesia by Gothic invaders; Gallus becomes Emperor and buys off the Goths.

253

- Aemilianus routs the Goths and is proclaimed Emperor; Gallus murdered; Aemilianus defeated and overthrown by Valerian.

260

- Valerian defeated and taken prisoner at Edessa by Sapor, King of Persia; his son Gallienus becomes sole Emperor. The Goths ravage the east of the Empire. General disorder and revolt (the so-called Thirty Tyrants). Postumus establishes a so-called Gallic Empire.

266

- Odenathus, after raising Palmyra to a position of power and repelling the Persians, is murdered; his widow, Zenobia, rules on behalf of her son and makes extensive conquests.

268

- Claudius becomes Emperor.

269

- Battle of Naïssus: Claudius defeats the Goths and saves the Empire from destruction.

270

- Aurelian becomes Emperor; Dacia granted to the Goths.

270

- St Anthony, the first Christian Monk, becomes an ascetic in Egypt.

271

- Battle of Châlons: Tetricus defeated and the 'Gallic Empire' ended.

272

- Aurelian destroys the power of Palmyra and takes Zenobia prisoner.

275

- Aurelian assassinated; Tacitus elected Emperor by the Senate.

276

- Probus becomes Emperor.

277

- Probus expels the Almanni from Gaul.

282

- Probus assassinated; Carus becomes Emperor.

283

- Carus succeeded by his two sons, Carinus and Numerian, as joint Emperors.

284

- Diocletian becomes Emperor.

286

- Maximian chosen by Diocletian as his colleague.

286

- Carausius appointed to protect British shore against Frank and Saxon pirates; proclaimed Emperor and recognised.

293

- Constantius Chlorus and Galerius created Caesars, with a share in governing the Empire: Rome ceases to be real capital, being replaced by the four towns of Nicomedia, Sirmium, Milan and Trier, one for each Augustus and Caesar. These four divisions afterwards become the Prefectures of the East, Illyricum, Italy and Gaul.
- Carausius murdered in Britain by Allectus.

296

- Allectus defeated and killed by Constantius Chlorus.

303

- Persecution of Christians.

304

- St Alban the first Christian martyr in Britain.

305

- Abdication of Diocletian and Maximian.

BARBARIAN INVASIONS

306

- Constantine the Great proclaimed Emperor at York, on the death of his father Constantius; Severus made joint Emperor by Galerius; Maxentius, son of Maximian, declared Emperor at Rome.

307

- Severus executed by Maximian; Licinius made joint Emperor by Galerius; Maximian also proclaimed Emperor; six Emperors at one time.

310

- Maximian executed by Constantine.

311

- Death of Galerius.

312

- Constantine invaded Italy; Maxentius's army defeated in Battle of Turin and in Battle of Verona.

312

- Battle of the Milvian Bridge (at Rome): Constantine captures Rome; death of Maxentius.

313

- Licinius defeats Maximin; death of Maximin soon afterwards.
- Edict of Milan grants freedom to Christians.

314

- Death of Tiridates, King of Armenia, who had become a Christian.

315

- Battle of Cibalis: Constantine defeats Licinius.

320
- Battle of Mardia: Licinius is again defeated; a Treaty of Peace concluded.

320
- St Pachomius founds the first Christian monastery in Egypt.

322
- Constantine defeats the Goths in Dacia.

323
- Battle of Adrianople: Liciunius defeated by Constantine.
- Battle of Chrysopolis: Licinius defeated by Constantine and dies soon afterwards.

324
- Constantine sole Roman Emperor; he adopts Christianity.

325
- Council of Nicaea, the first General Council of the Christian Church; held in the presence of Constantine; the doctrines of Arius condemned, chiefly through the influence of Athansius.

328
- Constantine founds a new capital at Byzantium under the name of Constantinople or New Rome.

330
- Constantinople dedicated.

332
- Constantius, son of Constantine, defeats the Goths in Moesia.

337
- Death of Constantine; his sons, Constantius, Constantine II and Constans, divide the Empire.

337
- The Empire at war with Persia under Sapor II.

340
- Constantine II killed in attacking the territories of Constans.

341
- Ulfilas begins the conversion of his fellow Goths to Arian Christianity; his translation of the Bible in Gothic is the oldest teutonic literary work.

348
- Battle of Singara: Romans defeated by Persians.

350
- Constans murdered in a revolt by Magnetius, who assumes the purple.
- Third Siege of Nisbis: Sapor II unsuccessful.
- Hermanric becomes King of the Goths and establishes a Gothic Empire in Central Europe.

351
- Battle of Mursa: Magnentius defeated by Constantius.

353
- Battle of Mount Seleucus: defeat of Magnentius, who then commits suicide; Constantius sole Emperor.

356
- Julian (the Apostate) begins campaign in Gaul against the Alamanni, Franks and others.

357
- Battle of Strassburg: Julian defeats the Alamanni.

359
- Amida captured by Sapor II.

359
- Julian subdues the Franks.

360
- Singara and Bezabde captured by Sapor II.

361
- Julian becomes Emperor; tries to restore Paganism as the state religion.

363
- Julian campaign against Persia leads to his death; Jovian Emperor.
- Jovian makes a humiliating peace with Persia.

364
- Valentinian I becomes Emperor.
- Valentinian divides the Empire into eastern and western, making Valens eastern Emperor.

365
- Revolt of Procopius against Valens.

366
- Procopius defeated and executed.
- Alamanni invade Gaul; defeated by Jovinus.
- War against the Visigoths under Athanaric begins.

368
- Valentinian defeats the Alamanni in the Black Forest and fortifies the Rhine.

369
- Theodosius drives back the Picts and Scots from southern Britain.

370
- Basil the Great, a pioneer of monasticism, becomes Bishop of Caesarea.

372
- St Martin, a pioneer of monasticism, becomes Bishop of Tours.
- Huns under Balamir begin westward movement from the Caspian steppes; they defeat and absorb the Alans.

373
- Theodosius suppresses revolt in Africa.

374
- Huns attack the Ostrogoths of Hermanric's kingdom and conquer them.
- War against the Quadi and Sarmatians.

- St Ambrose becomes Bishop of Milan.

375

- Huns attack Athanaric and the Visigoths.
- Gratian and Valentinian II, sons of Valentinian I, become western Emperors.

376

- Visigoths under Fritigern permitted by Valens to settle in Thrace; they successfully revolt because of oppression.

378

- The Alamanni defeated by Gratian near Colmar.
- Battle of Adrianople: Romans defeated by Goths and Valens killed.
- Massacre of Gothics in Asia by the Romans.
- Gregory Nazianzen accepts the mission of Constantinople.

379

- Theodosius the Great becomes eastern Emperor.

380

- Theodosius baptised in the Orthodox faith; suppresses Arianism in
- Constantinople and begins persecution of heretics.

381

- Second General Council of the Church, at Constantinople.

382

- Theodosius makes terms with the Goths and enlists them in his service.

383

- Revolt of Maximus in Britain; he invades Gaul and murders Gratian; treaty between Theodosius and Maximus, leaving the latter in possession of Gaul, Spain and Britain.

385

- Priscillian, a Spanish bishop, is executed at Träves for heresy by Maximus.
- St Jerome works on the Latin translation of the Bible (the Vulgate).

386

- Conversion of St Augustine.
- Ostrogoths defeated on the Danube.

387

- Sedition of Antioch severely punished by Theodosius.
- Maximus invades Italy; Valentinian flees to Theodosius.

388

- Maximus defeated and executed by Theodosius.

390

- Sedition of Thessalonica punished by massacre; Theodosius compelled by St Ambrose to do humble penance at Milan.
- Paganism prohibited under heavy penalties.

392

- Death of Valentinian II, strangled by Arbogast, a Frankish general in the imperial service; Eugenius usurps western Empire at the instance of Arbogast.

394

- Theodosius defeats Eugenius and becomes sole Emperor; Eugenius is killed and Arbogast commits suicide.
- Olympic Games finally abolished.

395

- Final division of the Empire into East and West: Honorius becomes western Emperor and Arcadius eastern Emperor.
- Death of Theodosius the Great.

396

- Alaric, the Visigothic leader, invades Greece.

397

- Alaric defeated in Greece by Stilicho, master-general of the western armies, of Vandal race.

398

- Alaric made master-general of eastern Illyricum and also proclaimed King of the Visigoths.
- St Chrysostom becomes Archbishop of Constantinople.

399

- Revolt of Ostrogoths in Asia Minor

under Tribigild: joined by Gainas, a Goth, who was military minister of the eastern Empire.

400

- St Ninian begins to Christianise the Picts of Galloway in Scotland.
- Alaric invades Italy; Honorius flees from Rome.
- Claudian, the last of the Roman poets, celebrates Stilicho's victories.

401

- Gainas defeated by Fravitta, a loyal Goth; beheaded later by the Hunnish King.

402

- Battle of Pollentia: Stilicho defeats Alaric.

403

- Battle of Verona: Stilicho again victorious over Alaric.

404

- Honorious makes Ravenna his capital.
- Gladiatorial contests abolished.

405

- Italy invaded by a Germanic host under the Pagan Radagaisus: Florence is besieged: the invaders are defeated and their leader is killed by Stilicho.
- St Patrick begins the conversion of the Irish.

407
- Revolt of British army: Constantine declared Emperor.

408
- Constantine acknowledged in Gaul and Spain.
- Theodosius II eastern Emperor; government conducted first by Anthemius, then by Pulcheria, sister of the Emperor.
- Stilicho disgraced and assassinated.
- Alaric besieges Rome; bought off.

409
- Second Siege of Rome by Alaric; Ostia captured: Attalus made Emperor by Alaric, with himself as master-general of the west.
- Spain invaded by Suevi, Vandals, Alans, etc.

410
- Alaric degrades Attalus; Rome besieged and sacked; Italy ravaged; death of Alaric.
- Edict of Honorius calling upon Britain to defend itself; Britain sets up a provisional government, as does Armorica (Brittany).

411
- Constantius regains Gaul for Honorius.

413
- Heraclian invades Italy from Africa; defeated and executed.

414
- Atawulf, successor of Alaric, after conquering in Gaul, marches to Spain in order to recover it for the Empire; he is assassinated next year at Barcelona.

418
- Visigoths under Wallia reconquer Spain for the Empire.

419
- Visigoths granted lands in Aquitania under the Empire: Visigothic kingdom of Toulouse established.
- Theodoric I King of the Visigoths.

422
- Eastern Empire successful against Persia.

423
- Death of Honorius; usurpation of the western Empire by John.

425
- Emperor John beheaded at Aquileia: Valentinian III becomes Emperor, with his mother Placidia as guardian.

427
- Chlodio first known King of the Franks, on the lower Rhine.
- Aëtius, a general of Valentinian III, deceives Boniface, another general of the Empire, into revolting in Africa.

428
- Boniface invites the Vandals to invade Africa.

429
- The Vandals under Gaiseric invade Africa from Spain.

430
- Boniface, repenting, opposes the Vandals unsuccessfully.

431
- Third General Council of the Church, at Ephesus.

437
- Burgundian kingdom on the Upper Rhine overthrown by Aëtius: the Burgundians granted lands in Savoy.

439
- Carthage taken by the Vandals.

440
- Leo I (the Great) Pope (d.461).

445
- Huns under Attila attack the eastern Empire.

446
- 'The Groans of the Britons': unsuccessful appeal of the Britons to Aëtius for help against the invading Saxons and others (traditional).
- Treaty between Attila and Theodosius.

448
- Meroveus King of the Franks – hence Merovingian dynasty.

449
- Jutes under Hengist and Horsa invade and settle in Kent.

450
- Marcian becomes eastern Emperor as husband of Pulcheria.

451
- Attila and the Huns, with Ostrogothic subjects, invade Gaul.
- Battle of Châlons or the Catalaunian Fields or Maurica: Aëtius in alliance with the Visigoths under Theodoric I and the Franks under Meroveus repel Attila and save western Europe from the Huns; Theodoric killed.
- Fourth General Council of the Church, at Chalcedon.

452
- Attila invades Italy and destroys Aquileia; the city of Venice originated with fugitives.

453
- Death of Attila and end of his Empire; the Ostrogoths free again.
- Theodoric II, King of the Visigoths.
- Aëtius murdered by Valentinian III.

455
- Valentinian III assassinated at the instance of Maximus: Maximus becomes Emperor.

456

- Gaiseric and the Vandals march against Rome; Maximus assassinated when attempting flight; Rome sacked by the Vandals.
- Avitus made Emperor by the Visigoths.

456

- Avitus deposed by Rikimer, a Goth in the service of the Empire who had defeated the Vandals by sea and land; he is recognised as Patrician of Rome.
- Sardinia occupied by the Vandals.
- Visigoths conquers most of Spain: Toledo becomes their capital.

457

- Rikimer makes Majorian western Emperor; Leo I becomes eastern Emperor.
- Childeric King of the Franks.

460

- Majorian's great fleet for invasion of Africa destroyed by Gaiseric in the Bay of Carthagena, through treachery.

461

- Rikimer compels Majorian to abdicate and makes Libius Severus a purely nominal Emperor; Marcellinus revolts in Dalmatia and Aegidius in Gaul.

465

- Death of Severus; no western Emperor for two years.

466

- Euric King of the Visigoths.

467

- Anthemius becomes western Emperor.

468

- Leo's expedition against the Vandals fails.
- Sardinia recovered from the Vandals.

469

- The Vandals occupy Corsica.

472

- Olybrius made western Emperor by Rikimer, who sacks Rome and massacres Athemius; deaths of Rikimer and Olybrius.
- Glycerius Emperor for a brief period; Julius Nepos made Emperor by Leo I.

474

- Leo II eastern Emperor; succeeded by Zeno.

475

- The Patrician Orestes leads the barbarian confederates against Nepos in Ravenna; Nepos flees to Dalmatia.
- Romulus Augustulus, son of Orestes, proclaimed western Emperor.
- Odoacer, a Goth, leads a revolt of the barbarian allies, who proclaim him King of Italy: besieges Orestes in Pavia and executes him.

476

- Romulus Augustulus forced to resign the Empire.
- Zeno, at the instance of the Senate, made Odoacer Patrician of Italy.
- Odoacer obtains Sicily from the Vandals for tribute.

477

- South Saxons under Ella settle in England.

478

- Ostrogoths under Theodoric the Great invade Greece.

480

- Julius Nepos assassinated in Dalmatia; no successor appointed. End of the western Empire.

THE GERMANIC KINGDOMS

481

- Dalmatia annexed by Odoacer.
- Clovis becomes King of the Franks; Tournai his capital.

484

- Sardinia recaptured by the Vandals.

485

- Death of Euric, King of the Visigoths; the Visigothic kingdom at its greatest extent.

486

- Battle of Soissons: Syagrius, son of Aegidius, Roman ruler of a kingdom with Paris as its centre, defeated by Clovis and his kingdom is annexed.

488

- Theodoric the Great commissioned by the Emperor Zeno to recover Italy for the Empire.

489

- Battle of Aquileia: Theodoric defeats Odoacer.

489

- Battle of Verona: Theodoric defeats Odoacer.

490

- Odoacer again defeated by Theodoric.

491

- Clovis subdues the Thuringi.
- Anastasius I becomes Emperor at Constantinople.

492

- Isaurian War begins and occupies Anastasius till 496.

493

- Theodoric captures Ravenna and puts Odoacer to death; beginning of Ostrogothic kingdom of Italy.

495

- West Saxons settle in England under Cerdic and Cynric.

496
- Clovis subdues the Alamanni.

496
- Clovis converts from Paganism to Catholicism.

500
- Scots under Fergus Mor cross from Ireland to found kingdom of Dalriada in Scotland.
- Clovis defeats Gundobald, King of the Burgundians, near Dijon.

502
- War between the Empire and Persia (ended 506).

504
- Theodoric's general Pitzia defeats the Gepids and makes them subject allies.

507
- Battle of Vouillé (near Poitiers): Clovis defeats the Visigoths and kills their king, Alaric II.

508
- Clovis made a Roman Consul by the Emperor Anastasius.
- Peace between Theodoric and the Empire after a short war arising out of the Gepid war of 504.

510
- Clovis annexes Aquitania from Visigoths.
- Theodoric checks Clovis, wins Provence for the Ostrogoths and saves a small part of Gaul for the Visigoths.
- Theodoric rules the Visigothic kingdom as protector of his grandson Amalaric: Gothic power at its height.

511
- Death of Clovis; the Frankish kingdom divided among his four sons, Thierry, Childebert, Chlodomir and Clotaire, with capitals at Metz, Paris, Orleans and Soissons.

516
- Battle of Mount Badon: Saxon advance in Britain is checked by the Britons.

518
- Justin I becomes Emperor.

520
- The dating of the Christian Era introduced about this time in Italy by Dionysius Exiguus.

522
- War between the Empire and Persia.

524
- Boethius the philosopher executed by Theodoric on a charge of treason.

525
- Symmachus, father-in-law of Boethius, executed by Theodoric the Great.

526
- Remorse and death of Theodoric the Great.

IMPERIAL REVIVAL UNDER JUSTINIAN

526
- Destructive earthquake at Antioch: great loss of life.
- East and Middle Saxons settle in England about this time.

527
- Accession of Justinian I to the Empire.

529
- Justinian suppresses the Athenian Schools of Philosophy.
- Justinian's Code of Civil Law is prepared under the direction of Tribonian.

530
- Gelimer becomes King of the Vandals.

531
- Chosroes I becomes King of Persia.
- The Franks subdue the Thuringians in central Germany; also the Bavarians.

532
- The Nika at Constantinople: a destructive revolt due to the rivalry of the Blue and Green circus factions. Belisarius' troops massacre 30, 000 of the rebels.

- Peace concluded between Justinian and Persia.
- Franks invade Burgundy.

533
- War between the Empire and the Vandals: Carthage captured by Belisarius and Gelimer taken prisoner.
- Justinian's *Institutes* published; also the *Pandects* or *Digest*.

534
- Conquest of Burgundy by the Franks: end of the Burgundian kingdom.
- Africa recovered for the Empire; the Vandal kingdom at an end.
- Malta becomes a province of the Byzantine Empire.

535
- Moors defeated in Africa by Solomon, colleague of Belisarius.
- Amalasuntha, Queen of the Ostrogoths; strangled by Theodatus; a pretext for Justinian's invasion.
- Belisarius subdues Sicily.

536
- Belisarius invades Italy and takes Naples; Witigis becomes King of the Sostrogoths; Belisarius enters Rome.

537
- Justinian builds and dedicates the Cathedral of St Sophia in Constantinople.
- The Ostrogoths, under Witiges, besiege Belisarius in Rome. The siege fails.

538
- Belisarius deposes the Pope Sylverius; the see sold to Vigilius.

538
- Siege of Rome raised.
- Burgundians destroy Milan; Franks invade Italy.
- Buddhism arrives at the court of the Japanese emperor.

539
- Belisarius takes Ravenna.
- Bulgarian invasion of Macedonia and Greece; Slavs invade Illyricum and Thrace.

540
- Recall of Belisarius.
- Chosroes I invades Syria.
- The Goths revolt in Italy.

541
- Justinian ends the Roman consulship.
- Chosroes I captures Antioch and expels many of its people; Belisarius sent to defend Asia against him.
- The Goths victorious in Italy under Totila. Byzantine rule in Italy brought to an end.

542
- Plague in Europe.
- Belisarius drives Chosroes across the Euphrates.
- Battle of Septa: Visigothic invasion of Africa defeated.

543
- Rebellion of the Moors begins (ends 558).

551
- Death of St Benedict, organiser of western monasticism at Monte Casino (in Italy).
- Franks invade Spain and besiege Saragossa; heavily defeated by the Visigoths.

544
- Belisarius again in Italy.

545
- The Turks ascendant in Tartary.

546
- Totila captures Rome.

547
- Belisarius recovers Rome.
- English kingdom of Bernicia founded by Ida.

548
- Final recall of Belisarius from Italy.

549
- The Goths again take Rome; Sicily, Sardinia and Corsica captured; Greece invaded.
- Siege of Petra begins (ends 551).
- Beginning of Colchian or Lazic War (ends 556).

551
- Germanus leads an army to Italy against the Goths; he dies.
- End of the Roman Senate.
- Introduction of silk cultivation into Europe.

552
- Narses made commander against the Goths.
- Battle of Tadino: Totila defeated and killed.

553
- Narses recovers Rome.
- Battle of Mons Lactarius: the Goths under Teias defeated and Teias killed.

553
- Fifth General Council of the Church, at Constantinople.
- Invasion of Italy by Frankish and Alamanni forces under Lothaire and Buccelin.

554
- Battle of Casilinum: The Alamannic invaders defeated by Narses.
- Part of southern Spain recovered for the Empire by this date.
- End of the Ostrogothic kingdom; Italy becomes the Exarchate of Ravenna under the Empire.

558
- Avar embassy to Justinian: the Avars employed against the Bulgarians and Slavs.
- Clotaire I sole King of the Franks.

559
- Bulgarians under Zabergan invade Macedonia and Thrace and threaten Constantinople; defeated by Belisarius.

560
- Kingdom of Deira founded in Britain by Aella.

561
- Frankish monarchy divided among the four sons of Clotaire I, Charibert I, Guntram, Sigebert I and Chilperic I (capitals, Paris, Orleans, Rheims and Soissons).

562
- Peace concluded between Justinian and Persia.
  DEATHS
  Procopius, Byzantine historian.

563
- St Columba lands in Iona to Christianise the Picts of Scotland.

565
- Death of Justinian.

RISE OF THE PAPACY

565
- Justin II becomes Emperor: the Empire becoming Greek instead of Latin.

566
- Avar embassy to Justin II.
- Lombards and Avars destroy the Gepid kingdom.

568
- The Lombards under Alboin begin to conquer in Italy and establish a kingdom.

- Leovigild becomes King of the Visigoths.

570
- Birth of Mohammed.
- The Persians conquer Yemen in Arabia.
- Beginning of the Avar Empire under Baian in the Danube lands vacated by the Lombards.
- St Asaph preaching Christianity in north Wales.

571
- The Lombards take Pavia and make it their capital; Italy now partly imperial and partly Lombard.

572
- Renewal of war between Persia and the Empire.

573
- Alboin murdered at the instance of his wife, Rosamond; Clepho becomes King of the Lombards.

573
- Battle of Arderydd: Christian party gains the victory in the kingdom of the Strathclyde Britons.

574
- Clepho murdered; the Lombards ruled for ten years by a number of independent dukes.

575
- Synod of Drumceatt in Ireland: Co-

lumba gets Aidan recognised as independent King of Dalriada.

577
- Battle of Deorham: The West Saxons under Ceawlin defeat Britons; Saxon advance resumed.

578
- Tiberius II becomes Emperor.

579
- Hormuz succeeds Chosroes I as King of Persia.

581
- Slavs invaded Greece and Thrace: defeated by Priscus.

582
- Maurice becomes Emperor.

584
- Autharis becomes King of the Lombards, but the duchies of Spoleto and Beneventum in the centre and south remain practically independent; three invasions of Franks and Alamanni repelled.

585
- Visigoths conquer and absorb the Suevic kingdom in northwest Spain.
- St Columba leaves Ireland to convert Burgundy.

586
- Reccared becomes King of the Visigoths: under him the Visigoths

abandon Arianism and become Catholic Christians.

588

- The kingdom of Northumbria formed by the union of Bernicia and Deira.

590

- Gregory the Great becomes Pope (till 604): greatly increases the powers of the Bishop of Rome by taking advantage of the confusion and disunion of Italy.
- Revolt of Bahram in Persia; Hormuz deposed: Chosroes II becomes King of Persia, but has to flee to the Romans for help; Roman general Narses (not the conqueror of Italy) defeats Bahram and recovers his kingdom for Chosroes II.

592

- Agilulf becomes King of the Lombards.

595

- The Emperor Maurice has to fight against the Avars (till 602).

597

- Augustine, sent by Gregory the Great, converts Ethelbert and the kingdom of Kent to Christianity; becomes first Archbishop of Canterbury.

601

- Death of St David, patron saint of Wales.

602

- Phocas becomes Emperor: Maurice executed.

603

- Death of Kentigern (or St Mungo), who converted the Strathclyde Britons.
- Battle of Degsastan: Northumbrians under Tethelfrith defeat Scots under Aidan.

609

- Mohammed preaches at Mecca.

610

- Heraclius overthrows Phocas and becomes Emperor; the Empire hard pressed by Persians, Avar and Slavs.

611

- Persians capture Antioch.

613

- Clotaire II sole King of the Franks.
- Persians take Damascus and overruns Syria.
- Battle of Chester: Northumbrians under Ethelfrith defeat Welsh.

614

- St Gall, from Ireland, settles in east Switzerland.

616

- Persians take Alexandria and subdue Egypt.
- Asia Minor conquered by the Persians.

617
- Persians capture Chalcedon, opposite Constantinople.

621
- Swinthila becomes King of the Visigoths; recovers Southern Spain from the Empire.

622
- Heraclius begins his great campaigns against the Persians under Chosroes II.
- The Hejira, or flight of Mohammed from Mecca to Medina.

626
- Constantinople unsuccessfully attacked by the Persians in league with the Avars.

627
- Battle of Nineveh: Heraclius's final victory over the Persians.
- Edwin, King of Northumbria, embraces Christianity under the influence of Paulinus, who becomes first Archbishop of York.

628
- Chosroes II deposed and murdered; peace between Persia and the Empire.
- Mohammed's message to all rulers calling upon them to embrace Islam.

629
- Submission of Mecca to Mohammed; first battle between Muslims and the Empire, near the Dead Sea.

630
- Dagobert I sole King of the Franks.

632
- Death of Mohammed: Arabia conquered by the Muslims by this date.

THE ADVANCE OF ISLAM

632
- Mohammed succeeded by Abubekr, the first Caliph; beginning of the Caliphate.
  DEATHS
  Mohammed, founder of Islam.

633
- Battle of Heathfield: Edwin, King of Northumbria, overthrown and killed by Penda, heathen King of Mercia, in alliance with Welsh under Caedwalla.

634
- Battle of Ajnadain (near Jerusalem): Muslims under Khaled defeat the army of Heraclius.
- Omar becomes Caliph.
- Battle of Hexham: Oswald defeats Caedwalla and becomes King of Northumbria.

635
- The Muslims capture Damascus.
- St Aidan goes to Lindisfarne from Iona to re-Christianise Northumbria.

636
- Battle of Yermuk: Muslim victory

over Imperial troops seals fate of Syria.
• Rotharis King of the Lombards; a great legislator.

637

• Battle of Cadesia: Muslims defeat the Persians and conquer western Persian provinces.
• Muslims capture Ctesiphon in Persia.
• Muslims capture Jerusalem: the Temple becomes a mosque.

638

• Muslims capture Aleppo and Antioch.

639

• Death of Dagobert I, last notable Merovingian King of the Franks; Mayors of the Palace become the real rulers in Austrasia (eastern division of kingdom), Neustria (western division) and Burgundy; nominal kings called *rois fainéants* ('do-nothing kings').

640

• Muslims begin conquest of Egypt under Amru.

641

• Heraclius succeeded in the Empire by his sons, Constantine III and Heracleonas.
• Battle of Nehavend: Muslims defeat Persians and overthrow the Sassanid Dynasty; last Sassanid King, Yezdegerd III, dies a fugitive in 651.

642

• Constans II Emperor.
• Muslims occupy Alexandria.
• Battle of Maserfeld (Oswestry): Oswald of Northumbria defeated and killed by Penda of Mercia.

644

• Othman becomes Caliph.

647

• Muslims begin conquest of Africa.

649

• Muslims conquer Cyprus.

653

• Aribert first Catholic King of the Lombards.

654

• Muslims conquer Rhodes.

655

• Great naval victory of Muslims over Greeks off Lycian coast.
• Battle of the Winwaed: Penda of Mercia defeated and killed by the Northumbrians under Oswy.

656

• Othman murdered; Ali becomes Caliph.

659

• Wulfhere becomes King of Mercia and restores Mercian power.

660

- Sect of Paulicians, followers of St Paul, founded in Armenia by Constantine.

661

- Ali murdered; Moawiya first of the Ommiade Caliphs, with seat at Damascus.

662

- Emperor Constans II goes to Italy and tries to recover part of it.

664

- Synod of Whitby: Oswy of Northumbria decides for Roman against Celtic Christianity.

668

- Constantine IV becomes Emperor, after Constans II is assassinated in Italy.
- Death of Samo, a Frank who had founded a Slav kingdom in the Danube valley, after a long reign.

669

- Theodore of Tarsus reaches England as Archbishop of Canterbury; introduces Greek learning and organises the English Church.

670

- English poet Caedmon flourishes at this time.
- Aquitaine about this time breaks away from Frankish rule.

671

- Egfrith King of Northumbria.

672

- Wamba the last great King of the Visigoths.

673

- First Arab siege of Constantinople begins.

675

- Slavs and Bulgars overrun Macedonia.

677

- Arabs abandon siege of Constantinople and agree to pay tribute; Greek fire used by defenders.

679

- Bulgarians under Isperich occupy Moesia and settle there.

680

- Sixth General Council of the Church, at Constantinople; continues into 681.

685

- Justinian II becomes Emperor.
- Battle of Nechtansmere: Egfrith of Northumbria defeated and killed by the Picts under Brude; Northumbria never recovers its power.

687

- Battle of Tertry: Pepin of Heristal, the Austrasian Mayor of the Palace,

defeats the Neustrian Mayor of the
Palace and becomes virtual ruler
over the whole Frankish kingdom.
DEATHS
St Cuthbert, Bishop of Lindisfarne.

688
• Ine first great King of Wessex.

689
• Pepin defeats the Frisians.

690
• St Willibrord, an Anglo-Saxon, becomes Bishop of Frisia, which he
  converts to Christianity.

693
• Battle of Sebastopolis: Greeks defeated by the Muslims.

695
• Leontius usurps the Empire.

697
• First Doge of Venice elected.

698
• Muslims capture Carthage.
• Tiberius III usurps the Empire.

705
• Justinian II recovers the Empire and
  perpetrates great cruelties.

709
• Pepin defeats the Alamanni.
  DEATHS
  St Wilfrid, Bishop of York.

710
• Muslim conquest of Africa complete.
• Muslims begin conquest of Tran-
  soxiana; they reach India.
• Roderick King of the Visigoths.
• First Muslim invasion of Spain.

711
• Second Muslim invasion of Spain
  under Tarik; Visigoth kingdom
  overthrown in Battle of Xeres or
  Guadalete or Lake Janda; Toledo,
  the capital, captured; oppressed
  Jews welcome invaders.
• Justinian II executed; Philippicus
  becomes Emperor.

712
• Liutprand King of the Lombards;
  aims at unifying Italy under the
  Lombard monarchy.

713
• Battle of Segoyuela: Muslims again
  victorious over Visigoths; King Roderick killed.
• Anastasius II usurps the Empire.

714
• Death of Pepin of Heristal.

716
• Theodosius III usurps the Empire.

717
• Leo III (the Isaurian) becomes Emperor.
• Second Arab siege of Constantinople begins by land and sea under

Moslemah, brother of the Caliph Soliman; Muslims routed in 718 with the help of the Bulgarians and by means of Greek fire.

- Battle of Vincy: Charles Martel, son of Pepin of Heristal, defeats the Neustrians and becomes virtual ruler of the Franks.
- Church of Iona confirmed to Roman Catholicism.

718
- Charles Martel ravages the country of the Saxons (in north Germany).

720
- Muslims cross the Pyrenees and capture Narbonne.

721
- Muslim attack on Toulouse repelled by Eudes (Eudo), Duke of Aquitaine.

722
- St Boniface, an Anglo-Saxon, goes as Papal missionary to Germany under the protection of Charles Martel.

724
- Charles Martel ravages Frisia.

725
- Muslims take Carcassonne and Nimes.
- Charles Martel fights the Bavarians.

726
- Leo III begins his campaign against the worship of images, promulgat-

ing the Iconoclastic controversy; he is opposed by Pope Gregory II.

731
- Pope Gregory III summons a council at Rome that condemns the Iconoclasts; this breach between the Pope and the Empire makes the Roman Republic virtually independent of the Empire but under Papal influence.
- Muslims under Abderrahman advance to conquer France.
- Bede's *Ecclesiastical History* completed.

732
- Battle of Tours or Poitiers: Charles Martel defeats and drives back the Muslims.

THE AGE OF CHARLEMAGNE

733
- Ethelbald of Mercia becomes ruler of Wessex.

737
- Angus MacFergus, King of the Picts, subdues the Scots of Dalriada.

739
- Pope Gregory III appeals to Charles Martel for help against the Lombards, who, under Liutprand, are besieging Rome.

740
- Constantine V becomes Emperor.

741
- Death of Charles Martel: Frankish kingdom divided between his sons Pepin the Short and Carloman.

747
- Carloman becomes a monk, leaving Pepin sole master of the Franks.

750
- Ommiade dynasty of Caliphs overthrown and replaced by the Ambassides.
- Cynewulf, Anglo-Saxon poet.

751
- Pepin the Short, with the consent of Pope Zacharias, is crowned King of the Franks at Soissons, superseding the nominal Merovingian Childeric III: beginning of the Carolingian Dynasty.
- Ravenna captured by the Lombards under King Aistulf: end of the Exarchate.

752
- Battle of Burford: Cuthred of Wessex defeats Ethelbald of Mercia.

754
- Pope Stephen II concludes an alliance with Pepin, whom he anoints as King of the Franks and Patrician of the Romans.
- Pepin invades Italy and repels the Lombards under Aistulf; he grants the lands of the Exarchate to the

Pope; beginning of the temporal power of the papacy.
- Iconoclastic Synod Constantinople.

755
- Abderrahman founds the Emirate (afterwards Caliphate) of Cordova in Spain as a secession from the Abbasside Caliphate.

756
- Pepin again in Italy to subdue the Lombards.
- Strathclyde subdued by Angus the Pictish King and Eadbert of Northumbria.

757
- Offa becomes King of Mercia and makes himself overlord of England.

758
- Pepin fights heathen Saxons between the Rhine and the Elbe.

759
- Pepin takes Narbonne from the Muslims.

760
- Pepin begins conquest of Aquitaine; completed in 768.

766
- The Abbassides remove the Caliphate to Baghdad.

768
- Death of Pepin; Frankish kingdom di-

vided between his sons Charlemagne (Charles the Great) and Carloman.

770
- Dissolution of the monasteries by the eastern Emperor.

771
- Death of Carloman; Charlemagne sole King of the Franks.

772
- Charlemagne begins his wars against the Saxons.

773
- Desiderius, King of the Lombards, attacks the Pope, Adrian I, who appeals to Charlemagne.

774
- Charlemagne captures Pavia and overthrows the Lombard kingdom; he is crowned King of the Lombards; renews Pepin's donation of territory to the Pope.

775
- Leo IV becomes Emperor.

776
- Charlemagne again in Italy to repress the Lombards.

777
- Battle of Bensington: Offa of Mercia defeats Cynewulf of Wessex.

778
- Charlemagne invades Spain and takes Pampeluna; origin of the Spanish March (established 795). His rearguard cut to pieces by Basques at Roncesvalles: Roland killed.

780
- Constantine VI becomes Emperor, with his mother Irene as regent. The latter opposes the Iconoclasts.

781
- Eastern Empire abandons claims to the pontifical state in Italy.

782
- Alcuin, a British scholar, goes to Aachen (Aix-la-Chapelle) to organise the palace school of Charlemagne.
- The eastern Empire pays tribute to the great Caliph Haroun-al-Raschid.

787
- Seventh General Council of the Church, at Nicaea.

788
- Charlemagne finally conquers Bavaria, Duke Tassilo is deposed.

789
- Constantin I King of the Picts.

790
- Constantine VI proclaimed sole Emperor.

793
- First Viking raid on Britain, at Lindisfarne.

795
• First Viking raid on Ireland.

796
• Charlemagne conquers the Avars.

797
• Irene blinds Constantine VI and rules alone.

798
• Vikings raid the Isle of Man.

800
• Charlemagne crowned Holy Roman Emperor by Pope Leo III in St Peter's at Rome on Christmas Day.

801
• Charlemagne receives an embassy from Haroun-al-Raschid.

802
• Nicephorus I dethrones Irene and becomes eastern Emperor.
• First Viking raid on Iona.

804
• Charlemagne completes the conquest of the Saxons and compels them to accept Christianity.
DEATHS
Alcuin, English scholar.

806
• The Vikings desolate Iona.

807
• The Vikings attack the west coast of Ireland.

810
• The Frisian coast is ravaged by Vikings.

811
• Nicephorus I killed in a war against the Bulgarians under Krum; Michael I becomes eastern Emperor, after Stauracius reigned a few months.
DEATHS
Abu Nuwas, Arab poet.

812
• Michael I acknowledges Charlemagne as western Emperor.

813
• Michael I defeated by Bulgarians and dethroned; Leo V becomes eastern Emperor.

814
• Death of Charlemagne.

EMERGENCE OF FRANCE AND GERMANY

814
• Louis I of France becomes King of the Franks and western Emperor on the death of his father Charlemagne.

817
• Partition of Aachen: Louis I divides his kingdom among his sons.

818
• Bernard, King of Italy, nephew of Louis I, revolts; he is defeated and executed.

820

- Eastern Emperor Leo V murdered; Michael II becomes eastern Emperor.
- Viking raids on Ireland.

824

- Iona raided by the Vikings for the third time.

825

- Battle of Gafulford: Egbert of Wessex conquers the West Welsh (in Cornwall).
- Battle of Ellandune: Egbert of Wessex defeats Beornwulf of Mercia. Kent conquered about same time and East Saxons submitted.

826

- Crete taken by the Muslims.

827

- Muslim conquest of Sicily begins.

829

- Theophilus becomes eastern Emperor. Egbert of Wessex conquers Mercia.

833

- The Field of Lies: Louis I compelled by his sons to abdicate.

834

- Viking raids in Britain: Sheppey attacked.
- Vikings sack Dorstadt and Utrecht.

835

- Louis I restored to his kingdom.

836

- Vikings sack Antwerp; attack Dorsetshire.

838

- Vikings under Thorgils capture Dublin, after desolating much of Ireland.
- Battle of Hengestesdun: Egbert of Wessex defeats a combination of Vikings and West Welsh.

839

- Ethelwulf becomes King of Wessex and England.

840

- Muslims made conquests in Southern Italy.
- Death of Louis I; Lothair I, the eldest son, becomes western Emperor.

841

- Vikings under Oscar sack Rouen.
- Battle of Fontenoy: Louis the German and Charles the Bald, sons of Louis I, defeat their brother Lothair I.

842

- Louis the German and Charles the Bald exchange the Oaths of Strassburg in Romance and German, the earliest document of the French and German languages.
- Muslims capture Bari in South Italy and make it their base.

843

- Michael III becomes eastern Emperor under the guardianship of his mother Theodora, who finally restores image-worship.

843

- Treaty of Verdun: the Frankish Empire partitioned between Louis the German (eastern or German part), Charles the Bald (western or French part; Charles II of France) and Emperor Lothair I (Italy and a part between France and Germany): the beginning of France and Germany as distinct states.

844

- Vikings raid Spanish coast, but are driven off.
- Kenneth MacAlpin, King of the Scots as well as King of the Picts: beginning of Scottish kingdom.

845

- Malachy, King of Meath, defeats and kills Thorgils, Norse King of Northern Ireland.
- Vikings destroy Hamburg; Paris partly destroyed by Vikings under Ragnar.
- Battle of Ballon: Charles the Bald defeated by Bretons.

846

- Vikings defeated in Somerset.
- Muslims sack Rome.

848

- Vikings take Bordeaux.

- Vikings defeated in Ireland.
- Battle of Ostia: Muslims defeated in naval battle at mouth of Tiber, largely owing to Pope Leo IV.

850

- John Scotus (Erigena), an Irish scholar and theologian, flourishes about this time at court of Charles the Bald.

851

- Battle of Juvardeil: Bretons defeat Charles the Bald.
- Great Viking attack on England under Roric; Canterbury burnt; London plundered.
- Battle of Aclea: Ethelwulf of Wessex routs Vikings.

853

- Vikings land in Thanet.

855

- Death of Emperor Lothair I; his son Louis II becomes Emperor and King of Italy; another son, Lothair, becomes King of Lotharingia or Lorraine (the central kingdom of his father); and a third son, Charles, becomes King of Provence.

858

- Ethelbald becomes King of Wessex and England.
- Nicholas I becomes Pope; final breach between eastern and western Churches.

860

- Ethelbert becomes King of Wessex and England.
- Donald becomes King of Scotland.
- Vikings under Weland capture Winchester, capital of Wessex; then are defeated.

862

- Swedish invasion of Russia under Rurik; a state founded with Novgorod as capital, afterwards Kiev, the origin of Russia; Swedes become absorbed by the Slavs.

863

- Death of Charles, King of Provence; his kingdom falls mostly to Emperor Louis II, King of Italy.

864

- Boris, King of Bulgarians, baptised as a Christian.

865

- Russian attack on Constantinople.

866

- Robert the Strong, count of Anjou, killed in battle against the Vikings.
- Ethelred I becomes King of Wessex and England.
- 'Great Army' of Vikings under Ingwar and Hubba in East Anglia.
- Emperor Louis II routs the Muslims.

867

- Michael III murdered; Basil I becomes eastern Emperor, founding Macedonian dynasty.
- Vikings capture York: Northumbrian kingdom overthrown.
- Scotland ravaged by Vikings from Ireland under Olaf the White, King of Dublin.

868

- Muslims capture Malta.

869

- Death of Lothair, King of Lorraine.

870

- Treaty of Mersen: Lorraine divided between Charles the Bald and Louis the German; France and Germany conterminous.
- Vikings from Northumbria invade East Anglia; death of St Edmund, King of East Anglia, in Battle of Hoxne.
- Eighth General Council of the Church, at Constantinople.

DEATHS
Al-Kindi, Arabian philosopher.
Gottschalk, German theologian and poet.

871

- Vikings invade Wessex; capture Reading; defeated in Battle of Ashdown; successful in Battle of Basing; Battle of Marden is indecisive.
- Alfred the Great becomes King of Wessex and England.
- Battle of Wilton: Alfred is defeated by the Vikings, who winter in London.

- Olaf the White, from Ireland, invades Strathclyde and takes Dumbarton.
- Emperor Louis II captures Bari, the Muslim headquarters in south Italy, with naval help from the eastern Emperor Basil I.

872
- Battle of Halfsfjord: Harold Haarfager becomes sole King of Norway.

874
- Iceland colonised by Norwegians.
- Vikings defeat Mercian kingdom.

875
- Death of Emperor Louis II; Charles the Bald becomes western Emperor.
- Norse Earldom of Orkney established by Harold Haarfager.
- Viking attacks on Wessex renewed.
- Thorstein the Red, son of Olaf the White, conquers a large part of Scotland.

876
- Death of Louis the German: Charles the Fat becomes German King.
- Battle of Andernach: Charles the Bald defeated.

877
- Death of Charles the Bald: his son, Louis II (the Stammerer), becomes King of France.
- Vikings divide up Mercia.
- Battle of Dollar: Constantin II of Scotland defeated by Vikings.

- Battle of Forgan: Constantin II defeated and killed by Vikings.

878
- Vikings under Guthrum attack Wessex.
- Battle of Ethandun: Guthrum defeated by Alfred.
- Treaty of Wedmore: peace between Alfred and the Vikings; Guthrum baptised as a Christian; England divided between the two peoples.
- Muslims take Syracuse, almost completing conquest of Sicily.

879
- Death of Louis II; Louis III and Carloman, his sons, become joint kings of France.
- Boso becomes independent King of Burgundy or kingdom of Arles.

881
- Charles the Fat crowned Emperor at Rome.
- Vikings sack Aachen.
- Battle of Saucourt: Louis III and Carloman defeat the Vikings.

882
- Death of Louis III; Carloman sole King of France.
- Treaty of Elsloo: Charles the Fat reaches agreement with the Vikings.

884
- Death of Carloman, King of France: Charles the Fat chosen King of France; reunion of most of Charlemagne's Empire.

885
• Vikings under Rollo besiege Paris.

886
• Paris saved from the Vikings by Odo, Count of Paris.
• Leo VI becomes eastern Emperor.
• Alfred recovers London from the Vikings.

887
• Charles the Fat deposed; final break-up of Frankish Empire.

VIKING AND MAGYAR SETTLEMENTS

887
• On deposition of Charles the Fat, Arnulf becomes King of Germany and Odo, Count of Paris, King of West Franks.
• Louis the Blind succeeds Boso as King of Cisjuran Burgundy (Arles); Rudolph I founds kingdom of Transjuran Burgundy farther north.

888
• Berengar of Friuli King of Italy.
• Third siege of Paris by Vikings; bought off by Odo.
• Odo defeats Vikings in Champagne.
• Muslims or Moors settle on Provençal coast and penetrate inland.

891
• Battle of Louvain: Arnulf, King of Germany, defeats the Vikings.
• Guido of Spoleto becomes Emperor and King of Italy after defeating Berengar.

893
• Civil War between Odo and the Carolingian Charles the Simple; the latter admitted to a share in the kingdom.
• Simeon founds a great Bulgarian Empire, which falls to pieces after his death.
• Great Viking invasion of England under Hastings; Vikings defeated at Farnham and Bemfleet.

895
• Arnulf overthrows Guido and becomes King of Italy.
• Alfred the Great captures the Viking fleet.
• Magyars under Arpad invade Hungary, where they settle permanently.

896
• Arnulf crowned Emperor at Rome.

898
• Charles the Simple King of France on the death of Odo.

899
• Arnulf succeeded as German King by Louis the Child.
  DEATHS
  Alfred the Great.

900
• Edward the Elder succeeds Alfred the Great.

- Constantin III King of Scotland.

901
- Louis the Blind (of Provence) crowned Emperor as Louis III.

902
- Battle of the Holme: Edward the Elder defeats the Vikings of Northumbria.

903
- Magyars reach the Elbe.

904
- Sergius III becomes Pope; degradation of the papacy under the influence of Theodora, wife of Theophylact, Consul of Rome and her daughter Marozia.
- Constantin III of Scotland expels the Vikings.
- Muslims raid Salonica.

905
- Louis the Blind blinded by Berengar.

906
- Magyars complete conquest of Hungary.

907
- Magyars invade Bavaria.
- Russian fleet under Oleg attacks Constantinople.

908
- Magyars ravage Thuringia.

909
- Magyars ravage Suabia.
- Fatimite Caliphate founded in North Africa by Obaidallah.

910
- Battle of Augsburg: Louis the Child defeated by the Magyars.
- Battle of Tottenhall: Edward the Elder severely defeats the Vikings.
- Foundation of Cluny Abbey in eastern France; becomes the centre of a monastic reformation.

911
- Conrad I of Franconia succeeds Louis the Child as German King.
- Charles the Simple acquires Lotharingia or Lorraine.
- Muslims destroy the Greek fleet.
- Treaty of St Clair-sur-epte; the Vikings, under Rollo, allowed by Charles the Simple to settle in the land that becomes Normandy.

912
- Constantine VII becomes eastern Emperor; his uncle Alexander being regent and joint Emperor.

913
- Kingdom of Leon founded.
- Magyars penetrate to Rhine.

914
- Bulgarians capture Adrianople.

915
- Berengar crowned Emperor.

916

- Battle of Garigliano: Muslims defeated by Romans under Theophylact and Alberic, husband of Marozia.
- Pope John X forms a league against the Moors in South Italy.
- Edward the Elder and his sister Ethelfled, the Lady of the Mercians, recover eastern Mercia from the Vikings.
- Battle of Tempsford: Danes heavily defeated by Edward the Elder.
- Battle of Maldon: Edward the Elder victorious over the Danes; East Anglia recovered.

917

- Edward the Elder's victories over the Vikings continue; death of Ethelfled.

918

- Henry I (the Fowler) becomes the German King; beginning of Saxon line.

919

- Romanus I becomes co-Emperor in the East with Constantine VII.
- Edward the Elder receives the homage of all the northern kings in Britain.

922

- Robert I, Duke of France, brother of Odo, crowned King of France, Charles the Simple having been displaced.

923

- Battle of Soissons: Robert I, King of France, killed, though victorious over Charles the Simple's supporters; Hugh the Great becomes Duke of France and Rudolph I of Burgundy King of France; Charles the Simple made prisoner.

923

- Muslim fleet destroyed at Lemnos.

DEATHS

Rhases, Arab physician.

924

- Nine years' truce between Henry I and the Magyars; Magyars ravage Italy.
- Berengar, Emperor and King of Italy, assassinated.
- Athelstan King of England.

926

- Hugh of Provence becomes King of Italy.

927

- William Longsword succeeds Rollo as Duke of Normandy.
- Odo becomes Abbot of Cluny and starts the Cluniac reformation.
- Death of Simeon of Bulgaria.

928

- Henry I takes Brandenburg from the Slavs.

929

- Emirate of Cordova becomes a

Caliphate; there now exist three Caliphates.

DEATHS

Al-Battani, Arab astronomer.

932

- Alberic, son of Marozia, expels Hugh of Provence from Rome and becomes head of the commune.

933

- Battle of Merseburg: Henry I defeats the Magyars.
- The two Burgundian kingdoms (Cisjuran and Transjuran) united.

934

- Haakon I becomes King of Norway.

936

- Otto I (the Great) becomes German King.
- Louis IV (d'Outremer) becomes King of France.

937

- Magyars invade Burgundy and Aquitaine.
- Battle of Brunanburh: Athelastan defeats a combination of Scots, Vikings and Northumbrians.

938

- Alan of the Twisted Beard expels Normans from Brittany.

939

- Otto I conquers Lorraine.

940

- Edmund becomes King of England.
- Harold Bluetooth King of Denmark.

941

- Russian raid defeated by Byzantine fleet.

942

- Richard the Fearless becomes Duke of Normandy.
- Malcolm I becomes King of Scotland on Constantin III's abdication.

943

- Dunstan becomes Abbot of Glastonbury.

944

- Battle of Wels: Magyars defeated by Bavarians.
- Romanus I deposed.

946

- Eadred becomes King of England.

DEATHS

Tsuraguki, Japanese poet.

947

- Magyars again invade Italy and Aquitaine.

948

- Eadred suppresses a Northumbrian rebellion.

950

- Berengar of Ivrea becomes King of Italy.

DEATHS
Al-Farabi, Arab philosopher.

951
- Otto I invades Italy and makes Berengar do homage.

954
- Death of Alberic, the head of the Roman commune.
- Lothair King of France.
- Malcolm I of Scotland killed in battle; succeeded by Indulph.

955
- Battle of Augsburg (Lechfeld): Otto I defeats Magyars and the Slavs. East Mark (afterwards Austria) refounded.
- Eadwig becomes King of England.

956
- Death of Hugh the Great; succeeded as Duke of France by his son, Hugh Capet.

958
- Romanus II eastern Emperor.

959
- Edgar becomes King of England.

960
- Dunstan becomes Archbishop of Canterbury.

961
- Otto I again in Italy; crowned King of Italy at Pavia.

- Nicephorus takes Crete from the Muslims.
- Haakon I of Norway killed in battle.

962
- Otto crowned western Emperor at Rome: revival of Holy Roman Empire after a period of decline.

THE SAXON EMPERORS

962
- Dubh becomes King of Scotland.
- Byzantine victories under Nicephorus over Muslims in Asia Minor.
- Mieczyslaw I becomes ruler of Poland; accepts Christianity in 966.

963
- Basil II eastern Emperor, with Nicephorus II (Phocas) and Constantine VIII as co-Emperors.

964
- Nicephorus Phocas begins conquest of Cilicia from the Muslims.

967
- Cuilean King of Scotland.

968
- Nicephorus Phocas conquers Northern Syria.

969
- Nicephorus Phocas murdered by his nephew John Zimisces, who becomes co-Emperor.

971

- John Zimisces drives back the Russians from Thrace and other Balkan lands.
- Kenneth II King of Scotland.

972

- Death of Sviatoslav, the Russian ruler.

973

- Otto II becomes Emperor in the West.

975

- Edward the Martyr King of England.

976

- Death of John Zimisces; Basil II came into power.
- Samuel becomes King of Bulgaria; he made extensive conquests and built up a Bulgarian Empire.
- Otto II deposes Henry the Quarrelsome, Duke of Bavaria.

978

- Murder of Edward the Martyr; Ethelred II (the Unready) becomes King of England.
- Lothair of France invades Lorraine.

980

- Otto II goes to Italy; aims at conquering southern Italy.
- Vikings attack Southampton, Thanet and Chester.
- Vladimir I (St Vladimir) becomes Russian ruler.
- Battle of Tara: Malachy II, King of Meath, defeats the Vikings in Ireland.

982

- Greenland discovered by the Norwegians.
- Otto II heavily defeated in Italy by combined Byzantine and Muslim forces.

983

- Otto III becomes German King.

985

- Duke Henry of Bavaria restored.

986

- Death of Harold Bluetooth of Denmark; Sweyn Forkbeard becomes Danish King.
- Louis V King of France.

987

- Death of Louis V; Hugh Capet, son of Hugh the Great, becomes King of France, with Paris as capital: founder of the long Capetian dynasty.

988

- Russian Duke Vladimir becomes a Christian.

990

- Pax Ecclesiae, restricting private warfare, introduced in southern France.

991

- Olaf Tryggveson of Norway raids the British Islands (till 994).
- Battle of Maldon: Vikings bought off by Ethelred II.

992
- Boleslaus I becomes ruler of Poland.

993
- Vikings sack Bamborough.

994
- Sweyn Forkbeard and Olaf Tryggveson attack London but are driven off.

995
- Olaf Tryggveson becomes Olaf I King of Norway; imposes Christianity on his people.
- Constantin IV King of Scotland.

996
- Richard the Fearless succeeded by Richard the Good as Duke of Normandy.
- Robert II (the Pious) becomes King of France.
- Otto III crowned Emperor at Rome.

997
- Vikings again attack Wessex.
- Kenneth III King of Scotland.
- Stephen I becomes ruler of Hungary.

998
- Battle of Veszprem: Stephen I of Hungary victorious over rebels; takes title of king, which the Pope confirms in 1001.
- Crescentius, patrician of Rome, executed: Otto III master of Rome.

999
- Gerbert of Aurillac becomes Pope as Silvester II.

1000
- Battle of Svold: Norwegians defeated in naval battle by combined Swedes and Vikings; Norway divided between the conquerors.
- Leif Ericsson discovers Vinland, part of Canada.
- Battle of Glenmama: Malachy II and Brian Boru, Irish rivals, combine and defeat the Vikings.
- Revival of legal studies at Bologna: celebrated university founded later.

1001
- Vikings again bought off from Wessex.

1002
- Henry II, son of Henry the Quarrelsome, becomes German King.
- Ardoin of Ivrea crowned King of Italy.
- The Muslims take Sardinia.
- Massacre of Vikings in England on St Brice's Day.

1003
- Boleslaus I of Poland conquers Bohemia.
- Sweyn again invade England.

1004
- Ardoin overthrown in Italy: Henry II becomes King of the Lombards.

1005
- Malcolm II King of Scotland.

1006
- Boleslaus I of Poland gave up Bohemia.

1007
- Vikings again bought off from England by Ethelred II.

1009
- Another Viking invasion of England.

1012
- Ethelred II again buys off Vikings.

1013
- Sweyn of Denmark again invades England; flight of Ethelred II; Viking conquest.

1014
- Death of Sweyn; his son Canute becomes King of England.
- Claf II (St Olaf) becomes King of Norway.
- Crushing defeat of Bulgaria by Basil II, followed by death of Samuel, King of Bulgaria; his Empire collapses.
- Battle of Clontarf: Vikings heavily defeated in Ireland by Brian Boru, but Brian himself killed.
- Henry II crowned Emperor at Rome.

1015
- Death of Vladimir I of Russia.

1015
- Duchy of Burgundy annexed to the French monarchy by Robert II.

1016
- Death of Ethelred II; Edmund Ironside fights against Canute, but defeated at Assandun; partition of kingdom arranged, but death of Edmund leaves Canute sole king.

1018
- Basil II, the Bulgar-slayer, completes the conquest of Bulgaria.
- Battle of Carham: Scotland annexes Lothian.

1022
- Catharist heretics burned at Orleans.

1024
- Death of Henry II.

THE FRANCONIAN EMPERORS

1024
- Conrad II elected German King: first of Franconian Emperors.

1025
- Constantin VIII sole eastern Emperor.
- Death of Boleslaus I, King of Poland.

1027
- Conrad II crowned Emperor at Rome.
- Truce of God, restricting private war, first proclaimed in southern France.

1028

- Romanus III eastern Emperor.
- Fall of Caliphate of Cordova.
- Ferdinand I (the Great) King of Castile.

1030

- Normans begin conquest of Southern Italy or Apulia.
- Battle of Stiklestad: Norway overthrown and annexed by Denmark.
- Seljuk Turks begin aggression in Asia Minor.
- Henry I King of France.

1032

- Lusatia recovered from Poland by Emperor Conrad II.
- Duchy of Burgundy bestowed on King Henry's brother Robert: line lasts till 1361.

1033

- Kingdom of Burgundy annexed to Emperor by Conrad II.

1034

- Duncan King of Scotland.
- Michael IV eastern Emperor.

1035

- William the Conqueror becomes Duke of Normandy.
- Canute's sons, Hardicanute and Harold, joint rulers of England.

1037

- Norway recovers its independence from Denmark.

- Harold King of all England.
- Bretislav I Prince of Bohemia (conquers Moravia, Silesia, much of Poland).

Deaths

Avicenna, Arab physician and philosopher.

1038

- Ferdinand I of Castile acquires Leon.

Deaths

Alhazen, Arab physicist.

1039

- Henry III German King.

1040

- Macbeth King of Scotland.
- Hardicanute King of England.

1041

- Bohemia made subject to the Empire.
- Michael V eastern Emperor.

1042

- Edward the Confessor King of England.
- Emperor Michael V deposed: Constantine IX eastern Emperor.

1043

- Unsuccessful Russian expedition against Constantinople.

1044

- Henry II defeats Hungarians.
- Seljuks capture Edessa.

1046
- Anarchy in Rome: three rivals for Papacy: Henry III called in and chooses Clement II, who crowns him Emperor.
- The Norman Robert Guiscard arrived in Italy.

1047
- Battle of Val-ès-Dunes: William of Normandy, aided by King Henry I, defeats rebel nobles.

1049
- Harold Hardrada King of Norway.

1050
- Emund succeeds Anund as King of Sweden.

1051
- Fall of Earl Godwin in England.
- Emperor Henry III subdues Hungary.

1052
- Earl Godwin's triumphant return.
- Edward the Confessor founds Westminster Abbey.

1053
- Battle of Civitella: Robert Guiscard, the Norman, defeats Papal forces; makes agreement with Pope Leo IX.

1054
- Scotland invaded by Siward in support of Malcolm Canmore; Macbeth defeated at Dunsinane.

- Battle of Mortemer: William of Normandy defeats the French royal forces.
- Death of Yaroslav the Great, Grand Duke of Russia.
- Breach between eastern and western churches complete.
- Theodora eastern Empress.

1055
- Seljuk Turks under Togrul Beg occupy Baghdad and restore authority of the Caliph.

1056
- Henry IV German King.
- Michael VI eastern Emperor: last of the Macedonian dynasty.

1057
- Malcolm III (Canmore) King of Scotland.
- Isaac I (Comnenus) eastern Emperor after dethroning Michael VI: first of the Comneni.

1058
- Battle of Varaville: William of Normandy defeats the French royal forces.
- Boleslaus II King of Poland.

1059
- Constantine (X) Ducas eastern Emperor.
- Method of papal election settled.
- Robert Guiscard obtains title of Duke of Apulia and Calabria from Pope Nicholas II, subject to Holy See.

1060
- Norman invasion of Sicily begins under Count Roger: Messina taken.
- Philip I King of France.
- Steinkel succeeds Emund as King of Sweden.

1063
- William of Normandy conquers Maine.

1064
- Seljuks conquer Armenia.
- Ferdinand I takes Coimbra from Portugal.

1065
- Alfonso VI succeeds Ferdinand I as King of Castile and Leon.

1066
- Battle of Stamford Bridge: Norwegian invasion defeated: Harold Hardrada killed.
- Haakon the Red King of Sweden: Olaf Kyrre King of Norway.
- Battle of Hastings: William of Normandy (William the Conqueror) defeats and kills Harold II and Norman conquest of England begins.

1067
- Michael VII and Romanus IV eastern Emperors.

1070
- Malcolm III of Scotland marries Margaret of the English royal family.

- Duchy of Bavaria given to Count Welf.

1071
- Battle of Manzikert: Seljuks under Alp Arslan defeat forces of Romanus IV, who is captured: Asia Minor lost to eastern Empire.
- Normans capture Bari, last Greek possession in Italy.
- Normans take Palermo.
- Norman conquest of England complete.

1072
- Malcolm III of Scotland pays homage to William the Conqueror.

1073
- Hildebrand becomes Pope as Gregory VII.
- Saxon revolt against the Empire.

1074
- Peace of Gerstungen between Henry IV and the Saxons.

1075
- Seljuks capture Jerusalem.
- Henry IV reduces the Saxons.
- Gregory VII issues his decrees on clerical celibacy and investiture of prelates.

1076
- Emperor Henry IV summons a synod of German bishops at Worms, which declares Gregory VII deposed; Gregory VII declares Henry

IV deposed and excommunicated.
- Sancho Ramirez of Aragon becomes King of Navarre.

1077
- Humiliation of Emperor Henry IV by Gregory VII at Canossa in Tuscany; Rudolph of Suabia elected German King; civil war results.
- Ladislas I (St Ladislas) King of Hungary.

1078
- Nicephorus III eastern Emperor, after displacing Michael VII.

1080
- Rudolph of Suabia defeated and killed. Seljuks capture Nicaea.

1081
- Alexius I (Comenus) eastern Emperor; beginning of continuous dynasty of Comneni.
- Battle of Durazzo: Normans under Robert Guiscard defeat Emperor Alexius I.

1083
- Henry IV enters Rome.
- Battle of Larissa: Emperor Alexius I defeats Normans.

1084
- Alfonso VI recovers Toledo from the Moors.
- Carthusians founded at Chartreuse, near Grenoble, by St Bruno.
- Henry IV crowned Emperor in Rome

by anti-pope Clement III; Gregory VII saved by Robert Guiscard; Rome sacked.

1085
- Emperor Alexius I recovers Durazzo from Normans.
- Death of Gregory VII.

1086
- The Domesday Book, a survey of England commissioned by William I, is completed.
- Battle of Zalaca: Alfonso VI defeated by Almoravides under Yusuf.

1087
- William II (Rufus) King of England.

1088
- Bohemia under Vratislav is made a kingdom by the Emperor.

1090
- Count Roger of Sicily takes Malta from the Moors.

1091
- Norman conquest of Sicily completed.
- Emperor Alexius I defeats the Petchenegs.

1092
- William Rufus annexes southern Cumbria to England.
- Seljuk Empire broken up into parts on death of Malik Shah.

1093

- Donald Bane King of Scotland.
- Anselm becomes Archbishop of Canterbury.
- Magnus Barefoot King of Norway.

1094

- Duncan King of Scotland, after overthrowing Donald Bane; overthrown and killed by Donald Bane and Edmund, who share the kingdom between them.
- Rodrigo Diaz, called El Cid, takes Valencia from the Moors.

1095

- Pope Urban II advocates a crusade, to recover the holy places, at Council of Clermont.
- Coloman, great reforming King of Hungary.
- Count Henry of Burgundy marries Theresa of Leon, receiving County of Portugal as dowry; beginning of Portuguese state.

1096

- First Crusade sets out: led by Godfrey of Bouillon, his brother Baldwin, Raymond of Toulouse, Bohemond of Otranto and a Tancred; preceded by popular forces under Peter the Hermit and Walter the Penniless.

1097

- Edgar King of Scotland.
- Frankish County of Edessa founded in Syria.

- Anselm, quarrels with William Rufus, leaves the kingdom.
- Crusaders capture Nicaea and win Battle of Doryloeum.

1098

- Crusaders take Antioch: Principality of Antioch formed under Bohemond.
- Cistercians founded by St Robert at Citeaux, near Dijon.
- Magnus Barefoot invades Orkneys and Sudreys.

1099

- Crusaders take Jerusalem.
- Crusaders win Battle of Ascalon.

1100

- Henry I King of England.
- Baldwin I succeeds his brother Godfrey of Bouillon as ruler of Jerusalem and takes title of King.

1102

- Magnus Barefoot devastates Sudreys and conquers Isle of Man: Scottish King Edgar recognises his claim to the western islands.
- Boleslaus III King of Poland.

1103

- Death of Magnus Barefoot.

1104

- Revolt of Henry, son of Henry IV (afterwards Henry V).
- Alfonso I (the Battler) King of Aragon.
- Crusaders capture Acre.

1106
- Henry V German King.
- Battle of Tinchebrai: Henry I of England defeats Robert, Duke of Normandy and gains the duchy.
- Lothair of Supplinburg appointed Duke of Saxony.

1107
- Alexander I King of Scotland.
- Battle of Durazzo: Emperor Alexius defeats the Normans under Bohemond.
- Council of Troyes.

1108
- Louis VI (the Fat) King of France.

1109
- Crusaders capture Tripoli (in Syria).
  DEATHS
  Anselm of Canterbury, philosopher.

1110
- Crusaders capture Beirut.

1111
- Henry V crowned Emperor at Rome.

1112
- Theresa rules alone over Portugal on death of Count Henry.

1114
- Saxon rebellion against Empire.

1115
- Peter Abelard begins teaching at Paris. St Bernard Abbot of Clairvaux.

- Death of Countess Matilda of Tuscany: her estates left to the papacy.

1116
- Henry V in Italy.

1118
- John II eastern Emperor.
- Alfonso I of Aragon captures Saragossa.

1119
- Order of Templars founded.
- Battle of Brenneville (Brémule): Louis VI defeated by the English under Henry I.

1120
- Knights of St John (or the Hospitallers) acquire a military character.
- Battle of Cutanda: Almoravides defeated by Alfonso I of Aragon.

1122
- Concordat of Worms settles the controversy between Empire and Papacy about investiture of bishops.

1123
- Emperor John II defeats the Serbians and exterminates the Petchenegs.
- First Lateran Council of the Church.
  DEATHS
  Omar Khayyam, Persian poet and scientist.

1124
- David I King of Scotland.

- Emperor John II defeats the Hungarians.
- Boleslaus III of Poland converts the Pomeranians.
- Christians, with help of Venice, captured Tyre.

1125

- Death of Emperor Henry V: end of Franconian line of Emperors.

The Hohenstaufen Emperors

1125

- Lothair of Supplinburg elected German King as Lothair II.

1126

- Emperor John II successful against Seljuks.
- Henry the Proud becomes Duke of Bavaria.
- Pierre de Bruys burned for heresy.

1127

- Death of Guilhem, Count of Poitiers, first of the Troubadour poets.
- Conrad of Hohenstaufen proclaimed German King in rivalry with Lothair II: flees to Italy.
- Roger II, Count of Sicily, becomes also Duke of Apulia.

1128

- Conrad crowned King of Italy.
- Theresa deposed in Portugal: Alfonso I becomes Count.

1130

- Roger II assumes style of King of Sicily as Roger I.

1133

- Lothair II crowned Emperor at Rome. Beginning of alliance between kingdom of Jerusalem and Emir of Damascus.

1134

- Conrad yields to Lothair II.
- Battle of Braga: death of Alfonso I of Aragon and Navarre: Navarre and Aragon again separated.
- Sverker King of Sweden: amalgamates Swedes and Goths.

1135

- Stephen King of England.
- Alfonso VII King of Castile and Leon.

1137

- Emperor John II defeats Armenians.
- Louis VII King of France.
- Queen of Aragon marries Raymond, Count of Barcelona; Aragon greatly extended.
- Henry the Proud of Bavaria obtains Duchy of Saxony.

1138

- Battle of the Standard: defeat of the Scots.
- Conrad III elected German King, never actually crowned Emperor: first of the Hohenstaufen line.
- Normans capture Naples.

1139

- Pope Innocent II compelled to recognise Norman kingdom of Sicily and South Italy.
- Second Lateran Council of the Church.
- Henry the Lion becomes Duke of Saxony.
- Death of Boleslaus III; his Polish realm is divided into four principalities.
- Battle of Ourique: Alfonso I of Portugal defeats the Moors and takes title of King.
- Geoffrey of Monmouth *History of the Britons*.

1140

- Beginning of Guelf versus Ghibelline contest in Germany about this time; later mostly in Italy.
- Vienna becomes capital of Austria.

1142

- Treaty of Frankfort between Conrad and his opponents: Henry the Lion confirmed in Duchy of Saxony and Bavaria given to Henry Jasomirgott, Margrave of Austria.

DEATHS

Peter Abelard, French theologian and philosopher.

1143

- Manuel I becomes eastern Emperor.
- Alfonso I of Portugal recognised by Peace of Zamora as independent of Spain.
- Democratic revolution at Rome against nobles and the pope's temporal power.

DEATHS

William of Malmesbury, English historian.

1144

- Turks recapture Edessa (end of the Christian principality).

1145

- Anold of Brescia at Rome to direct the revolution.

1146

- Second Crusade inspired by St Bernard.

1147

- Emperor Conrad III and Louis VII of France set out on Second Crusade. France governed by Abbé Suger.
- Henry the Lion, Duke of Saxony, conquers lands beyond the Elbe.
- Alfonso I of Portugal captures Lisbon.
- King Roger of Sicily invades Greece.
- Arnold of Brescia supreme in Rome.

1148

- Failure of Second Crusade against Damascus.

1149

- Normans expelled from island of Corfu.

1150
- Carmelites (White Friars) founded about this time at Mount Carmel by Berthold.
- University of Salerno founded, based upon a much older medical school.
- Approximate date of *Nibelungenlied*.
- Albert the Bear becomes Margrave of Brandenburg, the precursor of Prussia.
- Eric IX King of Sweden.

1151
- Henry of Anjou becomes Duke of Normandy.
- Henry the Lion becomes Duke of Bavaria.

1152
- Frederick I (Barbarossa) German King.
- Louis VII divorces Eleanor of Aquitaine; she marries Henry of Anjou and brings Aquitaine to him.

1153
- Malcolm IV King of Scotland.
- Treaty of Wallingford: succession of Henry of Anjou to English throne assured.

1154
- Henry of Anjou becomes King of England as Henry II.
- Frederick Barbarossa invades Italy.
- Nureddin, Turkish ruler of Mosul, captures Damascus.

- William I (the Bad) King of Sicily and Naples.
  DEATHS
  Geoffrey of Monmouth, English churchman and historian.

1155
- Arnold of Brescia hanged and burned at the command of Pope Adrian IV, to whom he had been handed over by the Emperor.
- Frederick Barbarossa crowned Emperor in Rome by the Pope.

1156
- Bavaria confirmed to Henry the Lion; Austria created as a duchy.
- Franche-Comté (County of Burgundy) gained for the Empire by marriage.

1157
- Castile and Leon separated at death of Alfonso VII.
- Waldemar I King of Denmark.

1158
- Bohemia finally made a kingdom under Vladislav II.
- Alfonso VIII King of Castile.
- Second invasion of Italy by Frederick Barbarossa.

1159
- Peter Lombard, noted theologian, Bishop of Paris.
- Milan besieged by Frederick Barbarossa.

1160
- Chrétien de Troyes, French poet, flourishes at this time.
- Frederick Barbarossa excommunicated by Pope Alexander III.

1162
- Frederick Barbarossa destroys Milan.
- Alfonso II King of Aragon.

1163
- Frederick Barbarossa invades Italy for the third time.

1164
- Somerled of the Isles invades southern Scotland: dies at Renfrew.

1165
- William I (the Lyon) King of Scotland.

1166
- Assize of Clarendon.
- Fourth Invasion of Italy by Frederick Barbarossa.
- William II (the Good) King of Sicily and Naples.

1167
- Oxford University founded.
- Lombard League formed against Frederick Barbarossa.
- Frederick Barbarossa enters Rome; forced to withdraw by plague.

1169
- Wendish pirates overthrown in Rügen.

1170
- Murder of Thomas à Becket, Archbishop of Canterbury.
- Waldensians founded in southern France by Peter Waldo.
- Invasion of Ireland by Strongbow.

1171
- Saladin becomes ruler of Egypt, superseding Fatimite dynasty and founding the Ayyubite.
- Henry II lands in Ireland and receives submission of many chiefs.

1173
- Frederick Barbarossa invades Italy for fifth time.
- Bela III made King of Hungary by the Emperor Manuel.

1174
- William the Lyon, King of Scotland, captured by England; released under Treaty of Falaise on doing homage for his kingdom.
- Saladin takes Damascus: Muslim power in Asia again consolidated.

1176
- Battle of Legnano: Lombard League completely defeats Frederick Barbarossa.

1177
- Treaty of Venice: a truce between Frederick Barbarossa, the Pope and the Lombard League.

1179
- Third Lateran Council of the Church.

1180
- Marie de France, French poetess, flourishes at this time.
- War between Emperor Frederick and Henry the Lion; Duchy of Bavaria given to Otto of Wittelsbach.
- Alexius II eastern Emperor.
- Philip II (Augustus) King of France.

Deaths

John of Salisbury, English scholar and cleric.

1182
- Banishment of Jews decreed in France.
- Canute VI King of Denmark.
- Massacre of Latins in Constantinople.

1183
- Peace of Constance: definite agreement between Emperor, Pope and Lombard League.
- Emperor Alexius murdered; Andronicus I becomes eastern Emperor.
- Turkish ruler Saladin takes Aleppo.

1185
- Emperor Andronicus I overthrown: Isaac II (Angelus) eastern Emperor.
- Sancho I follows Alfonso I as King of Portugal.
- William II of Sicily takes Salonica, but fails to keep it.

1186
- Guy of Lusignan King of Jerusalem.

- Saladin completes consolidation of Turkish power.
- Bulgarians recover independence of the Empire.

1187
- Battles of Tiberias and Hattin: Saladin victorious over Christians. Jerusalem taken by Saladin.

1189
- Henry II of England invades France.
- Richard I King of England: independence of Scotland bought back.
- Tancred King of Sicily and Naples.
- Third Crusade begins: joined by Emperor Frederick, Philip Augustus and Richard I. Siege of Acre begins.

1190
- Henry VI German King.
- Order of Teutonic Knights founded.
- Trouvères flourishes at this time at the court of Marie of Champagne.

Deaths

Chrétien de Troyes, French court poet.

1191
- Henry VI crowned Emperor at Rome.
- Henry VI invades southern Italy: fails against Naples.
- Richard I takes Cyprus and sells it to the Templars; resold to Guy of Lusignan, King of Jerusalem.
- Crusaders take Acre: King Philip returned to France.

1192
- Agreement between Richard I and

Saladin. Richard captured by Duke Leopold of Austria on his way home and handed over to the Emperor.

1193
• Death of Saladin.
• Philip Augustus attacks Normandy.

1194
• Richard I released.
• Henry VI conquers kingdom of Sicily and Naples (claimed in right of his wife) and annexes it to Empire.

1195
• Emperor Isaac II deposed: Alexius III eastern Emperor.
• Cyprus becomes a kingdom under Guy of Lusignan's brother Amaury.

1196
• Christians lose Jaffa.
• Peter II becomes King of Aragon.

1197
• Ottacar becomes King of Bohemia.

1198
• Philip Suabia and Otto IV of Brunswick rival Emperors.
• Innocent III becomes Pope.
• Frederick, son of Henry VI, crowned King of Sicily.
  DEATHS
  Averroes, Arabian scholar.

1199
• John King of England.

1200
• Mariner's Compass known in Europe soon after this date.
• Saxo Grammaticus, Danish historian, flourishes at this time.
• Walter Map, English author, flourishes at this time.
• Cambridge University founded.
  DEATHS
  Chu-Hsi, Chinese philosopher.
  Procopius, Byzantine historian.

1201
• Philip of Suabia under Papal ban.
• Fourth Crusade starts from Venice.
• Knights of the Sword founded to convert the Letts.
• Denmark conquers Holstein and Hamburg.
  DEATHS
  Archbishop Absalon, Danish statesman.
  Reynaud de Coucy, French poet.

1202
• Crusaders take Zara on behalf of Venice, at instance of the Doge Henry Dandolo. Waldemar II succeeded Canute VI as King of Denmark: captures Lübeck, Schwerin.

1203
• Wolfram von Eschenbach, German poet, flourishes at this time.
• Emperor Isaac II restored by Crusaders along with Alexius IV.

1204
• France conquers Anjou, Maine, Normandy from England.

- Alexius V is made eastern Emperor, then replaced by Baldwin I of Flanders, the first Latin Emperor: beginning of Latin Empire of Constantinople.
- Crete given to Venice.
  DEATHS
  Moses Maimonides, Jewish religious philosopher.

1205
- Emperor Baldwin defeated and captured by Bulgarians at Adrianople and executed.
- Andrew II King of Hungary.

1206
- Walther von der Vogelweide, German poet, flourishes at this time: the greatest of the Minnesingers.

1208
- Innocent III placed England under interdict.
- Philip of Suabia murdered: Otto IV sole western Emperor.
- Albigensian crusade begins: first crusade against heresy.

1209
- Otto IV in Italy: crowned Emperor at Rome.
- King John excommunicated.
- Cambridge University founded.

1210
- Godfrey of Strassburg, German poet, flourishes at this time.
- University of Paris founded about this time.

- Franciscan Order (Grey Friars) founded by St Francis of Assisi.
- Otto IV is excommunicated by the Pope, but successfully completes conquest of Sicily.
- Genghis Khan, Mongol leader, invades China.

1211
- Alfonso II becomes King of Portugal.

1212
- Battle of Navas de Tolosa: Almohades is defeated heavily by a combination of all the Christian kings of Spain and Portugal under Castile.
- Children's Crusade.
- Frederick II crowned German King.

1213
- Villehardouin, French historian of the Fourth Crusade, dies about this time.
- King John surrenders to Innocent III and does homage for kingdom.
- Battle of Muret: defeat of the Albigenses: Peter II of Aragon killed.
- James the Conqueror becomes King of Aragon.

1214
- Alexander II King of Scotland.
- Battle of Bouvines: Philip of France defeats John of England, Otto IV and others.
  DEATHS
  Alfonso VIII of Castile.

1215
- Dominican Order (Black Friars) founded at Toulouse by St Dominic.
- Magna Carta signed by King John.
- Fourth Lateran Council of the Church abolishes trial by ordeal.

1216
- Louis, heir of French king, called in by English barons against John. Death of John: Henry III King of England.

1217
- Fair of Lincoln: Prince Louis of France defeated.
- Ferdinand III (the Saint) King of Castile.
- Crusade led by Andrew of Hungary.
- Haakon IV King of Norway.

1218
- Death of Otto IV; Frederick I western Emperor.
- Waldemar II of Denmark captures Reval.
- Ivan Asen II Bulgarian King: conquers Albania, Epirus, Macedonia and Thrace; capital, Tirnovo.

1219
- Damietta taken by John de Brienne, King of Jerusalem.
- Genghis Khan's invasion.

1220
- Frederick II crowned Emperor at Rome.
- Approximate date of the *Owl and Nightingale* and of the *Queste del St Graal*.
  DEATHS
  Hartmann von der Aue, German poet.
  Saxo Grammaticus, Danish historian.

1221
- Dominicans settle at Oxford.
- Crusaders abandon Damietta.

1222
- Golden Bull, the Great Charter of Hungary.

1223
- Louis VIII King of France.
- Sancho II King of Portugal.
  DEATHS
  Giraldus Cambrensis, Welsh writer.

1224
- Franciscans settle at Oxford and Cambridge.
- Mongols advance into Russia; Russians defeated in Battle of Kalka.

1225
- English take Gascony.
- Frederick II assumes the title of King of Jerusalem in right of his wife.

1226
- Lombard League renewed against Frederick II.
- Louis IX (St Louis) King of France.
- Waldemar II of Denmark compelled to surrender most of Danish conquests.

DEATHS
Francis of Assissi

1227
- Battle of Bornhöved: Frederick II defeats Denmark.
- Ottoman Turks settle in Angora under Ertoghrul.
- Frederick II sets out on a crusade, then excommunicated.

DEATHS
Genghis Khan.

1228
- Frederick II sets out on Fifth Crusade.
- French King gives the County of Venaissin, near Avignon, to the Papacy.

1229
- Frederick II procures cession of Jerusalem to the Christians; crowned King of Jerusalem.
- James of Aragon conquers the Balearic Islands.
- Papal victory over Frederick II's troops in Italy.
- Treaty of Meaux: submission of the County of Toulouse and the Albigensians.

1230
- Franciscans in Paris.
- Teutonic Knights begins to settle in Prussia.
- Wenceslas I King of Bohemia.
- Final Union of Castile and Leon.

1231
- Privilege of Worms: German princes recognised by Emperor as virtually independent.

1232
- Pope Gregory IX establishes the monastic inquisition.

1235
- War against Lombard League.
- Bela IV King of Hungary.

1236
- Cordova conquered by the Christians.

1237
- Battle of Cortenuova: Lombard League defeated by Frederick II.
- Ryazan sacked by Mongols under Batu Khan.

1238
- James of Aragon conquers Valencia.
- The Mongols settle in Russia (The Golden Horde), with capital at Sarai; Kiev taken.

1239
- Frederick II excommunicated.

1240
- Mendovg ruler of Lithuania.

1241
- Invasion of Hungary and Poland by Batu Khan: Silesian princes defeated in Battle of Liegnitz; Pesth captured.

1242
- Mongols defeated at Olmütz and Neustadt.
- Battles of Taillebourg and Saintes: Louis IX defeats Henry III of England.

1244
- End of Albigensian Persecution.
- Christians finally lose Jerusalem.

1245
- First Church Council of Lyons.
- Frederick II excommunicated and declared deposed by Innocent IV.
  DEATHS
  Alexander of Hales, philosopher and theologian.

1246
- Provence joined to France.
- Henry Raspe, Landgrave of Thuringia, elected German King at the instigation of the Pope.

1247
- Frederick II besieges Parma (defeated 1248).
- Death of Henry Raspe; William II, Count of Holland, elected German King by Papal party.

1248
- Rhodes taken by Genoa.
- Earl Birger virtual ruler of Sweden; Stockholm founded.
- St Louis started Sixth Crusade.
- Christians conquer Seville.
- Alfonso III succeeds Sancho II of Portugal.

1249
- Alexander III King of Scotland.
- St Louis of France takes Damietta; then defeated and captured at Mansourah; released on giving up Damietta.

1250
- Conrad IV German King.
- Sorbonne founded in Paris.
- Beginning of Mameluke rule in Egypt.
- Manfred, natural son of Frederick II, regent of Naples and Sicily.

1251
- Emperor Conrad IV in Italy.
- Conrad and Manfred take Capua and Naples.
- Alfonso X King of Castile.

1252
- Innocent IV approves torture for the discovery of heresy.

1253
- Struggle between Venice and Genoa begins. Ottacar II King of Bohemia.
  DEATHS
  Robert Grosseteste, Bishop of Lincoln.

1254
- Death of Conrad IV; son Conradin proclaimed King of Sicily.
- St Louis returns to France.

1255
- League of Rhenish towns formed, supported by William of Holland.

- Bavaria divided into Upper and Lower.

1256
- St Bonaventura becomes general of the Franciscans.
- Death of William of Holland: double election to Empire of Richard of Cornwall and Alfonso X of Castile: the period 1256-73 known as the Interregnum in the history of the Empire.
- First form of Hanseatic League.

1258
- Provisions of Oxford forced by barons on King Henry III.
- Manfred crowned King of Sicily.
- Mongols capture Baghdad and destroy the Abbasside Caliphate.

1259
- Treaty of Paris: peace between Louis IX and Henry III.
- Death of Ezzelino de Romano, tyrant who supported Frederick II in Italy.
- Second Tatar raid on Poland.
  DEATHS
  Matthew Paris, English monk and historian.

1260
- Battle of Montaperti: Florentine Guelfs defeated by Ghibellines of Sienna; Ghibellines supreme in Florence.
- Mongols take Damascus.
- Battle of Kressenbrunn: Ottacar II of

Bohemia defeats Bela, King of Hungary and obtains Carinthia, Istria.

1261
- Tatar invasion of Hungary repelled by Bela IV.
- Latin Empire of Constantinople overthrown: Michael VIII becomes eastern Emperor: beginning of Palaeologian dynasty.
- Charles of Anjou accepts the crown of Sicily from the Pope.

1262
- First Visconti lord of Milan.

1263
- Norwegian disaster at Largs: Death of Haakon IV; succeeded by Magnus VI.
- Portugal reaches present limits and attains complete independence.

1264
- Mise of Amiens: Louis IX arbitrates between Henry III and the English barons, deciding in favour of former.
- Battle of Lewes: Henry III defeated by Simon de Montfort.
- Battle of Trapani: Venetian victory over Genoese fleet.

1265
- Burgesses first called to English parliament by Simon de Montfort.
- Battle of Evesham: Simon de Montfort defeated and killed by the royal army under Prince Edward.

- Christians conquer Murcia; only
  Granada left to Moors in Spain.

1266
- Hebrides ceded by Norway to Scotland.
- Battle of Benevento: defeat and death
  of Manfred; Charles of Anjou be
  comes master of Sicily and Naples.
- Ghibellines expelled from Florence.

1268
- Christians lose Antioch.
- Battle of Tagliacozzo: Conradin defeated by Charles of Anjou and after
  wards executed; end of Hohenstaufen line.

THE AGE OF DANTE

1270
- St Louis on Eighth Crusade: dies at
  Tunis; Philip III (the Bold) King of
  France.
- Stephen V King of Hungary.

1271
- Prince Edward of England goes to
  Acre (returned in 1272).
- Marco Polo, Venetian traveller, sets
  out on his journey to China.

1272
- Edward I King of England.
- Ladislas IV King of Hungary.

1273
- Rudolph of Hapsburg elected German King.

1274
- Dominicans settle at Cambridge.
- Second Church Council of Lyons
  effects a temporary union of the
  eastern and western Churches.
  DEATHS
  St Thomas Aquinas, scholastic the-
  ologian.

1275
- Magnus Ladulas King of Sweden.

1276
- Peter III King of Aragon.

1277
- Edward I invades Wales.

1278
- Battle of Marchfield, (Dürnkrut):
  Ottacar II of Bohemia killed; Czech
  Empire dismembered; Wenceslas II
  King of Bohemia.
  DEATHS
  Nicola Pisano, Italian sculptor.

1279
- Statute of Mortmain.
- Diniz becomes King of Portugal.

1280
- Trouvère poetry comes to an end.
- Eric II becomes King of Norway.
  DEATHS
  Albertus Magnus, German scholas-
  tic philosopher.

1282
- England conquers Wales.

- Andronicus II eastern Emperor.
- Sicilian Vespers: massacre of French in Sicily; Sicily separated from Kingdom of Naples and obtained by King of Aragon.
- Hapsburgs established in the Duchy of Austria.

1283
- Prussia subjugated by Teutonic Knights.
  DEATHS
  Saadi, Persian poet.

1284
- Battle of Meloria: Genoa crushes Pisa.
- Sancho IV King of Castile.
- Queen of Navarre marries the eldest son of Philip III of France: Navarre then joined to France till 1328.

1285
- Statute of Winchester and Second Statute of Westminster.
- Philip IV (the Fair) King of France.
- Charles II King of Naples; Alfonso III King of Aragon.

1286
- Margaret, Maid of Norway, Queen of Scotland.

1288
- Pope declares a crusade against Ladislas IV of Hungary.
- Osman I succeeds Ertoghrul as leader of Ottoman Turks.

1289
- Christians lose Tripoli.

1290
- Treaty of Brigham between Scotland and Edward I. Death of the Maid of Norway.
- Statue to Quia Emptores.
- Expulsion of Jews from England.
- Ladislas IV of Hungary murdered.

1291
- Fall of Acre: end of Christian power in Syria and Palestine.
- Death of Emperor Rudolph of Hapsburg.
- Everlasting League of Uri, Schwyz and Unterwalden: beginning of the Swiss Republic.
- James II King of Aragon.

1292
- John Baliol made King of Scotland by Edward I.
- Adolf of Nassau elected German King.

1294
- Boniface VIII becomes Pope.
- Death of Guiraut Riquier, last of the Troubadours.
- Guienne seized by France.
- Venetian fleet defeated by Genoa.
- The King of Aragon abandons Sicily, but Sicily under Frederick III refuses to be joined to Naples.
  DEATHS
  Roger Bacon, English philosopher and scientist.

Kublai Khan, founder of Mongol dynasty in China.

1295
- Model English Parliament summoned by Edward I, first representative parliament.
- Beginning of Franco-Scottish Alliance.

1296
- Bull of Clericis Laicos issued by Boniface VIII: extravagant Papal claims.
- John Baliol renounces the kingdom of Scotland.
- Ferdinand IV King of Castile.

1297
- Battle of Stirling: victory of Sir William Wallace over English.

1298
- Battle of Falkirk: Edward I defeats Wallace.
- Adolf of Nassau defeated and killed at Gelheim by Albert I, Duke of Austria, who had been elected German king.

1299
- Battle of Curzola: Venice defeated by Genoa.
- Treaty between Venice and the Turks.
- Haakon V King of Norway.

1300
- Wenceslas II of Bohemia becomes

King of Poland, later also of Hungary.
- Boniface VIII proclaims a Jubilee.

1301
- Albert of Austria ravages the Palatinate and Mainz.
- Charles of Valois overthrows the Bianchi (White) Guelfs in Florence and drives Dante into exile.

1302
- End of the War of the Sicilian Vespers; Frederick III recognised as King of Sicily by the Peace of Caltabellotta.
- French States-General meet for the first time.
- Battle of Courtrai: Flemish victory over France.
DEATHS
Cimabue, Italian painter.

1303
- Edward I again conquers Scotland.
DEATHS
Boniface VIII.

1305
- Betrayal and execution of Sir William Wallace.
- Wenceslas III King of Bohemia.

1306
- Robert the Bruce crowned King of Scotland.
- Jews expelled from France.
- Wenceslas III of Bohemia murdered: end of dynasty.

- Vladislas I becomes Duke of Great Poland: reunites Great and Little Poland.

1307
- Edward II King of England.
- Philip IV of France seizes the property of the Knights Templars.

1308
- Murder of Albert of Austria: Henry VII (of Luxemburg) elected German King. Henry VII conquers Bohemia (1308-10).

DEATHS

Duns Scotus, scholastic philosopher and theologian.

1309
- Robert King of Naples.
- Clement V begins residence in Avignon: beginning of Babylonish Captivity of Popes (till 1377).

1310
- Henry VII goes to Italy.
- Arpad dynasty in Hungary succeeded by dynasty of Anjou in person of Charles I.
- Knights of St John or Hospitallers seize Rhodes.
- John of Luxemburg, son of Henry VII, elected King of Bohemia.

1311
- Church Council of Vienna.

DEATHS

Arnold of Villanova, Italian physician and alchemist.

1312
- Henry VII crowned Emperor at Rome.
- Abolition of Templars finally decreed by Pope Clement V, under pressure from Philip IV of France.
- France obtains the Lyonnais.
- Piers Gaveston, favourite of Edward II, is murdered near Warwick Castle.

1313
- Alfonso XI becomes King of Castile.

1314
- Louis X King of France.
- Battle of Bannockburn: Scottish independence asserted by Robert the Bruce.
- Louis IV of Bavaria and Frederick Duke of Austria rival claimants of the Empire.

1315
- Battle of Morgarten: a great Swiss victory over Leopold, Duke of Austria.
- Gedymin ruler of Lithuania: annexes Kiev, Chernigov, etc.

1316
- Edward Bruce King of Ireland.
- Philip V (the Tall) King of France.

1318
- Battle of Dundalk: Edward Bruce defeated and killed.
- Truce between Swiss and Hapsburgs.

1319
- First Union of Sweden and Norway: Magnus VII common King.

1320
- End of War between France and Flanders.
- Vladislas I revives royal dynasty in Poland.

1321
- Death of Dante Alighieri, Italian poet.

1322
- Battle of Mühldorf: Frederick of Austria defeated and taken prisoner by Louis of Bavaria.
- Battle of Boroughbridge; Edward II defeats his kinsman Thomas of Lancaster.
- Charles IV (the Fair) King of France.

1323
- James I of Aragon conquers Sardinia from the Pisans.
- Emperor Louis IV, deposed and excommunicated by John XXII, appeals to a Council.

1324
- Death of Marco Polo, Venetian traveller.

1325
- Frederick of Austria relinquishes claim to Empire.
- Alfonso IV King of Portugal.

1326
- First Scottish Parliament (at Cambuskenneth).
- Gunpowder known by this date.
- Scots College founded in Paris.
- Brussa taken by the Ottoman Turks and becomes their capital.
- Orkhan succeeds Osman as leader of the Ottoman Turks.

1327
- Edward II agrees to abdicate; Edward III King of England. Ex-King Edward II then murdered at Berkeley Castle.
- Orkhan takes Nicomedia.
- Alfonso IV King of Aragon.
  DEATHS
  Eckhart, German mystic.

1328
- Treaty of Northampton: England recognises the complete independence of Scotland.
- Andronicus III eastern Emperor.
- Philip VI King of France: beginning of Valois dynasty: Navarre separated.
- Battle of Cassel: Flemish insurgents under Jacob van Artevelde defeated by Philip VI.
- Louis IV is crowned Emperor at Rome and deposes Pope John XXII.

1329
- David II King of Scotland.
- Battle of Pelekanon: Andronicus III defeated by Ottoman Turks.

1330

- Ottoman Turks take Nicaea: Janissaries organised.
- Battle of Kustendil: Bulgaria conquered by Serbia.
- Walachia begins to gain independence from Hungary.

1331

- King John of Bohemia in Italy.

1332

- Battle of Dupplin Moor: Scottish regent, Earl of Mar, killed. Edward Baliol crowned King of Scotland.
- Lucerne joins the Swiss League.
- Battle of Plowce: Vladislas I defeats the Teutonic Knights.

1333

- Edward Baliol again invades Scotland.
- Battle of Halidon Hill: Scots defeated by Edward III.
- Casimir III (the Great) King of Poland: acquires Galicia.

1335

- Edward III invades Scotland.
- Internal free trade established in England.
- Zurich joins the Swiss League.

1336

- Peter IV King of Aragon.

1337

- Peter II King of Sicily.
- Jacob van Artevelde forms a league

of Flemish cities with Ghent as leader; they join England in the war against France.

DEATHS

Giotto, Italian painter.

THE HUNDRED YEARS' WAR

1338

- Hundred Years' War between France and England begins.

1339

- Edward Baliol driven from Scotland.
- Battle of Laupen: Nobels overthrown in Berne.

1340

- Battle of Sluys: English naval victory over France.
- Edward III claims throne of France.
- Emperor Louis IV reunites Bavaria under him.
- Battle of Rio Salado: Spanish and Portuguese repel an African invasion.
- Waldemar IV King of Denmark.

1341

- John V eastern Emperor.

1342

- Louis the Great King of Hungary.
- Duke of Athens appointed head of Florentine state (expelled 1343).

1343

- Joanna I, wife of Andrew of Hungary, becomes Queen of Naples.

- Charles I (the Bad) King of Navarre.
- Haakon VI King of Norway.

1344
- Suabian League of cities formed.

1345
- Order of the Garter founded about this date.
- Andrew of Hungary assassinated.
- Jacob van Arteveide assassinated.
- Emperor Louis takes possession of Holland, etc.

1346
- Battle of Neville's Cross: Scots defeated and David II captured.
- Battle of Crécy: English victory over French: King John of Bohemia killed.
- Battle of Zara: Venetians defeat Hungarians.
- Charles King of Bohemia.

1347
- English take Calais.
- John VI (Cantacuzenus) becomes co-Emperor in the East.
- Cola di Rienzi becomes Tribune in Rome.
- Corsica transferred from Pisa to Genoa.

1348
- Charles IV (of Bohemia) German King.
- Great Plague in Italy.
- Battle of Epila: Peter IV of Aragon

establishes his power over the nobles.

1349
- Black Death in England.
- Bavaria again divided.
- Persecution of Jews in Germany.
- Fall of Rienzi.

DEATHS
William of Occam, nominalist philosopher.

1350
- The Black Death in Scotland.
- Dafydd ap Gwilym, greatest of Welsh poets, flourishes at this time.
- John King of France.
- Peter the Cruel King of Castile.
- Boccaccio *Decameron*.

1351
- Statute of Labourers in England attempts to regulate wages.
- Statute of Provisors in England.
- Zurich joins the Swiss League.

1352
- Glarus and Zug join the Swiss League.

1353
- Statute of Praemunire places restraints on Papal authority in England.
- Berne joins the Swiss League.
- Battle of the Bosphorus: Venice defeated by Genoa.

1354
- New League of the Rhine.

- Rienzi killed in a riot.

1355

- Charles IV crowned Emperor in Rome.
- Death of Stephen Dushan, King of the Serbians: break-up of Serbian Empire.
- Conspiracy of Marino Faliero in Venice foiled.

1356

- Battle of Poiters: English victory over France won by the Black Prince; King John of France a prisoner.
- The Burnt Candlemass: Edward III burns every town and village in Lothian, Scotland.
- The Golden Bull settles the mode of electing the Holy Roman Emperor.
- War between Venice and Hungary.

1357

- Pedro I King of Portugal.

1358

- Turks under Suleiman take Gallipoli.
- Peace between Hapsburgs and the Swiss League.
- Treaty of Zara: peace between Venice and Hungary: Venice makes large cessions.
- Revolution in Paris: Étienne Marcel, provost of Paris merchants, leads a reform movement.
- Battle of Sapienza: Venice defeated by Genoa.
- Jacquerie or Peasants' Revolt in France.

1359

- Amurath (Murad) I becomes Turkish Sultan.
- Turks cross the Hellespont.

1360

- Peace of Bretigny between England and France.
- Moldavia independent of Hungary by this date.

1361

- Battle of Adrianople: Turks defeat the Emperor and capture the town.
- Waldemar IV of Denmark recovers Scania and conquers Gotland.
- Duchy of Burgundy expires with Philip de Rouvre.

1362

- Turks conquer Philippopolis.
- English becomes language of Parliament and the Law Courts in England.
- *Piers Plowman*, English poem, attributed to William Langland.

1363

- Timour (Tamerlane), the Tatar leader, begins conquests in Central Asia.
- The King of France creates his son Philip the Bold Duke of Burgundy.

DEATHS

Ranulf Higden, English chronicler.

1364

- Charles V King of France.
- Crete revolts against Venice.

1365

- Peter I of Cyprus takes Alexandria, Tripoli, etc, but does not retain his conquests.
- Albert of Mecklenburg supersedes Magnus as King of Sweden.

1366

- Statue of Kilkenny: English attempt to suppress Irish nationality in Leinster.
- Peter the Cruel expelled from Castile by his brother Henry of Trastamara.
- Amadeus VI of Savoy takes Gallipoli from the Turks and Varna from the Bulgarians.

1367

- Battle of Navarete (Najara): Henry of Trastamara defeated and Peter the Cruel restored to Castilian throne with the aid of the Black Prince.
- Ferdinand makes Lisbon capital of Portugal.
- Adrianople becomes Turkish capital.

1368

- Battle of Montiel: death of Peter the Cruel; succeeded by Henry of Trastamara.

DEATHS

Orcagna, Italian painter, sculptor and architect.

1369

- Venetians repel Hungarian invasion.
- Charles V declares war against England.
- Flanders passes by marriage to the Duchy of Burgundy.

1370

- Limoges sacked.
- Louis of Hungary elected King of Poland.

1371

- Robert II first Stewart King of Scotland.
- Turks defeat Louis of Hungary.

1373

- Charles IV gains Brandenburg and Lower Lusatia by treaty.
- Bertrand du Guesclin reduces Brittany.

1374

- Death of Petrarch, Italian poet and pioneer of humanism.

1375

- Waldemar IV of Denmark succeeded by Margaret.

DEATHS

Giovanni Boccaccio, Italian writer.

1376

- *The Bruce* composed by Scottish poet John Barbour.

1377

- King Edward III dies; Richard II King of England: effective power lies with the royal council.
- John Wycliffe, English theologian and religious reformer, summoned before the Bishop of London.
- Pope Gregory XI returns to Rome.

1378
- Great Schism in the Papacy begins: Urban VI and Clement VII both elected and strongly supported.
- Wencelsas IV King of Bohemia.
- War of Chioggia between Venice and Genoa begins.

1379
- Battle of Pola: Venice defeated by Genoa. Chioggia taken.
- John I King of Castile.

1380
- Gerhard Groot founds Brethren of the Common Life at Deventer.
- John Wycliffe begins to attack Roman Catholic doctrine of transubstantiation.
- Venice wins Chioggia back and captures Genoese fleet.
- Charles VI King of France.
- Battle of Kulikovo: Russian victory over Golden Horde under Dimitri Donskoi of Moscow.

1381
- First English Navigation Act.
- Peasants' Revolt in England under Wat Tyler.
- Charles of Durazzo conquers Naples: Queen Joanna murdered in 1382.
- League of German Free Cities.
- End of the war between Venice and Genoa.
- Treaty of Turin between Venice and Hungary: Venice cedes Dalmatia.

1382
- Earthquake Council in London condemns Wycliffe.
- Death of Louis the Great of Hungary; period of disorder follows.
- Battle of Roosebeke: Philip van Artevelde and the Flemish insurgents defeated by the French: Philip killed.
- Moscow taken by Mongols.
- Maillotin Revolt in Paris, etc.

1384
- Union of Heidelberg: peace between Count of Würtemberg and the Suabian League.

  DEATHS

  John Wycliffe, English religious reformer.

1385
- Gian Galeazzo Visconti sole ruler of Milan.
- Battle of Aljubarrota: Portuguese victory over Castilians.
- John I King of Portugal.

1386
- Battle of Sempach: Swiss victory over Austria: Leopold of Austria killed.
- Charles VI of France declares war against England.
- Death of Charles III of Naples: anarchy follows.
- Vladislas II becomes both King of Poland and Grand Duke of Lithuania: beginning of Jagellon dynasty.

- Alliance between England and Portugal confirmed by Treaty of Windsor.

1387
- English poet Geoffrey Chaucer begins *The Canterbury Tales*.
- John I King of Aragon.
- Charles III (the Noble) King of Navarre.
- Sigismund King of Hungary.

1388
- Battle of Otterburn: Scottish victory over English under Sir Henry Percy (Hotspur).
- Battle of Naefels: victory of Swiss canton Glarus over Austrians.
- Count of Würtemberg defeats the Suabian League.
- Rhenish Towns defeated at Worms by Elector Palatine Rupert.

1389
- Battle of Kossovo: Serbians overthrown by Turks; Amurath I killed; Bajazet I succeeds him and obtains from the Caliph the title of Sultan.

1390
- Robert III King of Scotland; Duke of Albany Regent.
- Henry III King of Castile.

1391
- Manuel II eastern Emperor.
- Massacre of Jews in Spain.

1393
- Great Statute of Praemunire in England.
- Turks capture Philadelphia, in Asia Minor; also Tirnovo, in Bulgaria.

1394
- Hapsburgs recognise the independence of the Swiss League.

1395
- Gian Galeazzo Visconti obtains from Emperor title of Duke of Milan.
- Martin I King of Aragon.
- Timour conquers the Kipchaks on the Volga.
- Turks, after taking Salonica and Larissa, besiege Constantinople.

1396
- Turkish conquest of Bulgaria completed.
- Fight at the North Inch between the Clans Chattan and Kay.
- Battle of Nicopolis: Crusading army of Hungarians, etc, under King Sigismund, defeated by Turks.

1397
- Union of Kalmar between Norway, Sweden and Denmark: Eric VII (XIII of Sweden) recognised as King.

1398
- Timour conquers Northern India.
- Rome submits to complete authority of the Pope, who is supported by Ladislas, King of Naples.

1399
- Richard II forced to abdicate: Henry IV chosen King of England.

1400
- Revolt of Owen Glendower in Wales.
- Wenceslas of Bavaria is deposed: Rupert, Elector Palatine, elected German King.
  DEATHS
  Geoffrey Chaucer, English poet.

1401
- William Sawtrey burned in England for heresy under a new statute against heretics.
- Rupert fails in Italy.
- Compact of Vilna: partial separation of Poland and Lithuania.

1402
- Battle of Homildon Hill: Scots defeated by English under Sir Henry Percy.
- Battle of Angora: Timour defeats Bajazet I and makes him prisoner; Turkish pressure on the Empire relieved.

1403
- Revolt of the Percy family in England; defeated in battle at Shrewsbury.

1404
- John the Fearless becomes Duke of Burgundy.

1405
- Death of Timour; his Empire falls apart.

1406
- James I of Scotland captured by England; proclaimed King.
- John II King of Castile.

1407
- Duke of Orleans murdered by a Burgundian.
- Rome occupied by Ladislas of Naples.
  DEATHS
  John Gower, English poet.

1409
- Sicily joined to Aragon by marriage.
- Council at Pisa: both Popes deposed; Alexander V elected.

1410
- Battle of Tannenberg: Teutonic Knights overthrown by Poland and Lithuania.
- Ferdinand the Catholic King of Aragon.
  DEATHS
  Jean Froissart, French historian.

1411
- Battle of Harlaw: Scottish Highlanders under Donald, Lord of the Isles, defeated by a Lowland force under the Earl of Mar.
- Sigismund of Hungary elected German King.
- Battle of Rocca Secca: Louis of Anjou defeats Ladislas of Naples.

1412
- Treaty between Hapsburgs and Swiss League renewed.

- Jan Hus of Bohemia excommunicated.
- Battle of St Cloud: Burgundian party in France defeat Armagnacs (followers of Orleans); Treaty of Auxerre concluded.

1417
- Sir John Oldcastle, the Lollard leader, is burnt for heresy.
- Henry V captures Caen.
- End of Papal Schism: Martin V sole Pope.

1413
- Ladislas of Naples sacks Rome.
- Henry V King of England.
- Mohammed I Turkish Sultan.

1418
- End of Council of Constance, without touching the reform question.
- Burgundians capture Paris.

1414
- St Andrews University founded in Scotland.
- Council of Constance met.
- Treaty of Arras between Burgundians and Armagnacs.

1419
- Henry V captures Rouen.
- War between Empire and Bohemia begins.
- Duke of Burgundy murdered at Montereau; Philip the Good succeeds. Burgundians join the English.
- Sigismund King of Bohemia, but not accepted by the people.

1415
- Battle of Agincourt: Henry V defeats French.
- Council of Constance condemns Jan Hus, who is burned; Bohemian nobles protest.
- Count Frederick of Hohenzollern obtains Brandenburg and title of Elector.
- Portugal takes Ceuta.

1420
- Treaty of Troyes: Henry V of England recognised as heir to crown of France.
- Battle of Vysehrad: Bohemians defeat Sigismund.

1421
- Battle of Baugé: Scottish victory over English.
- Amurath II Turkish Sultan.
- Sigismund declared deposed in Bohemia.

1416
- Jerome of Prague, a follower of Huss, burned.
- Alfonso V (the Magnanimous) King of Aragon: also King of Sicily and Naples.

DEATHS
Owen Glendower, Welsh rebel.

1422
- Henry VI King of England on death of Henry V and of France on death

of Charles VI; Charles VII in France called 'King of Bourges'.
- Battle of Deutschbrod: Bohemian victory over Sigismund.

1423
- Sigismund crowned Emperor at Rome.
- *The King is Quair* by James I of Scotland.
- Battle of Crevant: French defeated by English.
- Francesco Foscari Doge of Venice.

1424
- James I of Scotland set free.
- Battle of Verneuil: Duke of Bedford defeats the French.
- Treaty between Venice and Florence against Milan.

1425
- John VII eastern Emperor.

1426
- Dom Henrique of Portugal (Prince Henry the Navigator) charts the west coast of Africa and engages in slave trade.
- Battle of Aussig: Bohemian victory over the Empire.
  DEATHS
  Hubert van Eyck, Flemish painter.

1427
- Bohemians under Procopius completely defeat the Empire: Germany invaded.

1428
- Siege of Orleans by English.
- Turks take Salonica.

1429
- Siege of Orleans raised by Joan of Arc.
- Charles VII crowned at Rheims.
  DEATHS
  Masaccio, Italian painter.

1431
- François Villon, French poet, born.
- Joan of Arc burned by English at Rouen.
- Battle of Taus: Bohemian victory over Empire.
- Council of Basle begins.

1432
- Carmagnola executed by Venetians for treason in the war against Milan.

1433
- Sigismund crowned Emperor at Rome.

1434
- Battle of Lipan: conflict between different Hussite parties in Bohemia; Procopius killed.
- Cosimo de' Medici in power in Florence.
  DEATHS
  Vladislav II of Poland.

1435
- Treaty of Arras between Burgundy and Charles VII.

- Alfonso the Magnanimous reunites the Two Sicilies.

1436
- Charles VII regains Paris.
- Council of Basle practically concedes the demands of the Bohemians.
- Sigismund recognised as King of Bohemia.
- Charles VIII elected King of Sweden.

1437
- James II King of Scotland.
- Council of Basle transferred by Pope to Ferrara.

1438
- Albert V of Austria becomes King of Hungary and Bohemia; elected also German King as Albert II.
- Pragmatic Sanction of Bourges: Charles VII of France establishes independence of French Church.
- Amurath II invades Hungary; opposed by John Huniades.
- Alfonso V King of Portugal.

1439
- Formal union of Greek and Latin Churches arranged by Council of Basle sitting in Florence.
- Pragmatic Sanction of Mainz.
- Eric VII of Denmark is deposed, Christopher III of Bavaria elected King.

1440
- Bruges crushed by Duke Philip.
- Frederick III German King.

- Praguerie revolt in France: nobles against King.
- The Azores discovered.
- Ladislas V (Postumus) King of Bohemia and Hungary; Vladislas III of Poland a rival in Hungary.
- Invention of Printing with movable types by Johan Gutenberg of Mainz.
- Frederick II Elector of Brandenburg.
  DEATHS
  Jan van Eyck, Flemish painter.

1441
- Thomas à Kempis *De Imitatione Christi* about this date.

1443
- Turks defeated by Albanians under Scanderbeg.
- Battle of Nissa: Turks defeated by John Huniades.

1444
- Peace of Szegedin: Amurath II surrenders control of Serbia, Walachia and Bosnia to Hungary.
- Battle of Varna: Turkish victory over Hungary; King Vladislas III killed.

1446
- Death of Brunelleschi, Italian pioneer of Renaissance architecture.

1447
- Amurath II defeated by Scanderbeg.
- Casimir IV King of Poland and Grand Duke of Lithuania.

1448
- Constantine XI eastern Emperor.
- French regain Anjou and Maine.
- End of the Union of Kalmar: Christian I King of Denmark.
- Concordat of Vienna between the Emperor Frederick III and the Pope: obedience of German people to Rome pledged.
- Battle of Kossovo: John Huniades defeated by the Turks.

1449
- End of the Council of Basle.

1450
- Rebellion of Jack Cade in England.
- Francesco Sforza becomes Duke of Milan.
- Battle of Formigny: English defeated by French: Normandy recovered.
- Papal Jubilee.

1451
- Glasgow University founded.
- French recover Guienne.
- Mohammed II Turkish Sultan.

1452
- Frederick III crowned Emperor by Pope Nicholas V in Rome: the last coronation of an Emperor at Rome.
- James II of Scotland murders Sir William Douglas.

1453
- Turks capture Constantinople: end of the Easter or Byzantine Empire.
- Austria created an Archduchy.

- Ladislas V of Hungary becomes King of Bohemia also.
- Battle of Castillon: English defeated: end of the Hundred Years' War.

THE BEGINNING OF MODERN EUROPE

1454
- Peace of Lodi between Venice and Milan.
- First known document printed from movable types: at Mainz.
- Prussia incorporated in Poland.
- Henry IV King of Castile.

1455
- Wars of the Roses begin in England: first Battle of St Albans: Yorkist victory.
- House of Douglas overthrown in Scotland.

  DEATHS
  Fra Angelico, Italian religious painter.
  Lorenzo Ghiberti, Italian sculptor.

1456
- Turkish attack on Belgrade repelled by John Huniades.

1457
- End of Foscari's dogeship: Venice begins to decline.
- Death of Ladislas V of Hungary and Bohemia.

1458
- Matthias Corvinus, son of John Huniades, elected King of Hungary;

George Podiebrad elected King of Bohemia.
- Death of Alfonso the Magnanimous: Two Sicilies again separated.
- John II King of Aragon. Ferdinand I King of Naples.

1459
- Turks conquer Serbia.

1460
- William Dunbar, Scottish poet, born.
- James III King of Scotland.
- Battle of Wakefield: Lancastrian victory.
- Turks conquers the Morea.
- Denmark obtains Schleswig and Holstein.

1461
- Empire of Trebizond destroyed by Turks.
- Second Battle of St Albans: Lancastrian victory.
- Battle of Mortimer's Cross: Yorkist victory.
- Battle of Towton: Yorkist victory makes Edward IV King of England.
- Louis XI King of France.
- Ivan III (the Great) ruler of Moscow.
- Pragmatic Sanction of Bourges revoked.

1462
- Battle of Puck: Polish victory; Prussia conquered.

1463
- War begins between Venice and the Turks.
- Turks acknowledge Scanderbeg as ruler of Albania.

1464
- Turks conquer Bosnia.
- Death of Cosimo de' Medici of Florence: succeeded by his son Piero.
  DEATHS
  Roger van der Weyden, Flemish painter.

1465
- League of Public Welfare formed by French nobles against Louis XI.

1466
- Treaty of Thorn between Poland and the Teutonic Knights; Poland dominant and master of Prussia.
  DEATHS
  Donatello, Italian sculptor.

1467
- Turks conquer Herzegovina.
- Charles the Bold Duke of Burgundy.

1468
- Orkney Islands annexed to Scotland.
- War declared against Bohemia by Hungary.

1469
- Shetland Islands annexed to Scotland.
- Matthias Corvinus, King of Hunga-

ry, crowned King of Bohemia by Papal legate.
- Lorenzo de' Medici begins rule in Florence along with his brother Giuliano.
- Marriage of Ferdinand of Aragon and Isabella of Castile.

1470
- Truce between Hungary and Bohemia.
- Turks take Negropont.
- Three northern kingdoms reunited under Christian I of Denmark.

1471
- Battle of Barnet: Yorkist victory.
- Battle of Tewkesbury: Yorkist victory.
- Death of George Podiebrad of Bohemia; Prince Vladislav of Poland elected King.
- Sixtus IV becomes Pope; notorious for nepotism and abuses.
- Ivan the Great conquers Novgorod.
  DEATHS
  Thomas à Kempis, author of the *Imitation of Christ*.

1472
- Philip de Comines joins Louis XI.

1473
- Venice obtains Cyprus.
- Charles the Bold consolidates Burgundian power in Netherlands.

1474
- Scutari successfully defended against Turks.

- Ferdinand the Catholic King of Castile.
- Everlasting Compact: Swiss independence recognised.

1475
- First book printed in English language (*Recuyell of the Histories of Troy* by William Caxton at Bruges.
- Edward IV invades France to help Charles the Bold: Treaty of Pecquigny arranged with Louis XI.
- Battle of Racova: Stephen the Great of Moldavia defeats the Turks.

1476
- William Caxton sets up his printing press at Westminster.
- Battle of Granson: Swiss defeat Charles the Bold.
- Battle of Morat: Swiss defeat Charles the Bold.
- Battle of Toro: Portugal defeated by Ferdinand of Castile.

1477
- Battle of Nancy: Charles the Bold defeated and killed; end of Duchy.
- Mary, daughter of Charles the Bold, marries Maximilian, afterwards Emperor.

1478
- Plot of the Pazzi in Florence: Giuliano de' Medici killed; Lorenzo's position strengthened.
- Treaty of Olmütz between Hungary and Bohemia: Moravia, Silesia and Lusatia ceded to former.

1479

- Treaty of Brünn between Poland and Hungary.
- Treaty of Constantinople between Venice and Turkey.
- Ferdinand the Catholic becomes Ferdinand II of Aragon: Aragon and Castile united.
- Battle of Guinegate: French defeated by Maximilian.

1480

- Turks occupy Otranto for a short time; fail against Rhodes.

1481

- Spanish Inquisition established by Ferdinand the Catholic, with Torquemada as its chief.
- John II becomes King of Portugal.
- Hand becomes King of Denmark.
- Bajazet II becomes Turkish Sultan.

1482

- Treaty of Arras between France and the Netherlands: Louis IX receives Duchy of Burgundy, Franche-Comté, Picardy, etc.

1483

- Edward V murdered; Richard III King of England.
- Charles VIII King of France.

1485

- Battle of Bosworth: Richard III defeated and killed. Henry VII King of England: first of the Tudor dynasty.
- Matthias Corvinus takes Vienna.

- The Mad War in France.
- Partition of Leipzig: henceforward two Saxon lines.
- Sir Thomas Malory *Morte D'Arthur.*

1486

- Bartholomew Diaz doubles Cape of Good Hope.
- Frederick the Wise Elector of Saxony.
- John becomes Elector of Brandenburg.

1487

- Revolt of Lambert Simnel against Henry VII.
- Matthias Corvinus master of Austria, Styria and Carinthia.

1488

- Battle of Sauchieburn: death of James III and accession of James IV of Scotland.
- Venice obtains Cyprus.
  DEATHS
  Verrocchio, Italian sculptor.

1490

- Death of Matthias Corvinus, King of Hungary; Vladislav II of Bohemia elected: Hungarians expelled from Austrian duchies by Emperor Maximilian.
- Maximilian obtains Tirol.

1491

- Maximilian invades Hungary: Treaty of Pressburg.
- France obtains Brittany by marriage.

1492

- Christopher Columbus discovers the West Indies.
- Henry VII invades France: Treaty of Étaples.
- Ferdinand the Catholic conquers Granada: end of Moorish power in Spain.
- Expulsion of Jews from Spain.
- Alexander VI becomes Pope: scandalous reign.
- Death of Casimir IV of Poland.
  DEATHS
  Lorenzo de' Medici.

1493

- Maximilian I becomes German King.
- End of the Lordship of the Isles.
- Pope Alexander VI divides newly explored lands between Spain and Portugal.
- Treaty of Senlis: France gives Maximilian Artois and the County of Burgundy.

1494

- Aldus Manutius printing at Venice.
- Turks driven out of Styria.
- The Medici expelled from Florence.
- Charles VIII of France invades Italy.
- Treaty of Tordesillas between Spain and Portugal.
- Sir Edward Poynings Lord Deputy of Ireland.
- Poynings' Law passed: Parliament of Ireland made entirely dependent on that of England.

DEATHS
Hans Memling, Flemish painter.
Pico de Mirandola, Italian painter.

1495

- Manuel King of Portugal.
- Charles VIII conquers Naples.
- Battle of Fornovo: French advance in Italy checked.
- Holy League against France between Ferdinand, the Pope, the Emperor, etc.

1496

- Magnus Intercursus: a commercial treaty between England and Netherlands.
- Philip, son of Emperor Maximilian I and Mary of Burgundy, marries Juana, daughter of Ferdinand and Isabella of Spain.

1497

- John Cabot discovers Labrador and Newfoundland.
- Perkin Warbeck, pretender to the English throne, captured.
- Turks devastate Poland.

1498

- Girolamo Savonarola executed in Florence.
- Erasmus at Oxford.
- Vasco da Gama reaches India by sea.
- Louis XII King of France.

1499

- Vicente Pinzon and Amerigo Vespucci reach America.

- Battle of Sapienza: Venetian fleet totally defeated by Turks.
- Louis XII conquers Milan; Ludovico il Moro overthrown.
- War between Ivan the Great and Alexander of Lithuania.
- Peace of Basle: Swiss League virtually recognised as independent of the Empire.

1500
- Battle of Vedrosha: Lithuanians routed by Russians.
- Poedro Cabral discovers Brazil.
  DEATHS
  Robert Henryson, Scottish poet.

1501
- France and Spain arrange joint conquest and partition of the kingdom of Naples; then fall out over the spoils.
- Alexander King of Poland: final union with Lithuania.

1502
- Massacre of the Orsini at Rome by Pope Alexander VI and his son Caesar Borgia.

1503
- Marriage of James IV of Scotland to Margaret Tudor, daughter of Henry VII.
- Battle of Garigliano: French defeated by Spanish in Italy.
- Julius II becomes Pope; Caesar Borgia overthrown.

1504
- Treaty of Blois between Louis XII and Maximilian I.

1505
- Almeida Portuguese Viceroy in India.
- Basil III Tsar of Moscow.

1506
- Sigismund I King of Poland.
- Philip, husband of Juana, recognised as King of Castile: died same year.
  DEATHS
  Chrisopher Columbus.
  Andrea Mantegna, Italian painter.

THE REFORMATION

1507
- Machiavelli in power at Florence.
- Margaret, daughter of Maximilian, becomes Governor-general of Netherlands.
- Louis XII takes Genoa.

1508
- Maximilian assumes at Trent the title of Roman Emperor elect, without waiting for coronation at Rome.
- League of Cambrai formed against Venice, comprising France, Empire and the Pope Julius II.
- Romance of Amadis de Gaul published.
- Michelangelo and Raphael working at Rome for Julius II: culmination of Renaissance Art.

1509

- Spaniards under Cardinal Ximenes defeat Barbary pirates and take Oran.
- Henry VIII King of England.
- Battle of Agnadello: Venetians defeated by French.
- Florence finally subdues Pisa.
- Great earthquake in Constantinople.
- Emperor Maximilian fails to take Padua.

1510

- Venice reconciled to the Pope.
- Albuquerque captures Goa in India for Portugal.
- Erasmus begins lecturing on Greek at Cambridge.
  DEATHS
  Sandro Botticelli, Italian painter.

1511

- Albuquerque takes Malacca.
- Holy League of Pope, Venice and Spain: joined by Henry VIII.

1512

- Selim I becomes Sultan.
- Imperial Diet at Cologne: last reforming Diet.
- Battle of Ravenna: Gaston de Foix victorious against Holy League but killed: artillery first decides a battle.
- Holy League restores the Medici in Florence.
- League between the Pope and the Emperor.

1513

- Leo X (de' Medici) becomes Pope.
- Franco-Venetian League renewed.

- Maximilian allies with Henry VIII against France.
- Battle of Novara: Swiss defeat the French.
- Battle of Guinegaste: English defeat the French.
- Battle of Flodden: English victory over Scots: James IV killed; James V becomes King of Scotland.
- Christian II King of Denmark.
- Vasco Núñez de Balboa discovers the Pacific Ocean.
- Machiavelli *The Prince*.

1514

- Greek New Testament of Erasmus.
  DEATHS
  Donato Bramante, Italian architect.

1515

- Francis I becomes King of France.
- Charles, grandson of Maximilian, becomes Governor of the Netherlands.
- Navarre incorporated with Castile.
- Congress of Vienna: marriage treaties between Maximilian and Vladislav of Hungary.
- Battle of Marignano: French defeat Swiss and recovered Milan.
- Cardinal Wolsey becomes Lord Chancellor of England.

1516

- Church Concordat between Francis I and Leo X.
- Death of Ferdinand the Catholic: Charles I (afterwards Emperor Charles V) becomes King of Castile, Aragon and other regions.

- Louis II becomes King of Hungary.
- Barbarossa, the pirate leader, captures Algiers.
- Treaty of Noyon: between France, Spain and the Holy Roman Empire.
- Everlasting League between the Swiss and France.
- Sir Thomas More *Utopia*.

DEATHS

Hieronymus Bosch, Dutch painter.

1517

- Turks occupy Cairo and overthrow the Mamelukes: Turkish Sultan henceforth Caliph.
- Treaty of Rouen between Scotland and France.
- Martin Luther publishes his Ninety-five Theses at Wittenberg: beginning of Reformation.

1518

- Melanchthon becomes Professor of Greek at Wittenberg.
- Zwingli becomes People's Priest at Great Minster of Zurich.

1519

- Death of Emperor Maximilian: Charles V elected King of the Romans.
- Ferdinand Magellan starts on voyage round the world.

DEATHS

Leonardo da Vinci, Italian artist.

1520

- Suleiman the Magnificent becomes Sultan.
- Luther excommunicated.

- The Meaux Preachers pioneer the Reformation in France.
- Field of the Cloth of Gold: interview between Henry VIII and Francis I.
- Christian II of Denmark, having overthrown Sten Sture, crowned King of Sweden.
- Stockholm Bath of Blood.
- Hernando Cortés conquers Mexico.

1521

- Luther at Diet of Worms: placed under the ban of the Empire.
- Battle of Villalar: Spanish revolt crushed by Charles V.
- Ferdinand, brother of Charles V, given the government of the Austrian Hapsburg dominions.
- Treaty of Bruges between Emperor Charles V and Henry VIII.
- Milan occupied by the troops of Charles V and the Pope.
- Turks capture Belgrade.

1522

- Adrian VI becomes Pope: last non-Italian Pope.
- Henry VIII created Defender of the Faith for answering Luther.
- Battle of the Bicocca (near Milan): French defeated by Imperialists and compelled to evacuate Lombardy: Francesco Sforza set up in Milan.
- Turks conquer Rhodes.
- Treaty of Windsor: between Charles V and Henry VIII.
- The Knights' War: Franz von Sickingen, a German Lutheran knight, fails to capture Trier.

1523

- Revolt against Christian II causes his flight from Denmark: Frederick I becomes King.
- Franz von Sickingen defeated and killed.
- Gustavus Vasa King of Sweden (Gustavus I): Union of Kalmar ends.
- Albert of Brandenburg, last Grand Master of Teutonic Order, becomes Lutheran.
- Charles Brandon, Duke of Suffolk invades France.
- French invasion of Lombardy (Bayard killed).
- Clement VII (of the Medici family) becomes Pope.

1524

- Catholic Swiss League formed.
- Beginning of Peasants' Revolt in Germany.
- Invasion of France by Duke of Bourbon; fails to take Marseilles; pursued to Italy.
- 'Erection' of James V in Scotland.
- Order of Theatines founded.

1525

- Clement VII's agreement with Francis I.
- Battle of Pavia: Francis I defeated by Charles V and made prisoner; hand firearms triumphant.
- Lefèvre's French New Testament condemned to be burned.
- Mass abolished at Zürich.
- Massacre of Weinsberg by revolting German peasants: rebels crushed in several fights.
- Peace between England and France.
- Albert of Brandenburg makes his dominions the hereditary Dukedom of Prussia.

1526

- Treaty of Madrid between Charles V and Francis I: Francis set free.
- Lutheran Alliance completed, with Landgrave Philip of Hesse as its moving spirit.
- League of Cognac against Emperor by Francis I, Pope, Florence, Venice and others.
- Milan surrenders to the Imperialists.
- Beginning of Danish breach with Rome.
- Battle of Mohács: Hungary overthrown by the Turks: King Louis II drowned.
- John Zapolya and Ferdinand of Austria both elected King of Hungary: Zapolya defeated by Ferdinand at Tokay.
- Ferdinand elected King of Bohemia.
- Order of Capuchins founded.
- Battle of Panipat: Muslim conquest of India by Babar begun: Mogul Empire founded.

1527

- Alliance between Henry VIII and Francis I.
- Sack of Rome by Imperialist troops under Duke of Bourbon.
- Second expulsion of Medici from Florence.

- Västeras Recess: beginning of official Swedish Reformation.
- French under Lautrec invade Italy.

1528
- England and France declare war against the Holy Roman Empire.
- Patrick Hamilton burned for heresy in Scotland.
- Naples besieged by French and Genoese.
- Genoese under Andrea Doria desert French, capture Genoa and establish a republic.

1529
- Diet of Speir: Protest against its decisions by Lutheran Princes and cities: hence name of Protestant.
- Berquin burned for heresy in France.
- Zurich declares war on Lucerne and Catholic allies: Peace of Kappel arranged.
- Treaty of Barcelona: between Pope and Emperor.
- Peace of Cambrai: between Francis I, Emperor and England: France abandons Italy, Flanders and Artois; Malta and Tripoli to Knights of St John.
- Conference of Marburg between Luther and Zwingli: failure.
- Unsuccessful siege of Vienna by Turks.
- Henry VIII's divorce trial begins: transferred to Rome by the Pope.
- Fall of Cardinal Wolsey.

THE COUNTER-REFORMATION

1530
- Compact between Charles V and Clement VII: Charles crowned Emperor by Pope at Bologna; the last to be crowned Emperor.
- Diet of Augsburg: Melanchthon prepares the anti-Zwinglian Confession of Augsburg.
- Tetrapolitana Confession (Zwinglian) prepared by cities of South Germany under influence of Bucer.
- Florence surrenders to the Medici after a long siege.
- Schmalkaldic League of Protestant German Princes formed.
- The Grisons League obtains the Valtelline.

1531
- Battle of Kappel: Catholic Swiss cantons victorious over Protestant: Zwingil killed.
- Second Peace of Kappel between the two religious parties in Switzerland.

1532
- 'Submission of the Clergy' to Henry VIII in England.
- Agreement of Nuremberg: Protestants guarantee peace till next Diet of General Council.
- End of Florentine Republic: Alessandro de' Medici made Duke.
- Francisco Pizarro conquers Peru.
- College of Justice founded by James V.
- Ariosto *Orlando Furioso*.

1533
- Thomas Cranmer becomes Archbishop of Canterbury.
- Death of Frederick I of Denmark: disputed succession.
- Anne Boleyn publicly named Queen of Henry VIII; Cranmer declares Catherine of Aragon's marriage null; Anne Boleyn crowned; Henry VIII excommunicated by Pope.
- Treaty of Peace between Turkey and Austria.
- Ivan IV (the Terrible) becomes Tsar.

1534
- Anabaptist revolution in Münster under John of Leyden (soon suppressed).
- Geneva adopts the Reformation.
- First Voyage of Jacques Cartier to Canada.
- Revolution in Lübeck under Wullenwever.
- Battle of Lauffen: Philip of Hesse, leader of the Schmalkaldic League, defeats Ferdinand's forces in Württemberg.
- Barbarossa II captures Tunis.
- Paul III becomes Pope.
- The Paris Placards against the mass: severe persecution.
- Luther's German Bible completed.
- Grevefeide or Count's War in Denmark.

1535
- Barbarossa II defeated and Tunis taken by Emperor Charles along with Andrea Doria, Venice, Knights of Malta and others.
- Act of Supremacy in England: Henry VIII Supreme Head of the English Church.
- Execution of Bishop Fisher and Sir Thomas More.
- The English Bible of Miles Coverdale (first complete one).
- Thomas Cromwell becomes Vicar-General for Henry VIII.

1536
- Treaty between Francis I and Suleiman.
- Dissolution of the monasteries ordered by Henry VIII in England.
- Savoy conquered by French.
- Calvin's *Institutes*.
- Anne Boleyn beheaded; Jane Seymour Queen of Henry VIII.
- Concord of Wittenberg between Luther and Zwinglians.
- Calvin at Geneva.
- Imperialists invade Province, but repelled.
- Christian III enters Copenhagen as King.
- Pilgrimage of Grace in England led by Robert Aske.
- William Tyndale burned for heresy in the Netherlands.

DEATHS
Erasmus of Rotterdam, humanist scholar.

1537
- Christian III takes possession of Norway.

- A Papal Commission reports on reform.
- Suleiman devastates Corfu in his war with Venice.
- End of Lübeck attempt at city-Empire: Wullenwever executed.

1538

- Defensive League against the Turks between the Emperor, Pope, Ferdinand and Venice.
- Calvin expelled from Geneva.
- Catholic League of Nürnberg.
- Truce for ten years between Francis I, Charles V and the Pope.
- Suleiman annexes part of Moldavia.
- Turkish fleet sails against India; Yemen captured.
- Naval flight in the Ambracian Gulf: Barbarossa defeats forces of Emperor, Pope, Venice and Genoa.

1539

- Act of the Six Articles against heresy in England.
- Society of Jesus (Jesuits) founded by Ignatius Loyola.

1540

- Charles V punishes Ghent severely for rebellion.
- Severe Edict of Fontainebleau against heresy.
- Thomas Cromwell executed.
- Peace between Venice and the Turks.
- Jacques Cartier exploring in the St Lawrence.

1541

- Religious Conference at Ratisborn: failure.
- Suleiman virtually annexes Hungary.
- Hernando De Soto discoverers the Mississippi.
- Henry VIII given the title King of Ireland by the Irish Parliament.
- Calvin finally settles in Geneva.
- Failure of Spanish attack on Algiers

1542

- Roberval attempts to found a French colony in Canada.
- French attack Artois and Flanders.
- Brunswick lands overrun by the Schmalkaldic League's forces.
- Imperialist forces under Joachim of Brandenburg fail to take Pesth from the Turks.
- Council of Trent opened.
- Battle of Solway Moss: English defeat Scots.
- Mary Stewart Queen of Scotland: Earl of Arran Regent.
- Inquisition set up in Rome.

DEATHS

Sir Thomas Wyatt, English poet.

1543

- Suleiman takes Gran, Stuhlweissenburg and others.
- Vesalius, the anatomist, publishes his chief work.
- Barbarossa and the French fleet capture Nice city, but not the citadel.
- Charles V victorious in his war against Duke William of Cleves.

DEATHS

Nicolas Copernicus, Polish astronomer.

1544

- Edict calling upon all subjects in the hereditary Hapsburg lands to accept Confession of Louvain.
- Battle of Ceresole: French defeat Spanish forces in Lombardy.
- Earl of Hertford invades Scotland; Edinburgh burned.
- Bologne taken by English.
- Peace of Crépy: between Emperor, England and France.

1545

- Battle of Ancrum Moor: Scottish victory.
- Massacre of the Waldenses.
- Brunswick territories appropriated by Schmalkaldic League.
- Council of Trent again opened.

1546

- Religious conference at Ratisbon: futile.
- George Wishart burned as a heretic in Scotland.
- Cardinal Beaton murdered to avenge Wishart and St Andrews Castle captured.
- Diet of Ratisbon: Protestants repudiate Council of Trent and demand a National Council.
- Anne Askew tortured and burned for heresy in London.
- Ban of the Empire against Philip of

Hesse and the Elector John Frederick of Saxony.
- Execution of the Fourteen of Meaux in France.
- Ernestine Saxony invaded and occupied by Maurice of Albertine Saxony and Ferdinand: Elector John Frederick recovers his territory and invades that of Maurice.

DEATHS

Martin Luther, German religious reformer.

1547

- Brittany united to French kingdom.
- Failure of revolt against Andrea Doria of Genoa.
- Earl of Surrey executed for treason.
- Edward VI becomes King of England: Earl of Hertford (created Duke of Somerset) becomes Protector of the realm.
- Practically all South German cities subdued by Emperor Charles by this date; Duke Henry regains Brunswick; Catholicism re-established in Cologne.
- Council of Trent removed to Bologna by the Pope.
- Execution of Jaime de Enzines at Rome: first Italian death for heresy.
- Henry II King of France.
- Battle of Mühlberg: Charles V defeats Elector John Frederick and takes him prisoner; the electoral dignity transferred to Maurice of Albertine Saxony.
- Philip of Hesse surrenders to Charles V.

- Capitulation of St Andrews: John Knox a French galley-slave.
- Inquisition established in Portugal.
- Battle of Pinkie: Somerset's victory over the Scots.
- Chambre Ardente created in France.
- Somerset repeals the English laws against heresy.
- English replaces Latin in English Church services.

1548
- Suleiman victorious against Persia.
- Sigismund II (Augustus) King of Poland.
- The Bohemian Brethren, expelled from Bohemia, settle in Poland.
- Interim religious compromise drawn up by a committee chosen by Charles V and proclaimed as an Edict.
- Mary Queen of Scots lands in France.

1549
- First Book of Common Prayer sanctioned by English Parliament.
- First Act of Uniformity in England.
- Edward Seymour, Duke of Somerset institutes social reforms in England: Enclosures Commission appointed.
- Ket's rebellion in eastern England suppressed.
- France declares war against England.
- Fall of Somerset: Warwick (afterwards Duke of Northumberland) in power.

- Parliament declares enclosures legal.

1550
- Julius III becomes Pope.
- Persecution of Catholics and heretics in England.
- Peace established between France and England: Boulogne given back to France.
- Dragut the corsair defeated by Charles and headquarters in Tunisia taken.
- Severe placard against heresy in the Netherlands.

1551
- Council of Trent resumed at Trent.
- Turks capture Tripoli from Knights of St John.
- Turco-Hungarian war renewed after a truce.
- Magdeburg capitulates to the Elector Maurice.

1552
- Somerset executed.
- Treaty of Chambord between Henry II and the Protestant German Princes.
- French invade and occupied Lorraine.
- Council of Trent suspended.
- Charles V's flight from Maurice of Saxony across the Brenner Pass.
- Treaty of Passau: Protestant position secured.
- Second Act of Uniformity in England.

- Second Book of Common Prayer.
- Kazan annexed by Ivan IV.

1553

- Sir Hugh Willoughby and Richard Chancellor set out in search of north-east passage.
- Death of Edward VI of England: Lady Jane Grey proclaimed Queen of Northumberland; Mary Tudor also proclaimed; Northumberland executed and Mary victorious.
- Battle of Sievershausen: Elector Maurice defeats Albert Margrave of Brandenburg, but killed.
- Battle of Steterburg: Albert of Brandenburg defeated by Duke Henry of Brunswick.
- Michael Servetus, an anti-Trinitarian, burned for heresy in Geneva by Calvin.

DEATHS

François Rabelais, French writer.

1554

- Sir Thomas Wyatt leads a rebellion in Kent.
- Execution of Lady Jane Grey and her husband; also of Suffolk and Wyatt.
- Mary of Lorraine Regent of Scotland.
- Battle of Schwarzach: Albert of Brandenburg defeated by Duke Henry of Brunswick and driven as a fugitive to France.
- Mary Tudor marries Philip, heir of Charles V.

- Cardinal Pole arrives in England: Parliament decides in favour of returning to Roman Catholicism.
- Astrakhan annexed by Ivan IV.

1555

- John Rogers burned for heresy in England; many others follow.
- Marcellas II becomes Pope; dies a few months later; Paul IV succeeds; Counter-Reformation in the Papal chair.
- Vaudois become Calvinists.
- Union of Bohemian Brethren and Calvinists in Poland.
- Latimer and Ridley burned in England.
- Religious Peace of Augsburg: Cujus regio, ejus religio.
- Charles V abdicates sovereignty of Netherlands at Brussels: Philip II succeeds.

1556

- Charles V abdicates sovereignty in Spain and Italy: Ferdinand I Emperor.
- Peace of Vaucelles between Philip and France.
- Thomas Cranmer burned at the stake.
- Battle of Panipat (second): Mogul conquest of India made secure.
- Akbar becomes Mogul Emperor in India.

DEATHS

Nicholas Udall, English playwright.

1557
- War declared between England and France.
- Battle of St Quentin: French defeated by Spanish under Duke of Savoy and Egmont.
- Colloquy of Worms: no result.
- First Bond of Lords of the Congregation: organisation of Scottish Protestantism.
- Livonia conquered by Ivan IV.

1558
- English expelled from Calais.
- Mary Queen of Scots marries the French Dauphin Francis.
- Battle of Gravelines: Egmont again defeated by the French.
- Deaths of Mary Tudor and Cardinal Pole; Elizabeth I becomes Queen of England.

1559
- Death of Christian III of Denmark: Frederick II succeeds.
- Colloquy of Westminster.
- Treaty of Cateau-Cambrésis: a European settlement between the Empire, France and England.
- Acts of Uniformity and Supremacy in England.
- John Knox returns to Scotland.
- Auto-da-fé at Valladolid: first one against heresy.
- Francis II King of France.
- First Papal Index of Prohibited Books: great opposition.
- Pius IV Pope.

- Philip leaves the Netherlands: Margaret of Parma Regent.

THE WARS OF RELIGION

1560
- Treaty of Berwick between Duke of Norfolk and the Scottish Lords of the Congregation.
- Tumult of Amboise.
- Elizabeth I sends Lord Grey with an army to help the Scottish Lords of the Congregation.
- Death of Mary of Lorraine, the Scottish Regent.
- Treaty of Edinburgh: French forces to quit Scotland.
- A Scottish Parliament abolishes Roman Catholicism in Scotland.
- Death of Gustavus Vasa, King of Sweden: succeeded by Erik XIV.
- Charles IX King of France.
- First Book of Discipline in Scottish Church.

1561
- Abortive Protestant Conference at Naumberg: Lutherans and Calvinists irreconcilable.
- Vaudois rebellion suppressed by Savoy.
- Reval becomes Swedish.
- Mary Queen of Scots lands in Scotland.
- The Colloquy of Poissy: a form of French National Church Council.
- Teutonic Order submits to Poland.

1562

- Edict of January: first legal recognition of Protestantism in France.
- Council of Trent resumes at Trent.
- Massacre of Vassy: First War of Religion in France begins.
- Huguenots take Orleans.
- Treaty of Hampton Court between Elizabeth and the Prince of Condé.
- Treaty of Prague between Emperor Ferdinand and Suleiman the Magnificent.
- English forces land to assist the Huguenots in France: Le Havre is occupied.
- French Royalists occupy Rouen.
- Battle of Corrichie: Earl of Huntly defeated by Moray and killed.
- Battle of Dreux: indecisive Royalist victory in France.
- Emmanuel Philibert of Savoy obtains Turin and makes it his capital.

1563

- Duke of Guise murdered in a suburb of Orleans.
- Edict of Amboise ends First War of Religion.
- Swedes defeat Danes off Bornholm.
- Havre evacuated by the English.
- Northern Seven Years' War declared by Denmark.
- Charles IX declared of age in France.
- End of Council of Trent: The Counter-Reformation complete.

1564

- Papal Decree confirming decrees of Council of Trent.

- Tridentine Index of Prohibited Books.
- Cardinal Granville recalled from the Netherlands.
- Treaty of Troyes between France and England.
- Maximilian II becomes Emperor.
- Philip orders decrees of Trent to be enforced in the Netherlands.
- Anti-Trinitarians in Poland.
- Calvinism established in Palatinate by the Elector Frederick III.
- Treaty of Lausanne adjusts boundaries between Berne and Savoy.

DEATHS

John Calvin, French theologian.

1565

- Failure of Turkish attack on Malta.
- Bayonne Conference between France and Spain.
- Mary Queen of Scots marries Henry Darnley; Moray flees to England.
- Trent Decrees and Placards against heresy begin to be enforced in Netherlands.
- Revival of Catholicism in Poland.
- First punishments of Puritans in England.

1566

- 'The Compromise' signed by many Netherland nobles, pledging them to oppose the Inquisition.
- Murder of David Riccio, confidential secretary to Mary Queen of Scots, at Holyrood Palace.
- 'The Request' presented to a Netherlands Assembly by Lewis of Nas-

sau and Brederode, embodying the principles of the 'Compromise'.
- The Culemberg Banquet in Brussels: Vivent les Gueux first heard.
- Iconoclastic outbreaks in the Netherlands.
- Conference at Dendermonde between William the Silent, Lewis of Nassau, Egmont, Horn; Egmont and Horn not prepared to resist Philip.
- Death of Suleiman the Magnificent in Hungary: Selim II succeeds as Sultan.

DEATHS

Nostradamus, French astrologer.

1567
- Murder of Lord Darnley.
- Rout of John de Marnix at Austruweel.
- Valenciennes taken by Royal forces.
- William of Orange goes into exile.
- Mary Queen of Scots marries James Hepburn, Earl of Bothwell.
- Shane O'Neill defeated and killed in Ireland.
- Murder of the Sture by Erik XIV of Sweden.
- Mary Queen of Scots taken prisoner at Carberry Hill, imprisoned in Lochleven Castle and compelled to abdicate.
- Arrest of Egmont and Horn after Alva had arrived in Netherlands as Captain-General; Council of Troubles created: Alva becomes Regent and Governor-General.
- Enterprise of Meaux.

- John Casimir, second son of Elector Palatine Frederick, leads a force into France to help the Huguenots.
- Battle of Saint Denis between Huguenots and Catholics: indecisive.
- Scottish Parliament declares Mary guilty of murder and to have forfeited the crown: James VI King of Scotland.

1568
- William of Orange proclaimed an outlaw.
- La Rochelle opens its gates to the Huguenots.
- Condé raises the siege of Orleans.
- Peace between the Emperor and the Turks.
- Peace of Longjumeau ends the Second War of Religion in France.
- Mary escapes from Lochleven: defeated by Moray at Langside; flees to England.
- Battle of Heiligerlee: Lewis of Nassau defeated Spanish.
- Execution of Egmont and Horn.
- Revolt of Moriscos in Granada: suppressed with great slaughter.
- Douay College founded by Father Allen.

1569
- Erik XIV deposed by Swedish Diet: John III becomes King.
- Spanish treasure ships seized at Falmouth and Southampton.
- States-General summoned at Brussels: Alva fails to get all his taxes.
- Beggars of the Sea first appeared.

- Battle of Jarnac: Huguenots routed: Condé captured and shot dead.
- Union of Lublin: Poland and Lithuania incorporated.
- Cosimo de' Medici created Grand Duke of Tuscany by the Pope.
- Battle of Moncontour: Huguenot defeat.

1570
- Assassination of Regent Moray; Lennox becomes regent of Scotland.
- Peace of Saint-Germain ends Third War of Religion: La Rochelle becomes Huguenot headquarters.
- Concensus of Sadomir: Union of Bohemian Brethren, Lutherans and Calvinists in Poland.
- Queen Elizabeth declared deposed by Pope.
- Northern Seven Years' War ended by Peace of Stettin.

1571
- Triple Alliance of Spain, Venice and Pope against Turks.
- Turks land in Cyprus.
- Beggars of the Sea forbidden to use English ports.
- Ridolfi conspiracy discovered by William Cecil.
- Thirty-nine Articles enacted in England.
- Beginning of penal legislation against Catholics in England.
- Battle of Lepanto: Don John of Austria wins naval victory over Turks.
- Regent Lennox murdered in Scotland: Earl of Mar Regent.

- Khan of Crimea invades Russia and burns Moscow.

1572
- Death of Sigismund II of Poland.
- Beggars of the Sea capture Brill; also Flushing, etc.
- Defensive alliance between France and England.
- Lewis of Nassau invades the Netherlands from France; takes Valenciennes and Mons.
- Edict of Rochelle ends Fourth War of Religion.
- William the Silent invades the Netherlands from the East: takes Roermond: Brussels shut against him.
- States of Holland at Dort recognise William the Silent as Stadtholder.
- Henry of Bourbon becomes King of Navarre.
- St Bartholomew's Day Massacre: Admiral Coligny murdered.
- Alva recovers Mons.
- Death of Regent Mar in Scotland: Morton succeeds.
- Sack of Malines, Zutphen and Naarden by Spanish troops.
- Siege of Haarlem begun by Don Frederick of Toledo.

1573
- Compact of Warsaw secures absolute religious liberty in Poland.
- Pacification of Perth.
- Edinburgh Castle surrendered by Kirkcaldy of Grange and Maitland of Levington.
- Venice cedes Cyprus to Turks.

- Duke of Anjou elected King of Poland.
- Surrender of Haarlem.
- Siege of Alkmaar: dykes cut: siege raised.
- Battle of Enckhuysen: Spanish fleet defeated by Dutch.
- William the Silent declares himself a Calvinist.
- Alva recalled from the Netherlands: Don Luis Requesens succeeds.

1574
- Huguenot rising begins Fifth War of Religion.
- Battle of Bergen: Dutch naval victory.
- Spaniards surrender Middelburg.
- Battle of Mookerheide: Lewis of Nassau killed.
- Plot of Vincennes.
- Henry III King of France.
- Flight of Anjou from Poland.
- Relief of Leyden after long siege.
- The Gerusalemme Liberata of Tasso.
- Murad III becomes Sultan.

1575
- Anjou declared deposed in Poland: Maximilian II elected by Senate, Stephen Bathory by Diet; latter victorious.
- Escape of Monsieur to join Huguenots.
- Battle of Dormans: Huguenot defeat.
- John Casimir again in France.

1576
- Henry of Navarre escapes to the Huguenots and abjures Catholicism.
- Death of Requesens: Don John of Austria Governor of Netherlands.
- Union of Holland and Zeeland completed.
- Edict of Beaulieu ends Fifth War of Religion (Peace of Monsieur).
- Rudolph II Emperor.
- The League formed by French Catholics.
- Pacification of Ghent.
- Revolt of Spanish troops in Netherlands: Sack of Antwerp and 'Spanish Fury'.

1577
- French King repudiates Edict of Beaulieu: Sixth War of Religion begins.
- Union of Brussels.
- 'Perpetual Edict': agreement between Netherlands and Don John of Austria.
- Don John seizes Namur.
- Peace of Bergerac: Edict of Poitiers: end of Sixth War of Religion.
- William the Silent enters Brussels.
- Francis Drake's voyage round the world begins.

1578
- State entry of Archduke Matthias into Brussels as Governor, with William the Silent as Lieutenant-General.
- Battle of Gemblours: Alexander of Parma's victory.

- Duke of Anjou accepted title of 'Defender of the Liberties of the Netherlands'.
- Battle of Alcazat-Kebir: King Sebastian of Portugal killed in Morocco; Henry succeeds.
- Battle of Verden: Poles and Swedes defeat Russians.
- Alexander of Parma becomes governor of Netherlands.
- Morton resigns the Regency of Scotland, but afterwards takes possession of the King.
- Fausto Sozzini (Socinus) in Transylvania and Poland.

1579

- League of Arras for protection of Catholic religion in Hainault, Douay and Artois.
- Union of Utrecht: Dutch republic formed.
- Edmund Spenser *Shepherd's Calendar*.
- John Lyly *Euphues*.

1580

- Philip of Spain obtains Portuguese crown on death of King Henry.
- Seventh War of Religion begins; ends in same year by Peace of Fleix.
- Robert Parsons and Edmund Campion, Jesuit missionaries, arrive in England.
- First collection of the *Essays* of Montaigne.
- Charles Emmanuel succeeds Emmanuel Philibert as Duke of Savoy.

DEATHS

John Heywood, English dramatist.

1581

- Philip puts a price on the head of William the Silent.
- Morton executed in Scotland.
- William the Silent provisionally accepts the title of Count of Holland.
- Philip II abjured by Brabant, Flanders, Utrecht, Gelderland, Holland and Zeeland.
- Poles and Swedes take Narva.
- Battle of Terceira: naval victory of Santa Cruz over Don Antonio.
- The Apology of William the Silent.
- Second Book of Discipline in Scotland.

1582

- Peace between Poland and Russia: former gained Livonia, etc.
- Anjou inaugurated at Antwerp as Duke of Brabant.
- Pope Gregory XIII introduces new style in dating by Bull.
- Anjou accepted as Lord of Friesland, Duke of Gelderland and Count of Flanders.
- Raid of Ruthven: James VI of Scotland a prisoner (till June 1583).

DEATHS

George Buchanan, Scottish scholar and historian.

1583

- 'French Fury' at Antwerp.
- Sir Humphrey Gilbert's voyage to found a colony in Newfoundland.

- Truce of Pliusa between Russia and Sweden.
- John Whitgift becomes Archbishop of Canterbury to suppress Puritanism.
- Execution of the rebel Earl of Desmond.
- William the Silent accepts the hereditary Countship of Holland and Zeeland.

1584

- William the Silent assassinated at Delft by Gérard.
- Association formed to protect Elizabeth.
- Episcopacy established in Scottish Church by James VI.
- Death of Ivan IV: succeeded by Theodore I, with Boris Godunoff as real ruler of Russia.

1585

- Treaty of Joinville against Henry of Navarre between Spain and the Catholic League.
- Sixtus V becomes Pope.
- Treaty of Nemours between Henry III and the Catholic League: latter victorious: Eighth War of Religion (War of the Three Henrys) follows.
- Papal Bull against Henry of Navarre and Condé.
- Drake commissioned for reprisals in West Indies.
- English Act against Jesuits, seminary priests, etc.
- Earl of Leicester lands in Holland with a force.

1586

- Leicester made Governor-General of United Provinces.
- Thomas Babington's Catholic plot exposed by Walsingham.
- Alliance between Elizabeth and James VI for the defence of Protestantism.

DEATHS

Sir Philip Sidney, English writer and soldier.

1587

- Execution of Mary Queen of Scots.
- Drake's expedition to Cadiz to delay sailing of Spanish Armada.
- Alexander of Parma captures Sluys.
- Leicester leaves Holland.
- Sigismund, son of John III of Sweden, elected King of Poland.
- Battle of Coutras: victory of Henry of Navarre.

1588

- Duke of Guise enters Paris: Henry III flees.
- Spanish Armada sets sail from Lisbon (20th May); defeated on 29th July.
- Guise murdered in Henry III's antechamber; his brother, the Cardinal, executed; other Leaguers arrested.
- Martin Marprelate tracts attacking Anglican bishops begin.
- Christian IV King of Denmark.

1589

- Duke of Aumale declared lieutenant-general of France; occupies Paris.

- Truce between Henry III and Henry of Navarre.
- Failure of Drake's expedition against Portugal.
- Henry III assassinated: Henry of Navarre becomes King as Henry IV; beginning of Bourbon Dynasty.
- Battle of Arques: Henry IV victorious.
- Galileo experiments with falling objects at leaning tower of Pisa.

1590
- Dutch capture Breda.
- Battle of Ivry: Henry IV triumphant.
- Savoyard forces invade Provence: Duke of Savoy enters Aix.

1591
- Torgau Alliance of Protestant princes to aid Henry IV.
- Henry IV excommunicated by the Pope.
- Dutch under Maurice and William Lewis of Nassau take Zutphen; then Deventer and Nimeguen.
- Murder of Tsarevitch Dimitri in Russia.
- Francis Vieta of Paris founds modern algebra.

1592
- Clement VIII Pope.
- Death of Alexander of Parma: Archduke Ernest succeeds in Netherlands.
- Sigismund King of Poland becomes King of Sweden also: Charles Regent of Sweden.

- Presbyterianism fully established in Scotland.

DEATHS
Michel de Montaigne, French author.

1593
- Upsala Council: Swedish Reformation.
- Maurice of Nassau takes Geertruidenburg.
- Henry IV's conversion to Catholicism: 'Paris vaut une messe'.
- Anti-Puritan Statute in England: many flee to Holland.
- English Acts against Popish recusants.

DEATHS
Christopher Marlowe, English playwright.

1594
- French invade Savoy.
- Henry IV enters Paris.
- Shakespeare *Comedy of Errors* and *Titus Andronicus*: earliest of his plays.

DEATHS
Tintoretto, Italian painter.

1595
- Henry IV declares war on Spain.
- Death of Archduke Ernest, Governor of Netherlands.
- Peace of Teusin between Sweden and Russia.
- Battle of Groenloo: Maurice of Nassau's victory.
- Henry IV absolved by the Pope.
- Peasant insurrection in Upper Austria.

DEATHS
Torquato Tasso, Italian poet.

1596
- Archduke Albert made Governor of Netherlands.
- Archduke Albert captures Calais.
- Henry IV takes La Fère.
- Triple Alliance between England, France and United Provinces.
- English expedition to Cadiz: Cadiz captured.
- Mohammed III defeats Archduke Maximilian in a three days' battle.
- Sir Robert Cecil becomes Secretary of State in England.
- Edmund Spenser *Faerie Queene*.

1597
- Battle of Turnhout: Maurice of Nassau's victory.
- Spaniards take Amiens (soon recovered).
- Polish suzerainty over Moldavia recognised by Sultan.
- Sully becomes Finance Minister of France.
- Serfdom introduced in Russia.
- Richard Hooker *Ecclesiastical Polity*.

1598
- Edict of Nantes: Protestant liberties secured in France.
- Netherlands erected by Philip II into a sovereign state under Archduke Albert; Albert marries Philip's daughter Isabel.
- Peace of Vervins between France and Spain.

- Philip III becomes King of Spain.
- Battle of Stangebro: Charles of Sweden defeats Sigismund.
- Death of Theodore I: Boris Godunoff becomes Tsar.

1599
- Earl of Essex becomes Lord Deputy of Ireland: disgraced on his return.
- Sigismund deposed in Sweden: Charles IX becomes King.
- Sweden conquers Finland.

DEATHS
Edmund Spenser, English poet.

1600
- Giordano Bruno, Italian philosopher, burned for heresy.
- Esthonia seeks the protection of Charles IX.
- Battle of Nieuport: Maurice of Nassau's desperate victory.
- Charles IX invades Livonia.
- Gowrie Conspiracy in Scotland.
- East India Company founded in England.
- Dr William Gilbert *De Magnete*, pioneering work on magnetism.

1601
- Valladolid becomes capital of Spain (till 1606).
- Rebellion and execution of Essex.
- Treaty of Lyons between France and Savoy: Savoy keeps Saluzzo, but cedes other territory.
- Dutch East India Company founded.
- Siege of Ostend begun by Spinola (surrendered 1604).

- Poland reconquers Livonia.
- English Poor Law Act passed.
- Spanish invasion of Ireland.
  DEATHS
  Tycho Brahe, Danish astronomer.
  Thomas Nashe, English poet and
  dramatist.

1602
- Battle of Kinsale: Spaniards and
  Irish rebels defeated.
- Execution of Marshal Biron.
- Treaty between France and the
  Grisons regarding the Valtelline.
- Arminius becomes a professor at
  Leyden: rivalry with Gomarus.
- Savoy fails to take Geneva.
- Shakespeare *Hamlet*.

1603
- Death of Elizabeth: James VI of
  Scotland becomes James I of Eng-
  land: Union of the Crowns.
- Earl of Tyrone submits: Ireland con-
  quered.
- The False Dimitri appears in Poland
  to claim Tsardom.

1604
- Hampton Court Conference fails to
  reach agreement between Puritans
  and Anglican High Churchmen.
- Maurice of Nassau takes Sluys.
- Peace between England, Spain and
  the Netherlands.
- The False Dimitri invades Russia.

1605
- Paul V becomes Pope.

- The False Dimitri accepted as Tsar
  on death of Boris.
- Battle of Kirkholm: Poles defeat
  Charles IX of Sweden.
- Gunpowder Plot to blow up Parlia-
  ment discovered in England.
- Cervantes *Don Quixote*.

1606
- Treaty of Venice between the Aus-
  trian Archdukes: Archduke Matthias
  becomes head of House of Austria.
- Venice under Papal Interdict.
- The False Dimitri killed: Vasili Shu-
  iski becomes Tsar.
- Peace of Zsitva-Torok between Em-
  pire and Turks: Imperial tribute to
  Turks abolished.
- Grand Remonstrances of Sandomir
  against Sigismund of Poland: its
  supporters suppressed.
  DEATHS
  John Lyly, English novelist and
  dramatist.

1607
- Battle of Gibraltar: Heemskerk de-
  stroys Spanish fleet.
- Earls of Tyrone and Tyrconnel leave
  Ireland for ever with their families.
- London Company colonises Virginia.
- Swedish power begins to be restored
  in Esthonia.

1608
- Alliance of Pressburg: Hungarian
  and Austrian Estates united against
  Emperor Rudolph.
- Evangelistic Union formed by Ger-

man Protestant Princes, headed by Christian of Anhalt.

- Emperor Rudolph cedes Hungarian crown and territorial dominion in Austria and Moravia to Archduke Matthias.
- Quebec founded by French under Champlain.

1609

- Alliance between Charles IX and Tsar against Poland.
- Death of Duke John William of Jülich and Cleves.
- Twelve Years' Truce between Spain and Holland: Spain concedes freedom of Indian trade.
- Rudolph's Letter of Majesty in Bohemia.
- Catholic Union (or League) formed at Munich under Maximilian of Bavaria.
- Edict against the Moriscos in Spain.
- Barbary Corsairs defeated at Tunis by Spain and France.
- Johannes Kepler begins publishing his astronomical laws.
- Galileo invents the telescope about this time.

1610

- James I and VI dissolves his first Parliament: constitutional struggle begins.
- Assassination of Henry IV of France: succeeded by Louis XIII.
- Battle of Klutsjino: Russians defeated by Poles and Tsar overthrown: Wladislav, son of Sigismund of Po-

land, crowned Tsar.

- Plantation of Ulster with English and Scottish colonists begins.
- Maurice of Nassau took Jülich.
- Frederick V becomes Elector Palatine.
- Dutch bring tea to Europe (from China) for first time.

DEATHS

Michelangelo Caravaggio, Italian painter.

1611

- War of Kalmar between Denmark and Sweden begins.
- Matthias crowned King of Bohemia and Emperor Rudoloph resigns Bohemian crown.
- Order of Baronets created.
- Gustavus Adolphus becomes King of Sweden: Oxenstierna his chief statesman.
- The Authorised Version of the Bible published.

1612

- Death of Emperor Rudolph II: Matthias elected Emperor.
- Evangelical Union of Princes conclude treaty with England.
- Turks recover Moldavia.
- James VI establishes Episcopacy in Scotland.
- English factory founded at Surat in India.

1613

- Peace of Knäred ends the War of Kalmar.

- Michael Romanoff becomes Tsar: Beginning of the Romanoff dynasty in Russia
- Frederick V, Elector Palatine, marries Elizabeth, daughter of James I and VI.

1614

- Last meeting of French States-General till 1789.
- Alliance between Sweden and United Provinces.
- Jülich and Cleves divided between the two claimants by treaty of Xanten.
- Addled Parliament in England.
- John Napier introduces logarithms.

1615

- Treaty between Empire and Turks.
- Sir Thomas Roe becomes resident English ambassador at court of Great Mogul in India.
- The Spanish Marriages: double alliance of French and Spanish royal families.
- Charles Emmanuel of Savoy defeated in Lombardy by Spanish viceroy.
- First newspaper (in Germany) appears.
- Dutch destroy Spanish fleet in East Indies and gain command of Moluccas.

1616

- Edict of Inquisition against Galileo.
- Fall of Somerset: Buckingham in power.
- Cardinal Richelieu becomes Foreign and War Minister.

- Dutch bring coffee to Europe (from Mocha) for the first time.

DEATHS

William Shakespeare, English poet and dramatist.

1617

- Peace of Stolbova between Sweden and Russia: Russia renounces Esthonia and Livonia; Sweden surrenders Novgorod.
- Richelieu out of office: Luynes in power.
- Ferdinand of Styria crowned King of Bohemia.
- Peace of Madrid between Austria and Bohemia.
- Treaty of Pavia between Savoy and Spain relating to Lombardy.
- War between Sweden and Poland.
- Henry Briggs introduces decimal notation.

THE THIRTY YEARS' WAR

1618

- Ferdinand of Styria proclaimed King of Hungary.
- Bohemian Protestants set up a provisional government.
- Failure of Osuna's conspiracy against Venice.
- Fall of Cardinal Klesl.
- Duke of Prussia added to Electorate of Brandenburg.
- The Five Articles of Perth accepted by a pseudo-General Assembly.
- Sir Walter Raleigh executed.
- Synod of Dort: the Arminian Re-

monstrants crushed in the United Provinces.

1619
- Death of the Emperor Matthias: Ferdinand II elected.
- Batavia founded as capital of Dutch East Indies.
- Execution of Oldenbarnveldt, the Dutch statesman.
- George William becomes Elector of Brandenburg.
- Emperor Ferdinand declared deposed from Bohemian throne and Elector Palatine Frederick V elected King of Bohemia.
- Bethlen Gabor of Transylvania, in alliance with Bohemians, occupies most of Upper Hungary.
- Agreement between Emperor Ferdinand and Maximilian of Bavaria.
- Slavery introduced in Virginia.
  DEATHS
  Nicholas Hilliard, English painter.

1620
- Frederick V ordered to quit the Emperor's dominions.
- Massacre of Protestants in the Valtelline.
- Tilly, the general of the Catholic League, enters Upper Austria.
- Spinola invades the Palatinate.
- Battle of the White Hill: Tilly defeated Christian of Anhalt and Thurn: Prague taken.
- Battle of Cécora: Poles heavily defeated by Turks when attempting to re cover Moldavia.

- Huguenots formulate their demands at La Rochelle: war followed.
- The Pilgrim Fathers set sail for New England.
- Francis Bacon *Novum Organum*.

1621
- Philip IV becomes King of Spain, with Olivarez as chief minister.
- Treaty of Madrid between Spain and France: the Valtelline restored to Grisons.
- Evangelical Union of Princes dissolved.
- Riga taken by the Swedes.
- End of Twelve Years' Truce between Spain and United Provinces.
- English Parliament attacks monopolies; dissolved after Protestation of Rights.
- Five Articles of Perth passed by Scottish Parliament.
- Fall of Francis Bacon.
- Dutch West India Company founded.

1622
- Articles of Milan: Grisons renounce the Valtelline.
- Battle of Wimpfen: Tilly victorious.
- Battle of Höchst: Tilly defeats Christian of Halberstadt.
- Battle of Fleurus: victory of Mansfield and Christain of Halberstadt.
- Treaty of Lindau: Austrian supremacy in the Valtelline strengthened.
- First English newspaper appears.
- Treaty of Montpellier between Louis XIII and Huguenots.

1623

- Ratisbon Conference: Maximilian got Frederick's electoral dignity.
- Treaty of Paris: France, Venice and Savoy unite to restore Valtellines.
- Prince Charles and Buckingham in Madrid.
- Expulsion of Protestant clergy from Bohemia.
- Battle of Stadtlohn: Tilly defeats Christian of Halberstadt.
- Dutch conquer Formosa.

  DEATHS
  William Byrd, English composer.

1624

- Monopoly Act in England: patents protected.
- Dutch take Bahia in Brazil from Portugal (soon recovered).
- Richelieu becomes Chief Minister of France.
- Massacre of Amboina.
- Protestants deprived of all rights in Bohemia.
- French occupy the Valtelline.

1625

- Huguenots seize Blavet and the royal ships.
- Charles I King of England, Scotland and Ireland.
- Frederick Henry Prince of Orange.
- Wallenstein becomes Imperialist commander-in-chief: enters Lower Saxony.
- English Parliament gives Charles I tonnage and poundage for one year only.

- Spinola takes Breda.
- Montmorency seizes islands of Ré and Oléron.
- Treaty of Southampton between England and the United Provinces.
- Swedes overrun Livonia.
- Failure of English expedition to Cadiz.
- Triple Alliance between England, Denmark and Holland.
- French colony of Cayenne founded; French also colonise St Kitts.

1626

- Battle of Wallhof: victory of Gustavus Adolphus over the Poles.
- English Treaty with Huguenots.
- Battle of Dessau Bridge: Wallenstein defeats Mansfield.
- Treaty of Monzon between France and Spain regarding the Valtelline.
- Impeachment of Duke of Buckingham.
- Swedish invasion of Prussia.
- Tilly takes Göttingen.
- Battle of Lutter: Tilly defeats Christian IV of Denmark.
- Forced loan in England; Sir John Eliot and others imprisoned.
- Peace of Pressburg between Wallenstein and Bethlen Gabor.
- English settlement of Barbados.

  DEATHS
  Francis Bacon, English philosopher and statesman.

1627

- War between England and France.

- Treaty of Alliance between France and Spain.
- Duke of Buckingham's expedition to La Rochelle in aid of Huguenots.
- Wallenstein occupies Schleswig and Jutland.
- Disputed succession in Mantua.

1628

- Treaty between Sweden and Denmark.
- Unsuccessful siege of Stralsund by Imperialist troops under Arnim.
- Petition of Right passed by Parliament and receives Royal Assent.
- Murder of Duke of Buckingham.
- Hein, Dutch naval leader, captures Spanish treasure fleet.
- Capitulation of La Rochelle: final failure of the Huguenot cause.
- William Harvey *On the Circulation of the Blood*.

1629

- Charles I dissolves Third Parliament; begins eleven years of personal rule.
- French invasion of Italy in support of Duke of Nevers' claim to Mantua.
- Edict of Restitution in Germany.
- Peace between England and France.
- Peace of Lübeck between Wallenstein and Denmark.
- Frederick Henry of Orange reduces Bois-le-Duc.
- Truce between Sweden and Poland for six years: Sweden gains Livonia and other territories.
- Spinola at war in Lombardy.

DEATHS
Cardinal Pierre de Berulle, French theologian.

1630

- Dutch take Pernambuco.
- French invasion of Savoy: Death of Charles Emmanuel.
- Gustavus Adolphus lands in Germany: conquers Pomerania.
- Mantua and Casale captured by Spain.
- Dismissal of Wallenstein.
- Treaty of Madrid between England and Spain.

1631

- Treaty of Bärwalde between France and Sweden.
- Protestant Convention at Leipzig.
- Gustavus Adolphus takes Frankfort-on-the-Oder.
- Spain's ignominious peace with France.
- Fall of Magdeburg to Imperialists.
- Battle of the Slaak: Dutch destroy Spanish fleet.
- Alliance between Gustavus Adolphus and John George of Saxony.
- Battle of Breitenfield: Tilly defeated by Gustavus Adolphus.
- Gustavus Adolphus conquers Franconia and takes Mainz.
- Saxons invade Lusatia and occupy Prague.
- Treaties of Cherasco: settlement of Mantuan succession.

DEATHS
John Donne, English poet.

1632

- Mannheim taken by Bernard of Weimar (in Swedish service).
- Gustavus takes Nürnberg.
- Battle of the Lech: Gustavus defeats Tilly, who is mortally wounded.
- Gustavus takes Augsburg and Munich.
- Wallenstein resumes command and recaptures Prague.
- Frederick Henry of Orange reduces Maestricht.
- Battle of Lützen: Gustavus victorious but killed: Pappenheim mortally wounded.
- Christina, daughter of Gustavus, becomes Queen of Sweden.
  Deaths
  George Herbert, English poet.

1633

- Alliance of Heilbronn: Palatinate restored to heir of Frederick V.
- Sir Thomas Wentworth (Earl of Strafford) becomes Lord Deputy of Ireland.
- French occupy Lorraine.
- Bernard of Weimar takes Ratisbon.
- Wallenstein invades Brandenburg and then Bavaria.
- Southern Netherlands reverts to Spain on death of Isobel.
  Deaths
  Philaret, Russian monk-statesman.

1634

- Wallenstein deposed (murdered soon after).

- King Ferdinand of Hungary recaptures Ratisbon.
- Battle of Nördlingen: Imperialist victory: Heilbronn Alliance broken up.
- Ship-money begins to be demanded by Charles I.
- Treaty of Paris between France and Sweden: Oxenstierna, Swedish Chancellor, against it.
- French Academy founded.
- William Prynne, English Puritan pamphleteer, condemned for his *Histriomastix*.

1635

- Alliance between France and the United Provinces.
- Treaty of Compiègne between France and Sweden.
- War declared by France against Spain.
- Treaty of Prague between the Emperor and Saxony: widely accepted: Sweden and France isolated.
- Battle of Livigno: Duke of Rohan's victory over the Austrian and Spanish forces in the Valtelline.
- Battle of Mazzo: Rohan's victory in the Valtelline.
- Compact at Stuhmsdorf between Sweden and Poland.
- Saxony declares war on Sweden.
- Compact between France and Bernard of Weimar.
- Imperialists take Mainz.
- Battle of Goldberg: Banér and Torstensson, Swedish generals, keep the Saxons out of Mecklenburg.

- Pierre Corneille *Medea*.
  DEATHS
  Lope de Vega, Spanish dramatist.

1636
- Brandenburg declares war on Sweden.
- Treaty of Wismar between France and Sweden.
- Battle of Wittstock: Banér's victory over Saxons and Imperialists.
- Pierre Corneille *Le Cid*.

1637
- Death of Ferdinand II; Ferdinand III elected Emperor.
- Rising of Grisons against France.
- William Laud's Liturgy published in Scotland: popular indignation.
- Frederick Henry of Orange recaptures Breda.
- Dutch conquests from Portuguese in West Africa.
- Descartes *Discours de la Méthode*.
  DEATHS
  Ben Jonson, English dramatist.

1638
- War declared by France against Austria.
- Battles of Rheinfelden (two): victories of Bernard of Weimar.
- Battle of Wittenweier: Bernard's victory.
- The National Covenant signed in Scotland.
- The Glasgow Assembly meets.
- Bernard of Weimar takes Breisach.

1639
- First Bishop's War: ended by Pacification of Berwick.
- 'Perpetual Peace' of Milan between Austria and the Grisons.
- Van Tromp destroys Spanish attacking Armada in the Downs.

1640
- The Short Parliament in England (April-May).
- Catalonia revolt against Spain.
- Second Bishops' War begins: ended by Treaty of Ripon: a Parliament is called.
- Long Parliament meets (November).
- Braganza proclaimed King of Portugal as John IV.
- Impeachment of Archbishop William Laud.
- Frederick William, the 'Great Elector', becomes ruler of Brandenburg.
- Van Diemen conquers Malacca.
  DEATHS
  John Ford, English dramatist.
  Peter Paul Reubens, Flemish painter.

1641
- Spanish royal forces repelled from Barcelona.
- Execution of Strafford.
- Truce of Stockholm between Brandenburg and Sweden.
- Charles I sets out for Scotland.
- Rebellion in Ulster.
- Grand Remonstrance voted and published by English Parliament.

1642
- Attempt to seize the Five Members of the Commons.
- Parliament seizes Hull: English Civil War begins.
- Conspiracy of Cinq-Mars against Richlieu discovered: Cinq-Mars executed: Richelieu dies shortly afterwards.
- Charles I raises his standard at Nottingham.
- Portsmouth surrenders to Parliament.
- Battle of Edgehill: drawn.
- General Assembly of Confederated Catholics in Kilkenny.
- Battle of Breitenfeld: Torstensson defeats the Imperialists.
- Abel Tasman's voyage begins.
- Richard Lovelace *To Althea, from Prison*.

1643
- Fall of Olivarez.
- English Parliament abolishes Episcopacy.
- Battle of Ross: Irish rebels defeated by Ormond.
- Louis XIV becomes King of France.
- Battle of Rocroi: D'Enghien's victory.
- John Hampden killed at Chalgrove.
- Battle of Adwalton Moor: Parliamentary forces under the Fairfaxes defeated.
- Westminster Assembly begins its sessions.
- Battle of Roundway Down: Waller's Parliamentary army destroyed.
- Royalists under Prince Rupert storm Bristol.

- French take Thionville.
- Severe defeat of Spanish fleet by French off Carthagena.
- Solemn League and Covenant: agreement between English Parliament and the Scots.
- Battle of Newbury: drawn: Falkland killed.
- Battle of Winceby: victory of Sir Thomas Fairfax and Oliver Cromwell.
- Torstensson, Swedish general, invades Denmark.

DEATHS

John Pym, Parliamentary leader.

1644
- Scots enter England under Alexander Leslie, Earl of Leven.
- Battle of Copredy Bridge; defeat of Waller.
- Battle of Kolberg Heath; defeat of Christian IV of Denmark in naval battle.
- Battle of Marston Moor: Parliamentary victory due to Cromwell, aided by Scots.
- Parliament captures York.
- French take Gravelines.
- Battle of Tippermuir: Montrose victorious.
- Battle of Freiburg: D'Enghien and Turenne defeat Imperialist general Mercy.
- Capitulation of Parliamentary army under Essex at Lostwithiel.
- Battle of Newbury (second): Parliamentary success.
- Turenne takes Mainz.

1645

- Execution of Archbishop Laud.
- Battle of Inverlochy: Montrose's victory.
- Uxbridge negotiations between Charles I and Parliament.
- New Model Army organised under Sir Thomas Fairfax.
- Battle of Jankau: Torstensson's victory.
- Battle of Auldearn: Montrose's victory.
- Battle of Herbsthausen: Mercy defeats Turenne.
- Royalists sack Leicester.
- Battle of Naseby: victory of Fairfax and Cromwell over Charles I and Rupert.
- Battle of Allerheim: D'Enghein and Turenne defeat Mercy (last killed).
- Battle of Alford: Montrose's victory.
- Battle of Kilsyth: Montrose's victory.
- Peace of Brömsebro between Sweden and Denmark and United Provinces.
- Fairfax takes Bristol.
- Swedish general Wrangel takes Bornholm.
- Battle of Philiphaugh: Montrose defeated by David Leslie.
- French conquests in Catalonia.

1646

- Fairfax takes Exeter and Oxford.
- Charles I surrenders to the Scottish army.
- D'Enghiem (Condé) takes Dunkirk.

1647

- Charles I handed over to English Parliament.
- William II succeeds Frederick Henry of Orange in United Provinces.
- Cornet Joyce abducts Charles I.
- Masaniello heads revolt in Naples against Spain.
- Quakers founded by George Fox.
- 'Heads of the Proposals' prepared by Henry Ireton.
- Army marches on London.
- 'The Agreement of the People' prepared by the Levellers.
- Charles I escapes to Carisbrooke Castle.
- 'The Engagement' between Charles I and the Scots.

1648

- Commons passes 'Vote of No Addresses'.
- Naples revolt suppressed by Don Juan of Austria.
- Frederick III King of Denmark.
- Battle of Zusmarshausen: Wrangel and Turenne defeat the Imperialists.
- Second Civil War begins in England.
- Assembly of the Hall of St Louis to discuss French situation.
- Battle of Preston: Cromwell defeats the Scots under Hamilton.
- Battle of Lens: Condé defeats the Spaniards.
- Rising in Paris.
- Fairfax takes Colchester.
- Peace of Westphalia ends Thirty Years' War.

- Declaration of Saint-Germain: demands of the Fronde granted.
- Failure of Newport negotiations between Parliament and Charles I.
- Charles I declines terms offered by the army.
- Pride's purge of Parliament.

THE AGE OF CROMWELL

1649
- First War of the Fronde in France (quickly ended by Treaty of Rueil).
- Execution of Charles I.
- Charles II proclaimed King of Scotland.
- English Parliament abolishes the House of Lords and the Monarchy.
- Cromwell storms Drogheda and captures Wexford.
- Sorbonne condemns Jansenism.

1650
- Arrest of Condé and other princes in France.
- Montrose captured by Davis Leslie and executed.
- Agreement of Breda between Charles II and the Scots.
- Cromwell leaves Ireland, leaving Ireton in command.
- Battle of Dunbar: Cromwell defeats the Scots under Leslie.

1651
- Charles II crowned at Scone.
- Parliament of Paris votes the release of Condé and the Princes and de-

mands dismissal of Mazarin; Princes released; Mazarin flees.
- Condé in revolt.
- Battle of Worcester: Cromwell defeats Charles II.
- Navigation Act passed by English Parliament.
- William III succeeds William II in United Provinces.

1652
- General Monck subdues Scotland.
- First War between England and Holland begins.
- Battle of Saint-Antoinne: Turenne against Condé.
- Provisional Fronde government in Paris: soon overthrown.
- Act for Settling of Ireland.
- English Admiral Robert Blake defeats De Ruyter in naval battle off coast of Kent.
- Capitulation of Barcelona.
- Van Tromp defeats Blake off Dungeness.
- Dutch settlement at Cape of Good Hope.
- France surrenders Dunkirk and Gravelines.
- Nukon, an ecclesiastical reformer, becomes Patriarch of Moscow.
DEATHS
Inigo Jones, English architect.

1653
- Mazarin returns to Paris.
- Van Tromp defeated by Blake off Portland.
- Rupert's Royalist fleet destroyed.

- Rump Parliament dissolved by Cromwell.
- Monck and Blake defeat Dutch off the Gabbard.
- Barebones Parliament meets.
- Monck defeats Dutch off the Texel: Van Tromp killed.
- John De Witt Grand Pensionary of Holland: the Orange family excluded.
- Cromwell accepts the Instrument of Government and becomes Protector.

1654
- Peace between England and Holland.
- Abdication of Christina of Sweden: Charles X King.
- Dutch lose Brazil.

1655
- Jamaica taken from Spaniards by Penn and Venables.
- Sweden declares war on Poland.
- Charles X takes Waresaw and Cracow.
- Treaty of Westminster between France and England.

1656
- Treaty of Königsberg between Charles X and Frederick William of Brandenburg; Treaty of Marienburg later and that of Labiau still later in same year.
- Warsaw recovered by Poles.
- Battle of Valenciennes: Turenne defeated by Condé and Don Juan.
- Battle of Warsaw: Poles defeated by

Swedes and Brandenburgers: Warsaw recaptured.
- Blake captures the Plate fleet.
- Mohammed Kiuprili becomes Vizier of Turkey.

1657
- Cromwell accepts the Humble Petition and Advice and assumes the title of Lord Protector after refusing that of King.
- Act of Union between Scotland and England: annulled at Restoration.
- Treaty of Paris between England and France.
- Death of Emperor Ferdinand III: Leopold I elected next year.
- Blake destroys Spanish fleet at Tenerife.
- Alliance between Austria and Poland.
- Denmark declares war against Sweden.
- Charles X invades Holstein.
- Treaty of Wehlau: Brandenburg joins Austria and Poland.

1658
- Swedes conquer most of Denmark.
- Peace of Roeskilde between Sweden and Denmark.
- Battle of the Dunes: Turenne defeats Condé and Don Juan and captures Dunkirk and Gravelines.
- League of the Rhine formed, including France.
- Second Danish War of Charles X.
- Death of Cromwell: Richard Cromwell Protector.

- Copenhagen relieved by the Dutch.
- Mohammed Kiuprili conquers Transylvania.
- Aurangzeb becomes Mogul Emperor in India.

1659
- Battle of Elvas: Portuguese defeat the Spaniards.
- Rump Parliament reassembled.
- Concert of the Hague: Holland, France and England against Sweden.
- Abdication of Richard Cromwell.
- Peace of the Pyrenees between France and Spain.
- Dutch takes Nyborg and captured a Swedish force.
- English Parliament resumed.

1660
- Long Parliament dissolved and a new Parliament called.
- Restoration of Charles II.
- Death of Charles X of Sweden.
- Peace of Oliva ends Swedo-Danish wars.
  DEATHS
  Velásquez, Spanish artist.

THE AGE OF LOUIS XIV

1661
- Death of Mazarin: Louis XIV assumes role of own minister.
- Savoy Conference fails to make agreement between Puritans and other churchmen.
- Treaty between England and Portu-

gal: England obtains Tangier and Bombay as a marriage dowry.
- Peace between Holland and Portugal.
- Episcopacy established in Scotland by decree.
- Peace of Kardis between Sweden and Russia.
- Corporation Act: first of a series of statutes against Puritans.

1662
- Alliance between France and Holland.
- Press Act in England.
- Act of Uniformity in England: leads to ejection of many clergy: beginning of English Nonconformity.
- Patronage restored by Scottish Parliament.
- Royal Society incorporated.
- Treaty between England and Holland.
- Act for the Settlement of Ireland.
- Dunkirk sold to France.
  DEATHS
  Blaise Pascal, French philosopher and scientist.

1663
- Battle of Amegial: Spaniards under Don Juan defeat the Portuguese and their English allies.
- Turks begins war against Austria.

1664
- French East India Company founded.
- Battle of St Gothard: Turks under

Ahmed Kiuprili defeated by Imperialists under Montecuculi.
- Jean Baptiste Colbert becomes chief minister under Louis XIV.
- Treaty of Vasvar between Turks and the Empire.
- First Conventicle Act in England.
- English expedition seizes New Netherland and changes New Amsterdam to New York.

1665
- Battle of Lowestoft: English naval victory over Dutch.
- Battle of Montes Claros: Portuguese defeat Spaniards.
- Great Plague in London.
- Charles II becomes King of Spain.
- Five Mile Act.
  DEATHS
  Nicolas Poussin, French painter.

1666
- Louis XIV declares war against England.
- Monck and Rupert defeated by De Ruyter in Four Days' Naval Battle.
- Dutch fleet defeated by Monck and Rupert.
- Great Fire of London.
- Quadruple Alliance: Holland, Brandenburg, Denmark and Brunswick-Lüneburg.
- Battle of Rullion Green: Scottish Covenanters defeated.

1667
- Act of English Parliament against Irish cattle trade.

- Dutch conquer Surinam and Tobago.
- Secret Treaty between Charles II and Louis XIV.
- War of Devolution in regard to Spanish Netherlands.
- Dutch fleet in the Thames.
- Peace of Breda between England and Holland.
- Lille taken by French.
- Fall of Clarendon in England: the Cabal ministry takes over.

1668
- Spain recognises independence of Portugal.
- France conquers Franche-Comté.
- Triple Alliance: England, Holland and Sweden.
- Peace of Aix-la-Chapelle between France and Spain.
- Abdication of John Casimir of Poland.

1669
- Michael Korybut Wisniowiecki becomes King of Poland.
- Turks conquer Crete.
- Ormond recalled from Ireland: restored in 1667.
- Secret Treaty between Louis XIV and the Elector of Brandenburg.
  DEATHS
  Rembrandt, Dutch painter.

1670
- Christian V becomes King of Denmark.
- Treaty between Holland and Brandenburg.

- Second Conventicle Act.
- Secret Treaty of Dover between Charles II and Louis XIV.

1671
- Leaders of a Hungarian Conspiracy executed.

1672
- Stop of the Exchequer in England.
- First Declaration of Indulgence issued.
- England declares war against Holland.
- Treaty between Sweden and France; also one between Sweden and England.
- War between France and Holland.
- Battle of Southwold Bay: De Ruyter defeats an Anglo-French fleet under the Duke of York.
- Alliance between the Emperor and Brandenburg.
- John de Witt resigns post of Grand Pensionary of Holland.
- Murder of John and Cornelius de Witt.
- Alliance between Emperor and Holland.

1673
- Test Act passed, barring Roman Catholics from holding public office.
- Charles II cancels Declaration of Indulgence.
- Battles of Schooneveld: De Ruyter against Rupert: both drawn.
- Battle of Kykduin: De Ruyter defeats Anglo-French fleet.

- Death of King Michael of Poland.
- Battle of Khoczim: John Sobieski defeats Turks.
- William of Orange takes Bonn: French have to evacuate Netherlands.
DEATHS
Molière, French playwright.

1674
- Peace between England and Holland.
- John Sobieski elected King of Poland.
- Franche-Comté conquered by France.
- Battle of Sinsheim: Turennne defeats the Imperialists and devastates the Palatinate.
- Battle of Seneff: indecisive conflict between William of Orange and Condé.
- Battle of Enzheim: Turenne's victory.
- Sweden at war with Brandenburg.
- Pondicherry founded by French in India.
- Sivaji crowns himself an independent Mahratta sovereign in India: wars with Aurangzeb.
DEATHS
John Milton, English poet.

1675
- Battle of Calmar: Turenne defeats the Great Elector and conquers Alsace.
- Battle of Fehrbellin: Great Elector's decisive victory over Sweden.
- Turenne killed.
- Shaftesbury organises an opposition

in English Parliament: beginning of Whig Party.
- Letters of Intercommuning in Scotland against Covenanters.
- Battle of Lemberg: Sobieski defeats the Turks.
- War of Scania begins between Sweden and Denmark.

1676

- Battle of Öland: Swedish naval disaster.
- Danes conquer Scania.
- Treaty of Zurawna between Turkey and Poland.
- Kara Mustafa succeeds Ahmed Kiuprili as Vizier of Turkey.
- Theodore II Tsar of Russia.
- French found Chandernagore in India.

1677

- Battle of Landskrona: Charles XI victorious over Danes.
- Marriage of William of Orange and Mary, daughter of James, Duke of York.
- Turkey at war with Russia.
- Stettin capitulates to the Great Elector.
  DEATHS
  Benedict Spinoza, Dutch philosopher.

1678

- Treaty between England and Holland.
- Peace between France and Holland.
- Titus Oates and the Popish Plot against King Charles II.

- Murder of Sir Edmund Berry Godfrey.
- Swedes expelled from Germany.

1679

- Archbishop Sharp murdered by Scottish Covenanters.
- Exclusion Bill introduced by English Parliament.
- Battle of Drumclog: Scottish Covenanters defeat Graham of Claverhouse.
- Battle of Bothwell Bridge: Covenanters defeated by Duke of Monmouth.
- Treaty of St Germain between Brandenburg and Sweden.
- Treaty of Fontainebleau between Denmark and Sweden.
- Peace of Nimeguen: treaties between France, Spain, Holland and Empire.
- The Great Elector makes an alliance with France.

1680

- Petitioners and Abhorrers for and against Exclusion Bill: beginning of English party system.
- House of Lords reject Exclusion Bill.
- Sanquhar Declaration: Charles II disowned by strong Covenanters.
- Battle of Aird's Moss, Ayrshire, Scotland: Covenanter Richard Cameron killed.

1681

- French occupy Strassburg.
- Donald Cargill executed in Scotland.

Pedro Calderon de la Barca, Spanish dramatist.

1682
- Revolt of Hungary.
- Death of Theodore II: Tsarevna Sophia becomes Regent for Ivan and Peter.

1683
- City of London charter forfeited.
- Rye House Plot against King Charles II discovered.
- Siege of Vienna by Turks under Kara Mustafa: relieved by John Sobieski.
- Battle of Parkány (Oct 7): Turks defeat Poles.
- Battle of Parkány (Oct 9): Turks defeated by Austrians and Poles: Gran captured.
- Kara Mustafa executed.
- Execution of English plotters Algernon Sidney and Russell.

1684
- Holy League against Turks between Austria, Poland and Venice.
- French take Luxemburg.
- Truce of Ratisbon between Louis XIV and Emperor Leopold.

1685
- Accession of James VII of Scotland and II of England.
- Alliance between Great Elector and Holland.
- Duke of Monmouth proclaims himself King.

- Battle of Sedgemoor: defeat of Monmouth.
- Judge Jeffreys and the Bloody Assizes in England.
- Execution of Monmouth.
- Execution of Earl of Argyle.
- Venetians under Francesco Morosini begin conquest of Morea.
- Battle of Gran: Charles of Lorraine defeats the Turks.
- Buda captured from the Turks.
- Revocation of Edict of Nantes in France: great emigration of the Huguenots.

1686
- Tyrconnel commander-in-chief in Ireland.
- Second Treaty between Frederick William and the Emperor.
- Augsburg Alliance to maintain Treaties of Westphalia and Nimeguen.

1687
- Tyrconnel Viceroy of Ireland.
- Second Declaration of Indulgence.
- Venetians capture Corinth
- Battle of Mohacs: Imperial victory by Charles of Lorraine and Lewis of Baden over Turks.
- Venetians take Athens.
- Mohammed IV supplanted by Suleiman II.

1688
- Frederick III Elector of Brandenburg.
- Acquital of Seven Bishops for opposing James II's policy of religious toleration.

- Invitation to William of Orange.
- Belgrade taken by the Elector of Bavaria.
- William of Orange lands in England: flight of James II to France: the 'Glorious Revolution'.
  DEATHS
  John Bunyan, English author.

1689

- House of Commons declare the English throne vacant: William and Mary declared joint sovereigns.
- The Palatinate devastated by forces of Louis XIV.
- Ex-King James II lands in Ireland.
- Louis XIV declares war against Spain.
- Scottish Parliament declare that James II has forfeited the Scottish crown: William and Mary chosen.
- Siege of Derry: ultimately relieved.
- Toleration Act in England.
- Battle of Killiecrankie: Claverhouse, Viscount Dundee, killed in hour of victory.
- Battle of Newtown Butler: James II's army defeated.
- Bill of Rights in England.
- Sophia's rule overthrown in Russia.

THE SPANISH SUCCESSION

1690

- Battle of the Boyne: James defeated and flees to France: Schomberg killed.
- Battle of Fleurus: French victory by Luxembourg over Dutch and allies.

- Battle of Beachy Head: French naval victory by Tourville over England and Holland.
- First Siege of Limerick.
- Belgrade recaptured by the Turks.
- Scottish Parliament abolishes the Lords of the Articles and Lay Patronage and re-establishes Presbyterianism: Scottish Parliament becomes a real power in Scotland.

1691

- French take Mons.
- Athlone taken by Ginkel.
- Battle of Aughrim: Ginkel defeats St Ruth (who is killed).
- Galway surrenders to William's forces.
- Second Siege of Limerick: capitulated.
- Battle of Szalankemen: Turks defeated by Lewis of Baden.

1692

- Massacre of Glencoe.
- Battle of La Hogue: Russell's naval victory over French.
- Louis XIV takes Namur.
- Battle of Steinkirke:Luxembourg defeats William of Orange.

1693

- Battle of Neerwinden: Luxembourg defeats William of Orange.
- Battle of Marsaglia: Duke of Savoy defeated by Catinat.
- Dutch take Pondicherry.
- National Debt created in England by Charles Montagu.

1694

- Bank of England founded by William Paterson.
- Triennal Act in England.
  DEATHS
  Queen Mary (England).

1695

- William III takes Namur.
- Freedom of Press established in England.
- Fénelon becomes Bishop of Cambrai.
- Darien Scheme proposed by Paterson.
- Anti-Catholic legislation in Ireland.
- Mustafa II Sultan.

1696

- Recoinage Act.
- Assassination Plot against William III discovered.
- Russia takes Azoff.
- Death of Ivan V: Peter the Great rules alone.
- Duke of Savoy joins France.

1697

- Charles XII King of Sweden.
- Irish Parliament refuses full ratification of the Articles of Limerick.
- Elector of Saxony elected King of Poland as Augustus II.
- Battle of Zenta: Turks defeated by Prince Eugene.
- Peace of Ryswick between France, England, Holland, Spain and the Empire.
  DEATHS
  John Aubrey, English author.

1698

- Revolt of the Strieltzy in Russia suppressed.
- First Treaty of Partition (of Spanish dominions) between Louis XIV and William III.
- New East India Company founded in England.

1699

- Treaty of Carlowitz between Austria, Venice, Poland and Turkey: Austria gains Hungary, Poland Podolia, Venice Dalmatia and Morea.
- Death of Joseph Ferdinand of Bavaria: Spanish Succession reopened.
- Second Partition Treaty.
- English legislation against Irish woollen industry.
- Frederick IV King of Denmark.
- Convention between Denmark and Russia.
- Alliance of Denmark and Poland against Sweden.
- Russia signs treaty with Poland for partition of Sweden.
  DEATHS
  Jean Racine, French dramatist.

1700

- Act of Resumption in Ireland.
- Thirty Years' Truce between Russia and Turkey.
- Great Northern war begins: Russia and Poland against Sweden.
- Peace of Traventhal between Denmark and Sweden.

- Last Will of Charles II of Spain makes Duke Philip of Anjou his heir.
- Death of Charles II of Spain: Louis XIV accepts the dead king's will: War of Spanish Succession begins.
- Battle of Narva: Charles XII defeats Russians.
  DEATHS
  John Dryden, English poet.

1701

- Brandenburg erected into the kingdom of Prussia: Frederick III first King as Frederick I.
- Prince Eugene invades Italy.
- Battle of Dünamunde: Charles XII defeats Russians and Saxons: Courland occupied.
- Battle of Chiari: Eugene defeats Villeroi.
- Grand Alliance concluded between England, Holland and the Holy Roman Emperor.
- Act of Settlement in England.

1702

- Battle of Errestièr: Swedes defeated by Russians.
- Eugene raids Cremona and captures Villeroi.
- King William III dies in a riding accident; Anne becomes Queen of Britain.
- Charles XII at Warsaw.
- The Allies take Kaiserswerth.
- Battle of Hummelshof: Swedes defeated by Russians.
- Battle of Klissow: Charles XII de-

feats Poles and Saxons: Cracow captured.
- Failure of English attack on Cadiz.
- English admiral Sir George Rooke destroys Plate fleet in Vigo.
- Battle of Friedlingen: Lewis of Baden defeated by Villers.
- English general Marlborough takes Liège.
- Camisard Rebellion (Huguenot) in central France.

1703

- Battle of Scharding: Austrians defeated by Bavarians.
- Battle of Pultusk: Charles XII defeats Saxons.
- Methuan Treaty between England and Portugal: another Methuan Treaty (commercial) later in same year.
- Marlborough takes Bonn.
- Battle of Höchstädt: Villars defeats Germans.
- Savoy joins Grand Alliance.
- Battle of Speyerbach: Allies defeated by Tallard.
- St Petersburg founded by Peter the Great.
- Act of Security in Scotland.
  DEATHS
  Samuel Pepys, English diarist.

1704

- Alien Act in England.
- Marlborough's victory at Donauwörth.
- Stanislaus Leszczynski made King of Poland by Charles XII.

- Russians take Dorpat and Narva.
- Rooke captures Gibralter.
- Battle of Blenheim: Marlborough and Eugene defeat Tallard and the Elector of Bavaria.
- Battle of Malaga: drawn naval battle between Rooke and Toulouse.
- Warsaw recaptured from Charles XII.
- Marlborough occupies Trier.

1705

- Death of Leopold I: Joseph I elected Emperor.
- Battle of Gemaurhof: Swedes defeat Russian attempt on Coutland.

1706

- Battle of Fraustadt: Swedish victory.
- Allies take Madrid (soon evacuated).
- Battle of Ramillies: Marlborough crushes Villeroi.
- Marlborough takes Ostend.
- Battle of Turin: Eugene defeats the investing army: French evacuate Piedmont.
- Peace of Altranstädt between Saxony and Sweden: Stanislaus recognised as King.
- Execution of Patkul.
- Battle of Kalisch: Swedes defeated by Russians and Saxons.
  DEATHS
  Pierre Bayle, French philosopher.

1707

- Convention of Milan: France abandons North Italy.

- Battle of Almanza: British defeated in Spain by Berwick.
- Treaty of Union between Scotland and England.
- Eugene abandons attempt on Toulon.
- Perpetual Alliance between Prussia and Sweden.
- Death of Aurangzeb: Mogul Empire in decline.

1708

- Whig Ministry in England.
- Battle of Holowczyn: Charles XII defeats Russians.
- Battle of Oudenarde: Marlborough defeats Vendôme.
- Battle of Lyesna: Swedes under Levenhaupt defeated by Russians.
- Leake and Stanhope take Minorca and Sardinia.
- Cossack leader Mazepa joined Charles XII.
- Lille taken by the Allies.
- Union of the two British East India Companies.

1709

- Battle of Pultawa: Charles XII defeated by Peter the Great and flees to Turkey.
- Alliance between Denmark and Augustus of Poland and Saxony.
- Battle of Malplaquet: victory of Marlborough and Eugene.
- Allies take Mons.
- New League against Sweden is formed between Augustus and Peter the Great.

- First Barrier Treaty between Britain and Holland.
- Danish invasion of Scania.

1710

- Battle of Helsingborg: Danes are defeated and driven out of Sweden.
- Russians take Viborg, Riga, Pernau and Reval.
- Battle of Almenara: defeat of Spaniards by Starhemberg.
- Impeachment by English parliament of Dr Henry Sacheverell for a sermon against religious toleration.
- Battle of Saragossa: Spaniards defeated by Starhemberg.
- Madrid again occupied by Allies.

1711

- War between Russia and Turkey.
- Death of Emperor Joseph: Charles VI elected Emperor.
- Peace of the Pruth between Russia and Turkey.
- Marlborough dismissed.

1712

- Peers created in British Parliament to pass peace clauses.
- Battle of Denain: Dutch defeated by Villars.
- Lay Patronage restored in Scottish Church against Scottish opinion.
- Battle of Gadesbusch: Swedish victory over Danes.

1713

- Second Barrier Treaty between Britain and Holland.

- Charles XII's defence against Turks at Bender.
- Death of Frederick I of Prussia: Frederick William I succeeds.
- Treaty of Utrecht ends War of Spanish Succession: Acadia, Newfoundland and other territories, ceded by France to Britain; Victor Amadeus of Savoy becomes King of Sicily.
- Pragmatic Sanction of Charles VI to settle Austrian Succession.
- Swedish forces capitulate at Oldenburg.
- Peace of Adrianople between Russia and Turkey.
- Papal Bull Unigenitus condemns Jansenism.

THE AUSTRIAN SUCCESSION

1714

- Peace of Rastadt between Austria and France: accepted by Empire in Peace of Baden.
- Accession of George I in Britain: beginning of Hanovarian dynasty.
- Peter the Great conquers Finland.

1715

- Louis XV becomes King of France.
- Jacobite rebellion in Scotland and northern England.
- Battle of Preston: Jacobites defeated and their army surrenders.
- Battle of Sheriffmuir between Jacobites and Royalists: indecisive
- Denmark cedes Bremen and Verden to Hanover.
- Third Dutch Barrier Treaty.

- Commercial treaty between Britain and Spain.

1716

- Commercial treaty between Britain and Holland.
- Prussia captures all Swedish Pomerania.
- Battle of Peterwardein: Turks defeated by Prince Eugene.
- John Law establishes Banque générale in France.
- Treaty of Westminster between Britain and the Emperor.
- Septenniel Act in Britain, life of Parliament extended from three to seven years.
- Triple Alliance: France, Britain and Holland.
- Turks conquer Morea.
  DEATHS
  Gottfried Wilhelm Leibnitz, German philosopher.

1717

- John Law founds the Louisiana Company.
- Spanish conquest of Sardinia.
- Bangorian controversy.
- Battle of Belgrade: Turks defeated by Prince Eugene.

1718

- Peace of Passarowitz between the Empire and the Turks.
- Charles VI joins Triple Alliance, making it a Quadruple Alliance.
- Battle of Cape Passaro: Byng destroys the Spanish fleet.

- Death of Charles XII of Spain.
- Victor Amadeus of Savoy becomes King of Sardinia instead of King of Sicily.
- Britain declares war against Spain.

1719

- France declares war against Spain.
- Treaty of Vienna between George I, Austria and Saxony.
- Treaty of Stockholm between Hanover and Sweden.
- Fall of the Spanish minister Alberoni.
- Daniel Defoe *Robinson Crusoe*.
  DEATHS
  Joseph Addison, English essayist.

1720

- Quadruple Alliance joined by Spain, Denmark and Poland.
- Failure of Law's Banque générale in France.
- Outbreak of Plague in Marseilles and southern France.
- South Sea Bubble.
- Francis Atterbury's plot to restore the Stuarts to English throne.
- Treaties between Sweden and Prussia and between Sweden and Denmark.

1721

- Treaty of Madrid between Spain and France.
- Sir Robert Walpole becomes prime minister.
- Peace of Nystad between Peter the Great and Sweden: Sweden ceases to be a first-rate power.

1722
• Peter the Great takes Baku.

1723
• Ostend East India Company chartered by Charles VI.

  DEATHS
  Christopher Wren, English architect.

1724
• Abdication of Philip V of Spain: Luis's short reign: re-accession of Philip V.
• Jonathan Swift begins publication of his *Drapier's Letters*.

1725
• First Treaty of Vienna between Austria and Spain.
• Alliance of Hanover between Britain, France and Prussia.
• Catherine I succeeds Peter the Great in Russia.

1726
• Alliance of Hanover joined by Sweden and Denmark.
• Treaty of Wusterhausen between Austria and Prussia.

1727
• Spain declares war against Britain.
• Peter II Tsar of Russia.
• George II King of Britain.
• First Indemnity Act for Nonconformists in England.

  DEATHS
  Isaac Newton, English scientist.

1728
• Convention of Pardo ends War between Spain and Britain.

1729
• Beginning of Methodist revival in Britain.
• Treaty of Seville between Britain, France and Spain.
• The Ostend Company abolished.

  DEATHS
  William Congreve, English dramatist.

1730
• Anne becomes Tsarina of Russia.
• Victor Amadeus, King of Sardinia, abdicates: succeeded by Charles Emmanuel.
• Christian VI becomes King of Denmark.

1731
• Spain denounces the Treaty of Seville.
• Britain and Holland guarantee the Pragmatic Sanction.
• Second Treaty of Vienna: Emperor ratifies Treaty of Seville: Spain afterwards accedes.

1733
• Death of Augustus II of Poland: Stanisláus Leszczynski elected king, also Augustus III: War of Polish Succession follows.
• Battle of Bitonto: Spanish victory in Italy over Austrian forces.
• Treaty of Turin between France and Sardinia.

- Treaty of the Escurial: First Family Compact between France and Spain.
- Prime Minister Sir Robert Walpole compelled to withdraw Excise Bill.
- Invention of fly shuttle by John Kay.
- Jethro Tull *The Horse-Hoeing Husbandry* encouraging improved agricultural techniques.

1735

- Abdication of Stanislaus Leszczynski: Augustus III elected King of Poland.
- War begins between Russia and Turkey.

1736

- Porteous Riots in Edinburgh.

1737

- Third Treaty of Vienna ends War of the Polish Succession: Don Carlos established as King of Naples.

1738

- Parties of Hats and Caps first appear in Sweden.

1739

- Peace of Belgrade: Austria sacrifices to Turks all the achievements of Peace of Passarowitz.
- Treaty of Constantinople ends Russo-Turkish war.
- War between Britain and Spain.
- Portobello in West Indies captured by Vernon.

1740

- Frederick II (Frederick the Great) becomes King of Prussia.
- Ivan VI becomes Tsar of Russia.
- Death of Charles VI: War of Austrian Succession begins, to prevent accession of his daughter, Maria Theresa.
- Invasion of Silesia by Frederick the Great.
- Samuel Richardson *Pamela*.

1741

- Battle of Mollwitz: Frederick the Great's victory over Austrians.
- Treaty of Breslau between France and Frederick the Great.
- Sweden declares war against Russia.
- Battle of Vilmanstrand: defeat of Swedes.
- Convention of Klein-Schnellendorf: Maria Theresa abandons Lower Silesia to Frederick.
- Frederick's allies capture Prague and Frederick invades Moravia.
- Elizabeth becomes Tsarina of Russia.
- Handel *Messiah*.
- Thomas Arne *Rule, Brittania!*

1742

- Fall of Sir Robert Walpole.
- Charles VII elected Emperor.
- Battle of Chotusitz: Austrians defeated by Frederick the Great.
  DEATHS
  Edmund Halley, English astronomer.

1743
- Battle of Campo Santo: Spanish defeat.
- Treaty of Worms between Austria, Britain and Sardinia.
- Battle of Dettingen: George II defeats the French.
- Peace of Berlin between Austria, Prussia and Saxony.
- Peace of Abo between Sweden and Russia.
- Treaty of Fontainebleau: Second Family Compact between France and Spain.

1744
- Union of Frankfort between Prussia, Hesse-Cassel and Elector Palatine.
- Henry Pelham Ministry in Britain.
- Invasion of Bohemia by Frederick the Great.
- War declared between Britain and France.
- Britain captures Louisburg from America.
  DEATHS
  Alexander Pope, English poet.

1745
- Death of Charles VII: Francis I, husband of Maria Theresa, elected Emperor.
- Treaty of Füssen between Austria and Bavaria.
- Jacobite rebellion in Britain.
- Battle of Prestonpans: Prince Charles Edward victorious.
- Battle of Fontenoy: defeat of British by Marshal Saxe.

- Alliance between Austria and Russia.
- Battle of Hohenfriedberg: Frederick the Great victorious.
- Battles of Sohr and Hennersdorf: Frederick the Great victorious.
- Battle of Kesselsdorf: Prussian victory over Austrians and Saxons.
- Battle of Basignano: French and Spanish victory in Italy: Milan captured.
- Treaty of Dresden between Prussia and Austria.
  DEATHS
  Jonathan Swift, English author.

1746
- Battle of Falkirk: Prince Charles victorious.
- Franco-Sardinian Alliance.
- Milan retaken from the French and Spaniards with aid of Charles Emmanuel of Sardinia: all Piedmont and Lombardy recovered.
- Brussels taken by Marshal Saxe.
- Frederick V King of Denmark
- Franco-Danish Alliance.
- Battle of Culloden: Jacobites finally crushed.
- Battle of Piacenza: Austrian victory.
- Treaty of St Petersburg between Russia and Austria.
- Britain takes Cape Breton.
- Ferdinand VI King of Spain.
- Battle of Roucoux: Marshal Saxe defeats the Allies: Netherlands secured.
- France captures Madras.

1747
- William IV Stadtholder of United Provinces.
- Treaty between Prussia and Sweden.
- Battle of Lauffeldt: French victory.

1748
- French take Bergen-op-Zoom.
- Treaty of Aix-La-Chapelle: War of Austrian Succession ended.

THE RISE OF THE BRITISH EMPIRE

1749
- Commercial Treaty of Aquisgran between Britain and Spain.
- Dupliex makes the Carnatic French.
- Henry Fielding *Tom Jones*.

1750
- Bill for the Prohibition of Colonial Manufactures before Parliament.
- Joseph becomes King of Portugal.
  DEATHS
  Johann Sebastian Bach, German composer.

1751
- Seizure and defence of Arcot by Clive.
- The *Encyclopédie* begins to appear in France.

1752
- Treaty of Aranjuez between Spain and Austria regarding Italy.
- Britain adopts the Gregorian calendar.

1755
- Convention of St Petersburg between Britain and Russia.
- Great Lisbon earthquake.
- English general Edward Braddock's forces destroyed by French and Indians in America.

1756
- Convention of Westminster between Britain and Prussia.
- Devonshire and Pitt (afterwards Earl of Chatham) forms a Ministry.
- Treaty of Versailles between France and Austria.
- France captures Minorca.
- Britain declares war against France: Seven Years' War begins.
- Surajah Dowlah seizes Calcutta: the Black Hole of Calcutta, in which many British prisoners are suffocated.
- Battle of Lobositz: Frederick the Great against the Austrians: indecisive.
- Russia adheres to Treaty of Versailles.

1757
- Clive captures Calcutta and Chandernagore.
- New Treaty of Versailles between France and Austria.
- Battle of Plassey: Clive's victory over Surajah Dowlah.
- Battle of Prague: Frederick defeats the Austrians.
- Battle of Kolin: Frederick defeated by Austrians under Daun.

- Battle of Hastenbeck: Hanoverians under Duke of Cumberland beaten by French.
- Battle of Gross-Jägerndorf: Prussians defeated by Russians.
- Convention of Klosterzeven: Hanoverian army to be disbanded.
- Battle of Rossbach: Frederick defeats the French.
- Battle of Breslau: Prussians defeated by Austrians.
- Battle of Leuthen: Prussian victory over the Austrians.

1758
- British capture Louisburg.
- Robert Clive becomes Governor of Bengal.
- Battle of Zorndorf: drawn between Frederick and the Russians.
- Battle of Hochkirch: Frederick defeated by Austrians.

1759
- Battle of Kay: Prussians defeated by Russians.
- Battle of Minden: French defeated by Ferdinand of Brunswick: Hanover saved.
- Battle of Kunersdorf: Frederick defeated by Russians.
- Battle of Quebec: Britain captures it from French: Wolfe and Montcalm killed.
- Charles III King of Spain.
- Jesuits expelled from Portugal and Brazil.
- Battle of Quiberon Bay: Hawke destroys French fleet.

1760
- Battle of Wandewash: Sir Eyre Coote defeats French in India: Pondicherry taken following year.
- Battle of Landshut: Prussian force annihilated: fall of Glatz.
- Battle of Leignitz: Frederick defeats the Austrians.
- Russians occupy Berlin.
- George III King of Britain.
- Capitulation of Montreal: Britain in control of Canada.
- Battle of Torgau: Frederick defeats the Austrians.

1761
- Battle of Panipat: Mahrattas defeated by Afghans in India: the Mogul Empire now only a shadow.
- Spaniards invade Portugal.
- Treaty of San Ildefonso: Third Family Compact between France and Spain.
- Fall of William Pitt the Elder, Prime Minister.
- Earl of Bute becomes Prime Minister.

1762
- Britain declares war against Spain.
- Peter III becomes Tsar of Russia; Catharine II Tsarina soon afterwards.
- Prussia concludes peace with Russia and Sweden: alliance between Russia and Prussia.
- Martinique, Havana, Manila and other territories, captured by Britain.

- Battle of Wilhelmsthal: British and Hanoverian victory over France.
- Battle of Lutternberg: British and Hanoverians defeat the French.
- Battle of Freiberg: Prussians defeat the Austrians.
- Jean Jacques Rousseau *Du Contrat Social*.

1763
- Seven Years' War ended by Peace of Hubertusburg between Prussia, Austria and Saxony and Peace of Paris between France, Spain and Britain: Britain gains Canada and other territories.
- Lord Bute resigns office in Britain: Granville Ministry formed.
- Whiteboy outbreaks in Ireland.

THE RISE OF THE UNITED STATES

1764
- John Wilkes expelled from House of Commons for attacks on the British monarchy.
- Stanislaus Poniatowski elected King of Poland.
- Jesuits expelled from France.
- Battle of Buxar: Britain gains Oude and other territories in India.
- Invention of Spinning Jenny by James Hargreaves.

1765
- Stamp Act passed by British Parliament.
- Joseph II becomes Emperor.

1766
- Repeal of Stamp Act, but Declaratory Act passed declaring Britain's right to tax the colonies.
- France annexes Lorraine.
- Oliver Goldsmith *Vicar of Wakefield*.

1767
- Spain expels the Jesuits.
- Treaty of alliance between Prussia and Russia.
- Tea and other duties imposed by British Parliament on America.

1768
- Corsica bought by France from Genoa.
- Renewal of alliance between Russia and Prussia.
- Confederation of Bar formed in Poland.
- Russia invades Poland.
- Turks declare war against Russia.
- Royal Academy established.
- The water frame invented by Richard Arkwright.

DEATHS
Laurence Sterne, English novelist.

1769
- Russians defeat Turks and occupied Moldavia and Bucharest.

1770
- Lord North becomes British Prime Minister.
- The 'Boston Massacre'.
- Spaniards attack Falkland Islands.

- Battle of Tchesmé: Turkish fleet destroyed by Russia.
- James Cook discovers New South Wales.
- Edmund Burke *Thoughts on the Present Discontents*.
  DEATHS
  Thomas Chatterton, English poet.

1771
- Parliament of Paris exiled.
- Gustavus III King of Sweden.
- Russia occupies the Crimea.
  DEATHS
  Tobias Smollet, Scottish novelist.

1772
- First Partition of Poland between Russia, Austria and Prussia.
- Royal Marriage Act in Britain.
- Gustavus III re-establishes absolutism in Sweden.
- Struensee, Danish reforming statesman, executed: Guldberg in power.

1773
- Alliance between France and Sweden.
- Jesuit Order suppressed by Pope Clement XIV.
- Indian Regulating Act passed.
- Warren Hastings becomes first Governor-General of Bengal.
- Pugachoff's insurrection in Russia.

1774
- Boston Tea Riot: retaliatory legislation by British Parliament.
- Louis XVI becomes King of France.

- Turgot becomes Finance Minister of France.
- Quebec Act passed.
- Battle of Shumla: Russians rout Turks.
- Treaty of Kutchuk-Kainardji between Russia and Turkey.
- Oxygen discovered by Joseph Priestley.
- Chlorine discovered by Karl Wilhelm Scheele.

1775
- Battle of Lexington: American victory.
- George Washington becomes commander-in-chief.
- Battle of Bunker Hill: Americans defeated.
- Spaniards attack Algiers.

1776
- Spaniards attack Sacramento.
- Parliament passes a Prohibitory Act against American commerce.
- Declaration of Independence by American colonies.
- Edward Gibbon begins *Decline and Fall of the Roman Empire*.
- Adam Smith *Inquiry into the Nature and Causes of the Wealth of Nations*.
  DEATHS
  David Hume, Scottish philosopher.

1777
- Maria I Queen of Portugal along with Pedro III.
- Necker becomes Finance Minister of France.

- General Burgoyne capitulates to Americans at Saratoga.

1778

- Treaty of Paris between France and America.
- Treaty of the Pardo between Spain and Portugal.
- Bavarian War of Succession begins.
- Treaty between Holland and America.
- Saville's Roman Catholic Relief Act.

  DEATHS
  Giambattista Piranesi, Italian etcher and architect.
  Voltaire, French writer.

1779

- Treaty of Teschen between Austria and Russia ends War of Bavarian Succession.
- Spain declares war against Britain.
- Siege of Gibraltar begins (relieved following year).
- The spinning mule invented by Samuel Crompton.

  DEATHS
  David Garrick, English actor.

1780

- Joseph II sole Emperor on death of Maria Theresa.
- Holland declares war against Britain.
- Armed Neutrality formed against Britain by Russia and Prussia.
- Alliance of Austria and Russia against Turkey.

- Hyder Ali conquers Carnatic.
  DEATHS
  Bernardo Canaletto, Italian painter.

1781

- French attack on Jersey defeated by Pierson.
- Rodney's victories in West Indies.
- French admiral De Grasse captures Tobago.
- Patent of Tolerance issued by Joseph II.
- Battle of Porto Novo: Sir Eyre Coote defeats Hyder Ali.
- Capitulation of Cornwallis in Yorktown to Americans.
- Serfdom abolished by Joseph II.

1782

- French capture Minorca and various West Indian islands.
- Spain suppresses rebellion in Peru.
- Evacuation of Barrier fortresses by Dutch.
- Rodney's victory over De Grasse in West Indies saves Jamaica.
- Declaration of Rights by Grattan: Irish legislative independence.
- Relief of Gibraltar by Howe.
- British inventor James Watt patents his steam engine.

1783

- Treaty of Versailles between Britain, France and America.
- Britain recognises independence of American colonies.
- Coalition Ministry of Fox and North.

- William Pitt the Younger in power in Britain.
- Catherine II annexes the Crimea.

1784
- Bernstorff in power in Denmark.
- India Act of William Pitt.
- Treaty of Constantinople between Russia and Turkey: Crimea finally passes to Russia.

1785
- Sweden declares war against Russia.
- Battle of Hogland: Russian naval victory over Sweden.
- The Fürstenbund (League of Princes) formed by Frederick the Great.
- Danish attack on Sweden.
- Treaty of Fontainebleau abrogates Barrier Treaty of 1715.
- The Diamond Necklace Affair in France.
- Power loom invented by Edmund Cartwright.
  DEATHS
  Samuel Johnson, English lexicographer.

1786
- Death of Frederick the Great: succeeded by Frederick William II.
- Commercial Treaty between Britain and France.
- Robert Burns *Poems Chiefly in the Scottish Dialect*.

1787
- Impeachment of Warren Hastings begins: Edmund Burke the leader.

- Disturbances in Austrian Netherlands.
- Invasion of Holland by Prussia.
- Assembly of Notables meet in France.
- Austria and Russia declare war against Turkey.

1788
- Triple Alliance between Britain, Holland and Prussia.
- First motion in House of Commons for abolition of slave trade.
- War between Sweden and Russia.
- Convention of Uddevalla: Danes evacuate Sweden.
- Charles IV King of Spain.
- Russians take Ochakoff from the Turks.

THE FRENCH REVOLUTION

1789
- Bread Riots in France.
- Gustavus III makes Swedish monarchy virtually absolute.
- States General meet in Versailles (4 May).
- Third Estate declares itself a National Assembly (17 June).
- Joseph II cancels the liberties of Brabant.
- Oath of the Tennis Court.
- Union of the Three Estates.
- Committee of the Constitution appointed.
- Fall of Necker.
- Fall of the Bastille (14 July).
- Battle of Focsani: Turks defeated by Austrians and Russians.

- King recalls Necker.
- Great reforming session of National Assembly on August 4: feudal tenures abolished, etc.
- Declaration of the Rights of Man.
- Battle of Rimnik: Turks defeated by Austrians and Russians.
- Émeute in Paris: mob marches to Versailles: King and National Assembly go to Paris (October).
- Austrians take Belgrade.
- Church lands nationalised by National Assembly (November).
- Assignats first issued (December).
- George Washington elected first President of the US.
- Selim III becomes Sultan of Turkey.

1790

- Belgian Republic constituted (January): suppressed in November.
- Alliance between Prussia and Turkey.
- French National Assembly deprives monastic vows of force and suppresses religious orders.
- Leopold II Emperor.
- Convention of Reichenbach: ends war between Austria and Turkey and Russia: war between Prussia and Austria averted.
- Suppression by France of a revolt in San Domingo.
- Treaty of Werelå between Russia and Sweden.
- Civil constitution of the clergy enacted in France.
- Resignation of Necker in France.
- Nootka Sound Convention between Britain and Spain.

- National Assembly issue a decree imposing an oath on the clergy.
- Edmund Burke *Reflections on the French Revolution*.

1791

- National Assembly decrees abolition of slavery in West Indies.
- New Polish constitution granted by Stanislaus Poniatowski: throne made hereditary.
- Flight of Louis XVI to Varennes.
- Massacre of the Champ de Mars.
- Treaty of Sistova between Austria and Turkey.
- Conference of Pillnitz between Emperor and Prussian King to arrange for support of Louis XVI.
- Fresh slave revolt in San Domingo.
- New French Constitution enacted (September).
- Union of Avignon and the Venaissin to France decreed.
- Louis XVI takes the oath to the new Constitution.
- End of National Assembly (30 September): Legislative Assembly begins next day.
- Treaty of Drottningholm between Sweden and Russia.
- Decree against the émigrés: vetoed by Louis XVI.
- Decree against non-juring priests: vetoed by Louis XVI.
- Joseph Priestley's house in Birmingham burned down by mob.
- Wolfe Tone founds the Society of United Irishmen.
- Constitutional Act for Canada.

- Thomas Paine *Rights of Man*: reply to Edmund Burke's *Reflections*.
  DEATHS
  Mirabeau, French political writer.
  Wolfgang Amadeus Mozart, German composer.

1792
- Treaty of Jassy: ends war between Russia and Turkey: Russia obtained Crimea.
- Tipu surrenders Seringapatam to the British: end of Second Mysore War.
- Alliance between Austria and Prussia.
- Francis II becomes Emperor.
- Assassination of Gustavus III of Sweden: Gustavus IV succeeds.
- A Jacobin ministry in power in France.
- 'Society of the Friends of the People' founded in Britain.
- France declares war against Austria (20 April).
- Russia invades Poland and Lithuania.
- Insurrection in the Tuileries at Paris: the Tuileries later taken by the mob.
- Longwy taken from the French by the Allies: then Verdun.
- September Massacres in Paris.
- Battle of Valmy: Dumouriez defeats Prussians.
- National Convention replaces Legislative Assembly (21 September).
- Monarchy abolished in France.
- French take Nice, Spires and Mainz.
- Battle of Jemappes: Dumouriez defeated Austrians: Brussels occupied by French.
- National Convention offers its protection to all nations struggling for freedom.
- Opening of Scheldt to commerce.
- Trial of Louis XVI begun.
- Outbreak of the bubonic plague in Egypt kills 800, 000.
- Mary Wollstonecraft *Vindication of the Rights of Women*.
- Rouget de Lisle *La Marseillaise*.
  DEATHS
  Robert Adam, Scottish architect.
  Sir Joshua Reynolds, English painter.

1793
- Committee of General Defence in France.
- Execution of Louis XVI (21 January).
- Second Partition of Poland.
- British Government declares war against France.
- France declares war against Britain and Holland.
- Royalist insurrection in the Vendée.
- French take Aix-la-Chapelle.
- Revolutionary Tribunal created in Paris.
- Battle of Neerwinden: French defeated by Austrians: Brussels evacuated by French.
- French evacuate the Netherlands.
- Dumouriez deserts to the Austrians.
- First Committee of Public Safety.
- The Girondists proscribed.
- Vendéans fail to take Nantes.

- Battle of Chatillon: Republican forces defeated in west of France by rebels.
- Second or Great Committee of Public Safety: more extreme. The Reign of Terror.
- Assassination of Marat by Charlotte Corday.
- Prussians take Mainz.
- Allies take Valenciennes.
- Toulon surrenders to Admiral Hood.
- French relieve Dunkirk.
- End of the Lyons revolt.
- Battle of Wattignies: French under Jourdan victorious over Austrians.
- Battle of Cholet: defeat of Vendéans.
- Execution of Marie Antoinette (16 October).
- Battle of Château Gontier: western French rebels victorious under La Rochejaquelin.
- Lyons massacres.
- The Girondists executed.
- Notre Dame consecrated to the worship of Reason.
- Diet of Grodno agrees to partition of Poland and revokes the new Polish constitution.
- New Republican Calendar comes into force in France.
- Battle of Kaiserslautern: Hoche fails against the Austrians in a three days' battle.
- Law of 14 Frimaire makes Committee of Public Safety supreme in France.
- Battle of Le Mans: Vendéans crushed.

- French recover Toulon: Napoleon Bonaparte distinguishes himself.
- Battle of Savenay: Kléber finally defeats the Vendéans.
- British take Tobago from the French.
- William Godwin's *Political Justice*.

1794
- Hoche master of the Palatinate.
- Execution of the Hébertists.
- Manifesto of Kosciusko in Poland against Prussia and Russia.
- Battle of Raslawice: Kosciusko defeats Russians.
- Execution of Dantonists.
- Russians evacuate Warsaw.
- Battle of the First of June: Howe defeats the French fleet.
- Jourdan takes Charleroi.
- Battle of Rawka: Poles defeated by Prussians.
- Feast of the Supreme Being in Paris organised by Robespierre.
- Law of 22 Prairial strengthens Revolutionary Tribunal.
- Prussians take Cracow.
- Battle of Fleurus: hard-won victory by Jourdan over Austrians under Coburg.
- The Ninth Thermidor: fall of Robespierre.
- Execution of Robespierre, Saint-Just and others.
- French capture Fuenterrabia.
- Britain captures Corsica.
- Battle of Maciejowice: Kosciusko routed and taken prisoner by Russians: Russians recapture Warsaw.

- Jacobin Club closed in Paris.
- French conquer all the North Catalonian fortresses.
- British capture Martinique, St Lucia and other territories.
  DEATHS
  Antoine Laurent Lavoisier, French chemist.

1795

- Treaty between Emperor and Catherine the Great of Russia for partition of Turkey, Venice, Poland and Bavaria.
- Peace of La Jaunaie with Royalist rebels in western France.
- British capture Ceylon and Malacca from Dutch.
- Insurrection of 12 Germinal in Paris: 'Bread and the Constitution of 1793'.
- Treaty of Basle between France and Prussia: Holland and Spain accede later.
- Insurrection of 1 Prairial in Paris.
- Revolutionary Tribunal abolished in France.
- 'White Terror' in southern France.
- Death of the French Dauphin in prison.
- Bilbao taken by French.
- Cape Town taken by British from Dutch.
- Orange Society founded in Ireland.
- Triple Alliance of Britain, Austria and Russia.
- Constitution of the Year III proclaimed (23 September).
- Belgium incorporated in France.

- Insurrection of Vendémiaire in Paris suppressed.
- The Directory installed in France (3 November).
- Battle of Loano: French victory over Austrian and Sardinian forces.
- Abdication of Stanislaus Poniatowski in Poland.
- French troops conquer Holland and establish the Batavian Republic.
- French recapture St Lucia.
  DEATHS
  James Boswell, Scottish author.

1796

- Napoleon Bonaparte appointed to command the Army of Italy.
- Armistice of Cherasco: neutrality of Sardinia.
- Conspiracy of Babeuf frustrated in Paris.
- Battle of Lodi: Bonaparte defeats Austrians.
- French occupy Milan, but abandon siege of Mantua.
- Battle of Solferino: Bonaparte defeats Austrians under Wurmser.
- Treaty of San Ildefonso between France and Spain.
- Archduke Charles defeats Jourdan in Bavaria and drives him across the Rhine.
- Cispadane Republic founded by Bonaparte: includes Modena, Bologna and Ferrara.
- Battle of Arcola: Bonaparte's desperate victory over Austrians under Alvintzy.
- Paul I Tsar of Russia.

- British evacuate Corsica.
- Battle of Lonato: Austrians defeated by French under Augereau.
- British reconquer St Lucia from French and take Demerara from the Dutch.
- John Quincy Adams elected President of US.

  DEATHS

  Robert Burns, Scottish poet.

1797

- Failure of Hoche's attempted invasion of Ireland.
- Third and Final Partition of Poland.
- Bonaparte takes Mantua.
- Battle of Cape St Vincent: Spanish fleet defeated by Jervis.
- Pope submits to Bonaparte.
- Mutiny in British fleet at Spithead: demands granted.
- Rising against French in Verona.
- Battle of Neuwied: Austrians defeated by Hoche.
- Preliminaries of peace at Loeben between Austria and Bonaparte.
- Mutiny in British fleet at the Nore: special legislation against it.
- French enter Venice.
- Genoa becomes Ligurian Republic under French influence.
- Cisalpine Republic established by Bonaparte in Lombardy.
- Cispadane Republic unites to Cisalpine Republic.
- Treaty between France and Portugal.
- Coup d'état of 18 Fructidor in France.

- Battle of Camperdown: Dutch fleet under De Winter defeated by Duncan.
- Peace of Campo Formio: Venice given to Austria: Ionian Islands to France: Austria surrenders Netherlands and recognises Cisalpine Republic.
- Valtelline annexed to Cisalpine Republic.
- Frederick William III King of Prussia.
- Paul I made Protector of the Knights of Malta.
- Congress of Rastatt.
- Britain takes Trinidad from Spain.

1798

- Roman Republic declared, with aid of France: temporal power of Pope overthrown.
- French occupation of Bern: Swiss Confederacy replaced by Helvetic Republic.
- Fall of Godoy in Spain.
- Sieyès elected a French Director.
- Bonaparte's Egyptian expedition sets sail: Malta taken.
- Bonaparte takes Alexandria.
- French occupy citadel of Turin.
- Battle of the Pyramids: French victory in Egypt: Bonaparte enters Cairo.
- Battle of the Nile: Nelson destroys French fleet under Brueys.
- France at war with Turkey: Russian fleet in Mediterranean to help Turks.
- Conscription introduced in France.
- Rebellion in Cairo.

- Paul I made Grand Master of the Knights of Malta.
- Ferdinand IV of Naples enters Rome: re-taken by French.
- Abdication of Charles Emmanuel IV of Savoy.
- Flight of Ferdinand of Naples.
- Alliance between Russia and Turkey: soon joined by Britain.
- Pitt introduces an Income Tax.
- English poets William Wordsworth and Samuel Taylor Coleridge *Lyrical Ballads*.
- Thomas Malthus *Essay on Population*.

1799
- French occupation of Naples: Parthenopean Republic created.
- Bonaparte's Syrian campaign begins: Jaffa taken.
- Austria declares war against France.
- Siege of Acre by French fails.
- Battle of Stockach: Jourdan defeated by Archduke Charles.
- British storm Seringapatam: Tipu killed.
- Congress of Rastatt ends without result.
- Milan taken by Russians and Austrians under Suvóroff.
- Allies enter Turin.
- Battle of Modena: French under Macdonald defeat Austrians.
- Naples capitulates to Bourbons.
- Suvóroff defeats Macdonald and overthrows the Italian republics.
- Battle of Aboukir: French victory in Egypt over Turks.

- Allies take Mantua.
- Battle of Novi: French routed: Joubert killed.
- British force lands in Holland under Duke of York.
- Battle of Bergen: British and Russians defeated in Holland.
- Battle of Zürich: Russians defeated by Masséna: Suvóroff driven out of Switzerland.
- Bonaparte deserts Egyptian army, leaving Kléber in command and lands in France.
- Convention of Alkmaar: Britain to evacuate Holland.
- 18 Brumaire: Directory overthrown by Bonaparte.
- Consulate established in France: Bonaparte, Cambacérès and Lebrun consuls.
- British take Surinam from Dutch.
- Repressive legislation in Britain against combinations and corresponding societies.

DEATHS
Joseph Black, Scottish chemist.
George Washington, first President of the USA.

NAPOLEON

1800
- Robert Owen establishes model industrial community in New Lanark, Scotland.
- Treaty of El Arish between Kléber and the Turks: French to evacuate Egypt.
- Pius VII becomes Pope.

- Battle of Heliopolis: Kléber defeats the Turks.
- Godoy restored in Spain at instance of Napoleon.
- Napoleon crosses the Great St Bernard Pass into Italy: occupies Milan.
- Masséna capitulates in Genoa.
- Assassination of Kléber in Egypt.
- Battle of Marengo: Austrian victory turned into French victory by Desaix, who is killed.
- Battle of Hochstädt: Moreau defeats Austrians under Kray.
- British capture Malta.
- Battle of Hohenlinden: Moreau defeats Austrians under Archduke John.
- Second Armed Neutrality: Russia, Sweden, Denmark and Prussia.
- Union of Britain and Ireland: abolition of Irish Parliament.
- Thomas Jefferson elected US President.

DEATHS

William Cowper, English poet.

1801

- British embargo on Russian, Danish and Swedish vessels in British ports.
- Toussaint L'Ouverture master of San Domingo.
- William Pitt the Younger resigns as prime minister.
- Peace of Lunéville between France and Austria: France gains Belgium, Luxemburg, Piedmont and other territories.

- Kingdom of Etruria founded by Napoleon in Tuscany.
- Treaty of Florence between France and Naples.
- Battle of Alexandria: Abercromby defeats French, but killed: Cairo surrenders to British: French evacuate Egypt.
- Paul I murdered: Alexander I Tsar.
- Danish embargo on British ships in Danish ports.
- Battle of Copenhagen: Parker and Nelson destroy Danish fleet.
- Constitution of Malmaison imposed on Switzerland by France.
- Treaty of Badajos between Spain and Portugal: Napoleon angry.
- Treaty of St Petersburg between Russia and Britain.
- Denmark accepts Russo-British Treaty.
- Chateaubriand's Génie de Christianisme: a Catholic revival.

1802

- Cisalpine Republic called Italian Republic.
- Peace of Amiens.
- Sweden accepts Anglo-Russian treaty.
- Concordat between Napoleon and the Pope.
- Legion of Honour created.
- Constitution of the Year X: Napoleon First Consul for Life (4 August).
- France annexes Piedmont.
- Treaty between France and Russia.
- French Marshall Ney sent to crush Switzerland.

- First British Factory Act.
- First practical steamboat: British engineer William Symington's *Charlotte Dundas*.

1803

- Act of Mediation replaces Helvetic Republic by a Swiss Confederation.
- Britain declares war against France.
- Robert Emmet, Irish rebel, hanged.
- United States purchases Louisiana from Napoleon, who had taken it from Spain.

1804

- Napoleon's legal legislation.
- Duc d'Enghien shot.
- William Pitt again prime minister.
- Empire established in France: Napoleon Emperor.
- Execution of Cadoudal and others for conspiracy in Paris.
- Napoleon makes Spain declare war against Britain.
- Revolt of Servia against Turkey: Kara George elected leader.

DEATHS

Immanuel Kant, German philosopher.

Joseph Priestly, English chemist.

1805

- Napoleon crowns himself King of Italy at Milan.
- Ligurian Republic annexed to France.
- Battle of Finisterre: Franco-Spanish fleet under Villeneuve defeated by Calder.

- Russo-Austrian Treaty.
- Parma and Piacenza annexed to France.
- Capitulation of Austrian general Mack in Ulm.
- Battle of Trafalgar: Nelson destroys the Franco-Spanish fleet, but is killed.
- Napoleon enters Vienna.
- Battle of Austerlitz: Napoleon defeats Austro-Russian army.
- Treaty of Vienna between France and Prussia: Prussia to get Hanover.
- Peace of Pressburg between France and Austria: Bavaria and Württemberg become kingdoms: Austria loses Venice and Tyrol.
- Sir Walter Scott *Lay of the Last Minstrel*.

DEATHS

Friedrich von Schiller, German writer.

1806

- Death of William Pitt: Ministry of All the Talents formed under Grenville and including Fox.
- New Treaty between France and Prussia.
- Venetia annexed to kingdom of Italy.
- Joseph Bonaparte declared King of the Two Sicilies.
- Prussia annexes Hanover.
- Prussia compelled to exclude British ships from Prussian ports: Britain declares war against Prussia.
- Louis Bonaparte becomes King of Holland.

- British occupy Buenos Aires, but forced by citizens to surrender.
- Battle of Maida: British defeat French in South Italy.
- Confederation of the Rhine formed by Napoleon: the confederated states secede from the Empire.
- Francis II resigns the Empire and becomes Francis I, Emperor of Austria: End of Holy Roman Empire.
- Death of Fox.
- Prussian ultimatum to Napoleon.
- Battle of Jena: Napoleon defeats Prussia.
- Battle of Auerstädt: Davout defeats Prussia.
- French occupation of Berlin: Prussia subdued.
- Napoleon's Berlin Decrees against Britain: The Continental System.
- Murat occupies Warsaw.
- Treaty of Posen: Saxony joins Confederation of the Rhine and becomes a kingdom.
- Russia suppresses Bucharest.

DEATHS

George Stubbs, English painter.

1807

- British Order in Council in reply to Berlin Decrees.
- Battle of Eylau: Napoleon against the Russians: indecisive.
- Bill passed by British Parliament abolishing the slave trade.
- Selim III of Turkey dethroned: Mustafa IV Sultan.
- Britain accedes to Convention of Bartenstein to help Prussia and Sweden.

- Battle of Friedland: Napoleon defeats the Russians.
- Treaty of Tilsit between France and Russia.
- British bombardment of Copenhagen: Danish fleet surrenders.
- Serfdom abolished in Prussia.
- Convention of Fontainebleau between Napoleon and Spain for partition of Portugal.
- Russian breach with Britain.
- French troops cross into Spain.
- Flight of Portuguese royal family to Brazil.
- British capture Montevideo.
- Kingdom of Westphalia founded by Napoleon for Jerome.

1808

- French seize Pampeluna and Barcelona.
- Russia invades Finland.
- Joachim Murat becomes King of Naples.
- Charles IV of Spain abdicates: Ferdinand VII becomes King.
- French under Murat in Madrid.
- National insurrection in Spain.
- Etrurian kingdom annexed to France.
- Papal States partly annexed to kingdom of Italy.
- Joseph Bonaparte made King of Spain.
- Palafox's defence of Saragossa: French repelled.
- French fail against Valencia.
- Capitulation of French at Baylen.
- Mahmud II Sultan of Turkey after murder of Mustafa IV.

- Joseph evacuates Madrid.
- British force lands in Portugal under Wellington.
- Battle of Vimiero: Wellington defeats Junot.
- Convention of Cintra: French evacuate Portugal.
- Convention of Erfurt: Napoleon and Russia.
- Napoleon takes Madrid.
- Frederick VI King of Denmark.
- Second siege of Saragossa (surrendered following year).
- James Madison elected US President.
- Goethe completes first part of *Faust*.

1809
- Peace of the Dardanelles between Britain and Turkey.
- Battle of Corunna: Moore defeats Soult, but is killed.
- Soult takes Oporto.
- Battle of Medellin: French under Victor defeat Spanish.
- Deposition of Gustavus IV of Sweden: Charles XIII succeeds.
- Battle of Abensberg: Napoleon defeats Austrians.
- Austrians occupy Warsaw for a time.
- Battle of Eckmühl: Napoleon defeats Archduke Charles.
- Wellington drives Soult out of Portugal.
- Napoleon in Vienna.
- Napoleon annexes Rome and Papal States to French Empire: Pius VII a prisoner.
- Battle of Aspern: Napoleon defeated by Archduke Charles: Lannes killed.

- Andreas Hofer and the Tyrolese take Innsbruck.
- Battle of Wagram: Napoleon defeats Austrians.
- Battle of Talavera: French under Victor defeated by Wellington.
- British Walcheren expedition: a failure.
- Revolts in Quito and other places in Spanish South America.
- Treaty of Fredrikshamn: Sweden cedes Finland to Russia.
- Peace of Schönbrunn between France and Austria.
- Battle of Alba de Tormes: Spaniards defeated.
- French take Gerona after long siege.
- Treaty of Jonköping ends war between Sweden and Denmark.
- Spencer Perceval becomes British Prime Minister.
- French naturalist Lamarck originates theory of evolution.

DEATHS

Thomas Paine, Anglo-American author.

1810
- Treaty between Sweden and France: Sweden adopts Continental System.
- Napoleon divorces Josephine.
- Soult takes Seville.
- Andreas Hofer shot.
- Caracas Junta appointed in South America.
- Revolution in Buenos Aires.
- Holland annexed to France.
- Ney takes Ciudad Rodrigo.
- Masséna invades Portugal.

- Battle of Busaco: Wellington defeated Masséna.
- Coimbra with its garrison taken by British.
- Wellington retires behind the lines of Torres Vedras.
- Fontainebleau Decrees by Napoleon against British goods.
- France annexes northwestern Germany.

1811

- French take Tortosa.
- France annexes Duchy of Oldenburg: leads to breach with Russia.
- Soult takes Badajoz.
- Masséna retreats from Portugal.
- Battle of Fuentes d'Oñoro: Masséna fails against Wellington.
- Wellington takes Almeida.
- Battle of Albuera: Beresford defeats Soult.
- Caracas Congress proclaims independence of Spain.
- Battle of Sagunto: Suchet defeats Spaniards.
- Massacre of the Mamelukes: Mehemet Ali supreme in Egypt.
- Chilian revolution.

1812

- French take Valencia.
- Napoleon occupies Swedish Pomerania.
- Wellington takes Ciudad Rodrigo.
- Caracas destroyed by earthquake.
- Wellington takes Badajoz.
- Assassination of Spencer Perceval:

- Lord Liverpool becomes prime minister.
- Treaty of Bucharest between Russia and Turkey.
- Napoleon invades Russia (24 June).
- Revolutionists capitulate under Miranda in Caracas.
- Battle of Salamanca: Wellington defeats Marmont.
- Wellington enters Madrid.
- Battle of the Borodino: Napoleon against the Russians under Kutusoff: drawn.
- Napoleon enters Moscow (14 September): city in flames.
- Napoleon evacuates Moscow (18 October).
- Crossing of the Berezina (26 November).
- Napoleon in Paris (19 December) ahead of the remnant of his army.
- War between Britain and US.

1813

- Russians invade Germany.
- Alliance between Russia and Prussia.
- Treaty of Stockholm between Sweden and Britain.
- Battle of Gross-Görschen: Napoleon defeats Russians and Prussians.
- Battle of Bautzen: Napoleon defeats the Russians and Prussians.
- Armistice of Pläswitz concluded at instance of Napoleon.
- Treaty of Reichenbach.
- Battle of Vittoria: Wellington defeats Jourdan and Joseph Bonaparte.
- French take Vilna.

- Battles of the Pyrenees: Wellington defeats Soult.
- Bolivar enters Caracas as Liberator.
- Austria declares war against Napoleon (12 August).
- Battle of Gross-Beeren: French defeated by Prussians.
- Battle of Katzbach: Blücher defeats Napoleon.
- Battle of Dresden: Napoleon defeats the Allies.
- Battle of Kulm: Allies defeat French.
- Battle of Dennewitz: Prussians defeat Ney.
- Turks reconquer Serbia: Kara George flees.
- Wellington takes San Sebastian.
- Battle of Leipzig (Battle of the Nations) (16-19 October): Napoleon defeated by the Allies: Leipzig taken.
- Wellington takes Pampeluna.
- Battles of the Nive: Wellington defeats Soult.
- Treaty of Valençay: Napoleon gives crown of Spain to Ferdinand.
- Wellington invades France (22 December).

- Allies occupy Paris (31 March).
- Battle of Toulouse: Wellington defeats Soult (10 April).
- Abdication of Napoleon (11 April).
- Treaty of Fontainebleau accepted by Napoleon: banished to Elba (13 April).
- Louis XVIII enters Paris (3 May).
- Ferdinand of Spain issues proclamation against the Constitution: Liberal deputies arrested.
- First Peace of Paris (30 May).
- Fall of Montevideo.
- Bolivar heavily defeated: abandons Caracas.
- Society of Jesus reconstituted by Pope Pius VII.
- Congress of Vienna opens.
- Peruvian invasion overthrows Chilian republic.
- Hetairia Philike founded at Odessa: Greek national movement begins.
- Treaty of Ghent ends war between Britain and the United States.
- Sir Walter Scott *Waverley*.

DEATHS

Marquis de Sade, French writer.

1814

- Battle of La Rothière: Blücher defeats Napoleon.
- Treaty of Kiel: Denmark surrenders Norway to Sweden.
- Battle of Orthez: Wellinton beats Soult.
- Battle of Laon: Allies defeat Napoleon.
- Treaty of Chaumont between Russia, Austria, Prussia and Britain.

1815

- Napoleon lands in France (5 March): the Hundred Days begin.
- William I of Holland becomes King of the Netherlands.
- Louis XVIII flees from Paris (19 March) and Napoleon enters next day.
- Second Serbian revolt against Turkey: under Milosh Obrenovitch.
- Spanish force lands at Cumaná in South America under Morillo.

- Brazil declared a separate kingdom.
- Battle of Tolentino: Murat overthrown in Italy.
- Revolt in the Vendée.
- Battle of St Gilles: Vendéans defeated and La Rochejaquelin killed.
- Final Act of Congress of Vienna (9 June).
- Battle of Quatre-Bras: Wellington defeated Ney (16 June).
- Battle of Ligny: Blücher defeated after hard fight (16 June).
- Battle of Waterloo: Napoleon defeated by Wellington and Blücher (18 June).
- Abdication of Napoleon (22 June).
- Allies enter Paris (7 July): Louis XVIII restored next day.
- Richelieu Prime Minister of France.
- Napoleon surrenders to the British (15 July): St Helena.
- Holy Alliance between Russia, Austria and Prussia.
- Concert of Europe established between Britain, Russia, Prussia and Austria.
- Alexander I grants a Polish constitution.
- Morillo invades New Granada: Bolivar flees.
- First Corn Law passed in Britain.

THE AGE OF METTERNICH

1816

- Death of mad Queen Maria I of Portugal: John VI proclaimed King of Portugal, Brazil and the Algarves.

- Independence of the Argentine provinces proclaimed.
- Radical meeting at Spa Fields broken up.
- Luddite anti-machinery riots.
- James Monroe elected US President.

1817

- Battle of Chacabuco: San Martin defeats the Royalists in South America.
- Seditious Meetings Act in Britain passed by Castlereagh, suspending Habeas Corpus Act.
- Simon Bolivar captures Angostura.
- Serbian autonomy recognised by Turkey.
- Ali Pasha of Janina at the height of his power.
- Acquittal of Hone.
- David Ricardo *Principles of Political Economy*.

DEATHS

Jane Austen, English novelist.

1818

- Battle of Maipú: Chilian independence.
- Charles XIV (Bernadotte) becomes King of Sweden and Norway.
- Prussia becomes a free trade area.
- Bavaria obtains a constitution: also Baden.
- Congress of Aix-la-Chapelle: France admitted to the Concert.
- Decazes chief minister in France.
- End of last Mahratta War in India: Mahratta power completely destroyed.

1819

- Radical meeting at Bonnymuir dispersed.
- Treaty of Frankfort completes work of Congress of Aix-la-Chapelle.
- Peterloo Massacre near Manchester.
- Carlsbad Decrees: reaction in Germany.
- The Six Acts in Britain restricting right of meeting, etc.
- Bolivar occupies Bogotá.

1820

- Spanish Revolution breaks out.
- George IV becomes King of Britain.
- Murder of the Duke of Berry in France.
- Fall of Decazes in France: Richelieu again chief minister.
- Cato Street Conspiracy against the Cabinet discovered: Thistlewood and others executed.
- Ferdinand of Spain decides to adopt the Constitution of 1812.
- Revolt in Naples.
- Congress of Troppau: Britain and France dissent from the reactionary protocol.
- Failure of George IV's Divorce Bill.
- Democratic insurrection in Lisbon.
- The Missouri Compromise on the slavery issue in the US.

1821

- Congress of Laibach.
- Prince Ypsilanti invades Moldavia to rouse the Greeks against Turkey.
- Battle of Rieti: Neapolitan constitutionalists defeated by Austrians.

- Revolt in Piedmont.
- Greek revolt in the Morea.
- Patriarch Gregorius and two Bishops hanged by Turks.
- John VI returned from Brazil to Lisbon.
- Death of Napoleon (5 May).
- Greeks under Ypsilanti defeated in Wallachia.
- San Martín enters Lima and proclaims independence of Peru.
- Battle of Carabobo: Bolivar defeats the Royalist forces and occupies Caracas.
- Richelieu resigns in France: Royalist reaction under Villèle.
- Iturbide declares for an independent Mexican Empire.
- Mehemet Ali begins conquest of Soudan.

DEATHS

John Keats, English poet.

1822

- Massacre in Scio by the Turks.
- Lima occupied by the Royalists.
- Battle of Pichincha: Sucre frees Quito.
- Iturbide proclaimed Emperor of Mexico.
- US recognises national independence of Colombia, Chile, Buenos Aires and Mexico.
- Dom Pedro proclaimed Emperor of Brazil.
- Suicide of Robert Stewart, Viscount Castlereagh: George Canning succeeds him.

- Brazil declared as an independent Empire.
- Congress of Verona: Britain dissents from coercion of Spain.
- Ali Pasha surrenders to the Turks and is murdered.

DEATHS

Antonio Canova, Italian sculptor.
Percy Bysshe Shelley, English poet.

1823

- France, Russia, Austria and Prussia demand the abolition of 1812 Constitution in Spain.
- Louis XVIII declares war against Spanish rebels.
- Britain recognises the Greeks as belligerents.
- The French invade Spain and enter Madrid.
- Bolivar enters Lima.
- Leo XII becomes Pope.
- President Monroe's message: beginning of Monroe Doctrine.
- Iturbide abdicates in Mexico owing to military revolt of Santa Ana.

1824

- Mehemet Ali takes part against the Greeks.
- Dom Miguel assumes government of Portugal, but compelled by the Powers to withdraw.
- Conference of St Petersburg on Eastern Question between Russia and Austria.
- Battle of Junin: Bolivar victorious.
- Charles X King of France.

- Battle of Ayacucho: Sucre decisively defeats Royalists.
- Laws against combinations repealed in Britain.
- John Quincy Adams elected US President.

DEATHS

George Gordon, Lord Byron, English poet.

1825

- Britain recognises independence of Buenos Aires, Colombia and Mexico.
- Ibrahim, son of Mehemet Ali, lands in Morea to help Turkey.
- Consecration of Charles X at Reims.
- Nicholas I becomes Tsar.
- December rising in Russia suppressed.
- Financial crisis in Britain.
- Navigation Laws partly repealed.
- Stockton and Darlington Railway opened.

1826

- Death of John VI of Portugal.
- Russian ultimatum to Turkey demanding evacuation of principalities of Moldavia and Wallachia.
- Protocol of St Petersburg regarding Greece: between Britain and Russia.
- End of defence of Missolonghi.
- Revolt of the Janissaries in Constantinople crushed.
- Chief Decembrists hanged in Russia.

- Massacre of the Janissaries in Constantinople.
- Jesuits return to France.
- Treaty of Akkerman: Turkey agrees to Russian demands.

1827

- George Canning becomes Prime Minister: Whig coalition.
- Press Censorship established in France.
- Treaty of London regarding Greece: between Britain, Russia and France.
- Death of Canning: Goderich Prime Minister.
- Battle of Navarino: Turkish fleet destroyed by allied fleet under Codrington.
- Martignac chief minister in France.
- Turkey denounces Treaty of Akkerman.

DEATHS

Ludwig van Beethoven, German composer.

William Blake, English poet and artist.

1828

- Capodistrias elected Greek President.
- Wellington becomes Prime Minister.
- Dom Miguel lands at Lisbon as Regent.
- Russia invades Turkey.
- Dom Miguel takes title of King of Portugal: reign of terror.
- Protocol of London: Britain, France and Russia.

- Ibrahim evacuates the Morea.
- Repeal of Test and Corporation Acts.
- O'Connell elected for Clare.
- Andrew Jackson elected US President.

1829

- Pius VIII becomes Pope.
- Polignac becomes chief minister in France.
- Catholic Emancipation Act passed in Britain.
- Treaty of Adrianople between Russia and Turkey: Greece recognised as independent: Serbian autonomy secured: Danubian principalities practically independent states.
- Fourth marriage of Ferdinand of Spain (to Maria Christina of Naples): beginning of Carlist movement.
- William Lloyd Garrison begins the abolitionist movement in US.
- The Rainhill locomotive trials: victory of George Stephenson's *Rocket*.

DEATHS

Sir Humphry Davy, English chemist.

1830

- William IV becomes King of Britain.
- The July Revolution in Paris: Louis Philippe becomes King.
- Belgian revolt against Holland: Belgian provinces proclaim their independence.

- Wellington succeeded by Earl Grey as Prime Minister.
- Algiers captured by France.
- Insurrection in Poland.
- Milosh hereditary prince of Serbia.
- Conference of London recognises Belgian independence.
- Victor Hugo *Hernani*.
  DEATHS
  William Hazlitt, English author.

1831

- Polish Diet declares the Romanoffs excluded from the sovereignty.
- Gregory XVI becomes Pope.
- Revolution in the Papal States.
- Battle of Grochov: Russians defeat Poles.
- Casimir Périer ministry in France.
- Second Reading of first Reform Bill carried in House of Commons by majority of 1 (21 March); hostile amendment carried (April); Parliament dissolved (22 April); majority for reform elected.
- Austrian troops help Pope to suppress rising in Bologna.
- Abdication of Pedro I in Brazil: Pedro II succeeds.
- Leopold of Saxe-Coburg elected as Leopold I, King of the Belgians.
- French squadron in the Tagus: Portuguese fleet surrenders.
- Dutch invasion of Belgium.
- Assassination of Capodistrias.
- Polish revolution crushed: the kingdom ended.
- House of Lords rejects first Reform Bill in its second form (8 October).

- Mehemet Ali invades Syria: siege of Acre.
- Charles Albert becomes King of Sardinia.
- Young Italy founded by Giuseppe Mazzini.
  DEATHS
  Georg Wilhelm Friedrich Hegel, German philosopher.

1832

- Kingdom of Greece erected by Convention of London: Otho of Bavaria becomes King.
- Ibrahim takes Acre.
- First Reform Act Passed (7 June).
- Ibrahim takes Damascus.
- Pedro's expedition lands in Portugal.
- Ibrahim conquers all Syria.
- The Pope condemns the teaching of Lamennals.
- Soult ministry in France, including the doctrinaires (Guizot, Thiers, etc).
- Antwerp capitulates to French.
- Battle of Konich: Ibrahim defeats Turks.
- General Election: Whig triumph.
- Crete placed under Egypt.
  DEATHS
  Jeremy Bentham, English philosopher.
  Johann Wolfgang von Goethe, German writer.
  Sir Walter Scott, Scottish novelist.

1833

- Russian squadron in the Bosphorus.
- Convention of Kutaya: Mehemet Ali

recognised by Turkey as Pasha of Syria, etc.
- Battle of Cape St Vincent: Napier destroys the Miguelist fleet.
- Treaty of Unkiar Skelessi: alliance between Russia and Turkey.
- Terceira defeats Miguelists near Lisbon.
- Siege of Oporto raised by Miguelists.
- Dom Pedro enters Lisbon.
- Death of Ferdinand of Spain: succeeded by his daughter Isabella II.
- Convention of Münchengrätz between Russia, Austria and Prussia in aid of Turkey (secret).
- Act for Emancipation of British colonial slaves.
- Treaty of Berlin between Austria, Prussia and Russia.
- Thomas Carlyle *Sartor Resartus*.

DEATHS
Edmund Kean, English actor.

1834
- Treaty between Britain, Spain, Portugal and France: Austria, Russia and Prussia become Carlist.
- Battle of Asseiceira: Miguelists finally defeated by Pedroists in Portugal: Maria II established as Queen.
- Poor Law Act in England.
- The Veto Act passed by the Scottish General Assembly.

1835
- Ferdinand I becomes Emperor of Austria.
- Carlists failed to capture Bilbao.
- Municipal Reform Act.

- Electric telegraph invented.

DEATHS
James Hogg, Scottish poet.
John Nash, English architect.

1836
- Thiers ministry in France: then Guizot ministry.
- Bilbao again relieved by Espartero from Carlist attack.
- Orange Lodges dissolved.
- Beginning of Chartist movement.
- Beginning of Great Trek of Boers away from British territory in South Africa.
- Martin Van Buren elected US President.

1837
- Molé ministry in France.
- Reign of Queen Victoria begins.
- Rebellion in Canada under Papineau and Mackenzie.
- Charles Dickens *Pickwick Papers*.

DEATHS
John Constable, English painter.
Giacomo Leopardi, Italian poet.
Alexander Sergeievich Pushkin, Russian poet.

1838
- Massacre of Boers by Zulu chief Dingan.
- People's Charter published.
- Anti-Corn Law League founded by William Cobden and John Bright.
- Dingan's Day: Boer revenge on Zulus.
- National Gallery opened.

1839

- Durham's Report on Canada submitted to British Parliament.
- War renewed between Sultan of Turkey and Mehemet Ali: Sultan's army invades Syria.
- Soult ministry in France.
- Treaty of London: final adjustment of Belgian frontiers and recognition by Holland.
- Battle of Nezib: Ibrahim's decisive victory over the Turks.
- Abdul Mejid becomes Sultan of Turkey.
- Prince Milosh abdicates in Serbia.
- French conquest of Algeria completed.
- First Afghan War begins (ends 1842).
- Christian VIII King of Denmark.

1840

- Penny postage introduced in Britain.
- Treaty of Waitangi between Captain Hobson and Maori chiefs.
- Thiers ministry in France.
- O'Connell revives the Repeal Association.
- End of the Carlist war in Spain.
- Frederick William IV King of Prussia.
- Convention of London: four Powers to Act against Mehemet Ali.
- Reactionary constitution imposed in Hanover.
- Beirut bombarded by Sir Charles Napier.
- Christina abdicates the Regency in Spain.
- Resignation of Thiers.

- Crete restored to Turkey.
- Acre taken by allied fleet.
- Union Act for Canada: responsible government granted.
- End of convict transportation to New South Wales, Australia.
- War between Britain and China on opium question.
- Abdication of William I in Holland: William II succeeds.
- William Henry Harrison elected US President.
- David Livingstone begins his work in Africa.

1841

- Mehemet Ali submits to Sultan: becomes hereditary Pasha of Egypt.
- Espartero becomes Spanish Regent.
- John Tyler becomes President of US on death of Harrison.
- Hong Kong ceded to Britain by China.
- James Baird discovers hypnosis

1842

- Death of Duke of Orleans: Regency Act in France.
- Alexander Karageorgevich becomes Prince of Serbia.
- Treaty between Britain and China: several ports opened.
  DEATHS
  Thomas Arnold, English educator.
  Stendhal, French novelist.

1843

- Entente Cordiale between France and Britain.

- Natal declared British.
- Battle of Miani: Napier conquers Sind.
- Counter-revolution in Spain: flight of Espartero: Narvaez in power.

1844
- Oscar I King of Sweden and Norway.
- France annexes Tahiti.
- Otto compelled to grant a constitution in Greece.
- Railway Act.
- Bank Charter Act.
- James Knox Polk elected US President.

1845
- Catholic Sonderbund formed in Switzerland.
- Failure of the potato crop in Ireland.
- First Sikh War.

1846
- Pius IX becomes Pope.
- Repeal of the Corn Laws.
- Entente Cordiale between Britain and France broken off on question of Spanish marriages.
- Austria absorbs Cracow.
- War between US and Mexico, due to annexation of Texas by former.

1847
- Austrian occupation of Ferrara.
- Federal Diet in Switzerland declares dissolution of Sonderbund.
- Swiss Federal general Dufour takes Fribourg and Lucerne and crushes the Sonderbund.

- Ten Hours Act in Britain.
- Mexico occupied by US troops.
- French defeat and capture Abd-el-Kader in Algeria.
- William Makepeace Thackeray *Vanity Fair*.

1848
- Austrians crush disturbances in Milan.
- Rising in Palermo: Sicily soon freed, except fortress of Messina.
- Constitutional edict in Naples.
- Frederick VII King of Denmark.
- Orange River Sovereignty named by Sir Harry Smith.
- Demand for a German National Parliament formulated in Baden Chamber.
- Constitution granted in Tuscany.
- February Revolution in Paris: Republic proclaimed: Lamartine a leader.
- Guizot dismissed.
- Louis Philippe abdicates.
- Neuchâtel proclaimed a Republic.
- Constitution granted in Piedmont.
- Insurrection in Vienna: resignation and flight of Metternich: End of Absolutist Reaction.
- Constitution granted in Rome: Republic proclaimed, with Mazzini at its head.
- Hungary gains the People's Charter: virtual autonomy.
- Successful insurrection in Berlin.
- Successful revolution in Milan.
- Venice proclaimed a Republic.
- Charles Albert invades Lombardy (25 March).

- Tuscany declares war against Austria.
- Chartist demonstration in London a fiasco.
- Tuscan forces invade Lombardy.
- Pope disclaims the Italian cause.
- Prussia occupies Schleswig and invades Jutland.
- Neapolitan constitution dropped.
- Flight of Emperor Ferdinand.
- German National Assembly at Frankfort.
- Battle of Goito: Piedmontese victory over Austrians.
- Radetzky overruns Venetia.
- National Workshops in Paris: soon abolished.
- Cavaignac suppresses a Paris insurrection.
- Archduke John elected Reichsverweser by Frankfort Assembly.
- Reichstag meets at Vienna.
- Battle of Custozza: Charles Albert defeated by Radetzky.
- Union of Venetia and Piedmont declared: soon overthrown.
- Radetzky reoccupies Milan.
- Salasco armistice.
- Truce of Malmoe between Denmark and Prussia.
- Battle of Boomplatz: Boers defeated by Sir Harry Smith.
- New Swiss Federal constitution.
- Hungary invaded by Jellachich, Ban of Croatia.
- Austria declares war against Hungary.
- Vienna again in revolution.
- Battle of Schwechat: defeat and retreat of Hungarian army.

- Vienna falls to Windischgrätz.
- New Dutch constitution.
- Flight of Pius IX to Gaeta.
- Ferdinand forced to abdicate: Francis Joseph becomes Austrian Emperor.
- Prince Louis Napoleon Bonaparte elected President of France for four years.
- Second Sikh War erupts in India: Punjab annexed.
- Transportation of leaders of Young Ireland.
- Treaty of Guadalupe Hidalgo cedes New Mexico, California and Texas from Mexico to the US.
- Gold discovered in California.
- Zachary Taylor elected US President.

REVOLUTION AND NATIONALISM

1849
- Battle of Kápolna: Hungarians defeated in bloody battle.
- William III King of Holland.
- Battle of Novara: Radetzky defeats Charles Albert.
- Battle of Chilianwala: Gough defeats the Sikhs.
- Battle of Gujrat: Gough crushes the Sikhs.
- Punjab annexed to British India.
- Charles Albert abdicates in favour of Victor Emmanuel II.
- Frankfort Assembly chooses King of Prussia as German Emperor: King of Prussia declines.
- Schleswig-Holstein War re-opened.

- Twenty-eight German States accept Frankfort Constitution of the Empire.
- Hungary declares itself a republic, at instance of Kossuth.
- Prussia rejects the Frankfort Constitution.
- French under Oudinot land in Italy to suppress Roman Republic: Garibaldi repels them at first, but Rome falls.
- Russia helps Austria to suppress Hungarian revolution.
- Revolt in Bavarian Palatinate.
- Prussians suppress revolt in Dresden.
- Revolt in Baden: Provisional Government formed.
- Sicilian revolution crushed by Naples.
- Haynau's brutality at Brescia.
- Austrians enter Florence.
- Garibaldi repulses the Neapolitans.
- Hungarians under Görgei take Budapest.
- Windischgrätz suppresses the Prague insurrection.
- Austrians take Budapest.
- Prussians suppress Baden revolution.
- Battle of Segesvár: Hungarians under Bem routed.
- Death of Mehemit Ali: Abbas I succeeds in Egypt.
- Battle of Szöreg:Haynau defeats Hungarians.
- Battle of Temesvar: Hungarians defeated.
- Abdication and flight of Kossuth.

- Surrender of Görgei and a Hungarian army at Világos.
- Venice surrenders to Austrians.
- Flight of Pope to Gaeta.
- Complete repeal of Navigation Laws in Britain.

DEATHS

Edgar Allan Poe, US author.

1850
- Erfurt Parliament called by Prussia.
- Saxony and Hanover withdraw from the Three Kings' League.
- Pius IX returns to Rome.
- Dispute between Greece and Britain over Don Pacifico.
- Peace of Berlin ends Schleswig-Holstein War.
- Cavour Prime Minister in Piedmont.
- Olmütz 'Punctuation': Austria and Prussia adjust Hesse-Cassel question.
- Millard Fillmore becomes US President on death of Taylor.
- Tennyson *In Memoriam*.

DEATHS

Sir Robert Peel, British statesman.

1851
- Secret Alliance between Austria and Prussia.
- First Australian goldfield opened.
- Louis Napoleon's coup d'état in France: victorious on a plebiscite.
- Palmerston dismissed from Foreign Office for unauthorised recognition of the French coup d'état.
- Austrian constitution abolished.

- Catholic hierarchy restored in Britain and Holland.
- The Great Exhibition in London.
  DEATHS
  William Turner, English painter.

1852

- Sand River Convention: Britain recognises independence of Transvaal.
- Hereditary Empire restored in France: Louis Napoleon becomes Napoleon III (November 22).
- Enrico Tazzoli hanged in Italy: 'Mantuan Trials'.
- Annexation of Lower Burma by Britain.
- Fall of Derby ministry.
- Franklin Pierce elected US President.
- Harriet Beecher Stowe *Uncle Tom's Cabin*.

1853

- Montenegrins defeat Turkish expedition against them.
- American naval commander Perry in Japan.
- Pedro V King of Portugal.
- Orange River Sovereignty abandoned by Britain.

1854

- German Zollverein practically complete.
- Orange Free State established.
- British and French troops occupy the Piraeus.
- Said Pasha ruler in Egypt.
- Revolt in Madrid: Espartero becomes premier.

- British and French troops land in the Crimea: beginning of Crimean War.
- Battle of the Alma: Russians defeated.
- Siege of Sebastopol begins.
- Battle of Balaklava: drawn: Charge of the Light Brigade.
- Battle of Inkerman: Russians defeated.
- Missouri Compromise repealed in US.

1855

- Sardinia joins Britain and France in Crimean War.
- Alexander II Tsar of Russia.
- Fall of Sebastopol.
  DEATHS
  Charlotte Brontë, English novelist.

1856

- Treaty of Paris ends Crimean War.
- Annexation of Oude to British India.
- James Buchanan elected US President.
  DEATHS
  Heinrich Heine, German poet.

1857

- Arrow incident in China leads to war: Palmerston defeated in Parliament: appeals to the country and obtains a majority.
- Outbreak of Indian Mutiny at Meerut.
- Prussia relinquishes control over Neuchâtel.
- Massacre of Cawnpore.

- Havelock's relief of Lucknow.
- British take Delhi palace.
- Campbell relieves Lucknow.
- Bank Charter Act suspended.
  DEATHS
  Honoré de Balzac, French novelist.

1858

- Orsini's attempt on life of Napoleon III.
- Occupation of Lucknow.
- Treaty of Aigun: Russia obtains from China a large part of Amur basin.
- Cavour and Napoleon III meet at Plombières.
- Sir Hugh Rose takes Gwalior.
- US treaty with Japan.
- Government of India transferred to the Crown: title of Viceroy given to Lord Canning.

1859

- Milosh restored as Prince of Serbia.
- War between Austria and Piedmont: Austria invades Piedmont.
- Battle of Montebello: Austrians defeated by Piedmontese.
- Battle of Palestro: Austrians defeated by Piedmontese.
- Battle of Magenta: French defeated Austrians and freed Milan.
- Battle of Melegnano: French defeat Austrians.
- Battle of Solferino: Austrians defeated by French and Piedmontese.
- Peace of Villafranca between France and Austria; Italy gains Lombardy.
- The duchies declare for union with Piedmont.

- Union of Moldavia and Wallachia under Prince Cuza: joint state becomes known as Romania.
- Spain at war with Morocco.
- Treaty of Zürich completes the Villafranca peace.
- Charles XV King of Sweden and Norway.
- John Brown's attack on Harper's Ferry.
- Charles Darwin *Origin of Species*.
  DEATHS
  Thomas de Quincey, English author.
  Alexis de Tocqueville, French author.

1860

- Commercial Treaty between Britain and France negotiated by Richard Cobden.
- Tuscany and Emilia declare for union with Piedmont.
- Treaty of Turin between France and Piedmont: France given Nice and Savoy.
- Revolution in Sicily: Garibaldi lands.
- Battle of Calatafimi: Garibaldi's victory.
- Garibaldi enters Palermo.
- Battle of Milazzo: Garibaldi victorious.
- Garibaldi invades Italy: enters Naples, from which Francis II had fled.
- Piedmontese army in kingdom of Naples.
- Naples and Sicily voted for annexation to Piedmont.
- Meeting of Garibaldi and Victor Emmanuel II: former salutes latter as King of Italy.

- Marches and Umbria vote for annexation to Piedmont.
- The Liberal Decrees in France.
- Michael becomes Prince of Serbia.
- Treaty of Tientsin ends war in China: more ports opened.
- Abraham Lincoln elected US President.
- Secession of Southern States: Civil War in US begins.
- John Ruskin *Modern Painters*.

1861

- William I becomes King of Prussia.
- Confederate States constituted in southern US: Jefferson Davis President.
- Fall of Gaeta.
- First manifesto of serf emancipation in Russia.
- Kingdom of Italy proclaimed (17 May).
- Fort Sumter capitulates to the Confederates: first shot in American Civil War.
- Lebanon constitution.
- Battle of Bull Run: Northern army defeated by Confederates.
- Abdul Aziz becomes Sultan of Turkey.
- France, Britain and Spain intervened in Mexico.
- Luiz I King of Portugal.

DEATHS

Elizabeth Barrett Browning, English poet.

Count Camillo Cavour, Italian statesman.

1862

- Battle of Shiloh: Confederates defeated by Halleck.
- French troops enter Mexico: Maximilian of Austria proclaimed Emperor.
- Seven Days' Battles: Federal victories.
- Garibaldi at Palermo.
- *The Alabama* sets out from Britain.
- Cotton famine in Lancashire.
- Garibaldi invades southern Italy.
- Battle of Aspromonte: Garibaldi defeated and taken prisoner.
- Second Battle of Bull Run: Confederates under Lee defeat Northern army.
- Montenegrin war ended by Convention of Scutari.
- Speke and Grant discovered sources of the Nile.
- Bismarck becomes Prussian minister.
- Battle of Antietam: Confederates under Lee and Northern army under McClellan: drawn.
- Lincoln's first Emancipation Proclamation.
- King Otho deposed in Greece.
- Battle of Fredericksburg: Northern army under Burnside completely defeated.

DEATHS

Henry David Thoreau, US author.

1863

- Battle of Murfreesborough: Confederates defeated by Rosecrans.
- Uprising in Poland against Russia.

- Ismail Pasha succeeds in Egypt.
- New constitution proclaimed for Schleswig and Holstein: indignation in Germany.
- Prince William of Schleswig-Holstein elected King of Greece as George I.
- Battle of Chancellorsville: Lee defeats Northern army under Hooker: Stonewall Jackson killed.
- Battle of Gettysburg: Lee defeated by Northern army under Meade.
- Vicksburg captured for the North by Ulysses S. Grant.
- Battle of Chickamauga: Northern army defeated in fierce battle.
- Christian IX King of Denmark.
- Battle of Chattanooga: Confederates defeated by Grant.
- Saxon and Hanoverian troops invade Holstein.
- Fenian Secret Society founded in Ireland to set up Irish republic.

DEATHS

Ferdinand Delacroix, French painter.
W. M. Thackeray, English novelist.

1864

- War declared against Denmark by Prussia and Austria.
- Battles of the Wilderness and Spotsylvania: indecisive struggles between Lee and Grant.
- Britain cedes the Ionian Islands to Greece.
- Battle of Cold Harbour: Grant defeated by Lee.
- Russia completes subjugation of the Caucasus.

- Geneva Convention regarding sick and wounded in war.
- End of Taiping Rebellion in China.
- Danish government hands over Schleswig and Holstein to Prussia and Austria.
- Atlanta captured by Sherman.
- Pius IX issued the Bull Quanta Cura and the Syllabus: Papal war against modern enlightenment and progress.
- Battle of Franklin: Confederates under Hood crushingly defeated.
- Battle of Nashville: Hood defeated by Northern army under Thomas.
- Sherman captures Savannah.
- International Working Men's Association founded in London.

DEATHS

John Clare, English poet.

1865

- Richmond evacuated by the Confederates.
- Lee surrenders at Appomattox: end of American Civil War.
- Assassination of Lincoln: Andrew Johnson becomes US President.
- Convention of Gastein between Prussia and Austria.
- Thirteenth Amendment of US Constitution abolishes slavery.
- Leopold II King of the Belgians.
- Russia acquires Tashkent.

1866

- Habeas Corpus Act suspended in Ireland.
- Treaty between Prussia and Italy.

- Austria declares war against Prussia.
- Italy declares war against Austria.
- Battle of Custozza: Italians defeated by Austrians.
- Battle of Lissa: naval defeat of Italians by Austrians.
- Hanoverians capitulate to Prussia.
- Battle of Königgrätz (Sadowa): Austrians under Benedek defeated by Prussians.
- Preliminaries of Nikolsburg between Austria and Prussia.
- Treaty of Prague between Prussia and Austria ends Seven Weeks' War.
- Treaty of Vienna between Austria and Italy: Italy obtains Venetia.
- Prince Charles becomes ruler of Romania.
- French withdraw from Rome.
- First Atlantic cable successfully laid.

1867

- Turkey agrees to withdraw her garrisons from Serbia.
- French withdraw from Mexico.
- British North America Act creates Dominion of Canada.
- Luxemburg made neutral.
- Title of Khedive granted by Sultan to the Viceroy of Egypt.
- Maximilian shot in Mexico.
- North German Confederation formed.
- Russia sells Alaska to US.
- Battle of Mentana: French help to defeat Garibaldi.
- Second Reform Act passed in Britain.

- Fenian outrages in London, Manchester, etc.
- Karl Marx *Das Kapital*.
- Louisa May Alcott *Little Women*.
  DEATHS
  Charles Pierre Baudelaire, French poet.
  J.A.D. Ingres, French painter.

1868

- Shogunate abolished in Japan: Mikado resumes the government.
- Benjamin Disraeli becomes British Prime Minister.
- Prince Michael of Serbia assassinated: Milan becomes Prince.
- Treaty between Russia and Bokhara giving Samarkand to former.
- Isabella II dethroned in Spain.
- Liberal triumph in general election in Britain: William E. Gladstone prime minister.
- President Andrew Johnson impeached in US: Ulysses S. Grant elected President.
- Hungarian autonomy established.

1869

- Suez Canal opened.
- Disestablishment and disendowment of Irish Church.
  DEATHS
  Hector Berlioz, French composer.

1870

- Ollivier ministry in France.
- Bulgarian Exarchate established.
- Leopold of Hohenzollern accepts offer of Spanish crown: candidature

soon withdrawn: France insists on promise not to renew it.
- Bismarck modifies the Ems telegram.
- France declares war (14 July): beginning of Franco-Prussian War.
- Battle of Wörth: Macmahon defeated by Crown Prince Frederick.
- Battle of Spicheren: French defeated.
- Battle of Colombey: German failure: battle drawn.
- Battle of Vionville: drawn.
- Battle of Gravelotte: Bazaine defeated.
- French troops finally abandon Rome: Rome occupied by Italian troops and becomes capital of the kingdom.
- Battle of Sedan: Capitulation of French army under Macmahon: the Emperor a prisoner.
- Republic proclaimed in France.
- Revolution in Paris: Provisional government of National Defence.
- Capitulation of Bazaine in Metz.
- Russia denounces Black Sea clauses of Treaty of Paris.
- Germans driven out of Orleans, but re-occupy it later.
- Irish Land Act.
- Education Act for England and Wales.
- Prim assassinated in Madrid.
- Amadeo I King of Spain.
- Red River Rebellion in Canada under Louis Riel: suppressed by Wolseley.

DEATHS

Charles Dickens, English novelist.

RELATIVE PEACE AND STABILITY

1871
- German Empire created at Versailles.
- Conference of London modifies Treaty of Paris of 1856.
- Bombardment of Paris: capitulation.
- Battle of Le Mans: Germans defeat Chanzy.
- Armistice between France and Germany.
- Bourbaki's army disarmed in Switzerland.
- National Assembly at Bordeaux: ratifies peace and deposes Napoleon III.
- Paris Commune set up: notable buildings destroyed.
- Treaty of Frankfort between France and Germany.
- Treaty of Washington: Alabama claims submitted to arbitration.
- Paris Commune suppressed with great cruelty.
- Thiers becomes President of the French Republic.
- Beginning of legislation legalising trade unions in Britain.

1872
- League of the Three Emperors.
- Oscar II King of Sweden and Norway.
- Geneva award in Alabama case.
- Education Act for Scotland.
- Ballot Act passed.
- Rebellion against Spain in the Philippines.

- Self-government in Cape Colony.
  DEATHS
  Grillparzer, Austrian dramatist.
  Samuel F.B. Morse, US inventor.

1873
- Abdication of Amadeo in Spain: Republic proclaimed.
- Russia takes Khiva.
- The Kulturkampf in Germany.
- Macmahon President in France.
- German troops evacuate France after indemnity had been paid.
  DEATHS
  David Livingstone, Scottish explorer.

1874
- Disraeli prime minister after general election.
- New Federal Constitution for Switzerland.
- Treaty between Germany and Russia.
- Patronage Act repealed in Scotland.
- Alfonso XII King of Spain.

1875
- Insurrection in Herzegovina.
- Britain annexes the Fiji Islands.
- Russia obtains Sakhalin.
- Treaty between Japan and Korea.
- Telephone invented by Alexander Graham Bell.

1876
- Disraeli buys Khedive's shares in Suez Canal for Britain.
- International control begins in Egypt.

- Russia annexes Khokand.
- Bulgarian massacres.
- Serbia declares war against Turkey.
- Murad V becomes Sultan on deposition of Abdul Aziz: soon replaced by Abdul Hamid II.
- Rutherford Hayes elected US President.
  DEATHS
  George Sand, French author.

1877
- Queen Victoria proclaimed Empress of India.
- Russo-Turkish War begins.
- Romania declared independent.
- Siege and capture of Plevna.
- Britain annexes Transvaal.
- Satsuma rebellion in Japan.
- Porfirio Diaz becomes President of Mexico.
- Great Indian famine.
- Sir Henry Morton Stanley explores the Congo.
  DEATHS
  Gustave Courbet, French painter.

1878
- Humbert I King of Italy.
- Russians take Adrianople: Montenegrins take Antivari, Dulcigno, etc.
- Leo XIII becomes Pope.
- Austria occupies Bosnia and Herzegovina.
- Treaty of San Stefano between Russia and Turkey.
- Treaty of Berlin replaces Treaty of San Stefano: Serbia and Romania in

dependent; Bulgaria autonomous; Macedonia restored to Turkey.
- Cyprus placed under British administration.
- Second Afghan War begins (ends in 1880).

1879
- Zulu War.
- Prince Alexander first Prince of Bulgaria.
- The dual control in Egypt: Britain and France.
- Alliance of Austria and Germany.
- Grévy President in France.
- Henry George *Progress and Poverty*.

1880
- Gladstone prime minister after a general election.
- Britain recognised Abdurrahman as Amir of Afghanistan.
- Turkey cedes part of Thessaly to Greece.
- Montenegro obtains Dulcigno.
- Revolt of Boers in the Transvaal.
- James Garfield elected US President.

DEATHS
Jacques Offenbach, French composer.

1881
- Battle of Majuba Hill: British defeated by Boers.
- Murder of Tsar Alexander II: Alexander III succeeds.
- France occupies Tunis.

- Transvaal independence recognised.
- Irish Land Act.
- Murder of President Garfield: Chester Arthur becomes President of US.
- Gambetta chief minister in France.
- Romania declares itself a kingdom.
- Revolt of the Mahdi in the Sudan.
- French protectorate on Upper Niger.

DEATHS
Fyodor Mikhailovich Dostoyevsky, Russian novelist.

1882
- Triple Alliance formed: Austria, Germany and Italy.
- Serbia declares itself a kingdom.
- War between Serbia and Bulgaria.
- Phoenix Park murders in Dublin.
- Arabi Pasha Egyptian minister: national revolt against misgovernment.
- British fleet bombard Alexandria.
- Battle of Tel-el-Kebir: Wolseley defeats Arabi Pasha.

DEATHS
Ralph Waldo Emerson, US poet.
Henry Wordsworth Longfellow, US poet.

1883
- Destruction of Egyptian army under Hicks Pasha near El Obeid.
- French protectorate in Annam.
- Germany begins national insurance.

DEATHS
Gustave Doré, French artist.
Edouard Manet, French painter.
Ivan Turgenev, Russian novelist.
Richard Wagner, German composer.

1884

- Sir Evelyn Baring (Lord Cromer) Consul-General in Egypt.
- Three Emperors' League revived.
- Gordon in Khartoum: besieged.
- Russia annexes Merv.
- Germany and Britain appropriate parts of New Guinea.
- French in Tonkin.
- Berlin Conference of the Powers regarding Africa.
- Convention of London between Britain and the Transvaal: Boer independence strengthened.
- Third Reform Act.
- Stephen Grover Cleveland elected US President.

1885

- Fall of Khartoum: Gordon killed: British and Egyptians evacuate the Sudan.
- Congo Free State constituted by the Powers.
- Russians and Afghans in conflict at Penjdeh.
- Treaty of Tientsin between France and China.
- Regency of Maria Christina in Spain.
- Italians occupy Massowah.
- Bulgaria absorbs eastern Roumelia.
- 3rd Marquis of Salisbury prime minister.
- Serbia declares war against Bulgaria and suffers defeat.
- Second Rebellion in Canada under Louis Riel: Riel executed.
- Daimler invents his petrol engine.

1886

- William Gladstone becomes prime minister.
- Alfonso XIII born to be King of Spain.
- Gladstone introduces his first Home Rule Bill for Ireland: defeated in Commons.
- The Plan of Campaign in Ireland.
- Treaty of Bucharest settles Serbo-Bulgarian War.
- Abdication of Prince Alexander in Bulgaria: Stambuloff the leading statesman.
- Britain annexes Upper Burma.
- Royal Niger Company formed.
- Canadian Pacific Railway completed.
- Gold discovered in the Transvaal.

1887

- Jubilee of Queen Victoria.
- First Colonial Conference.
- Prince Ferdinand elected ruler of Bulgaria.
- Treaty between France and China.
- Marie François Carnot President in France.

1888

- Frederick III German Emperor: soon succeeded by William II.
- British protectorate declared over parts of Borneo.
- Treaty between Russia and Korea.
- County Councils created in Britain.
- Parnell Commission.
- William Henry Harrison elected US President.

1889

- Abdication of Milan in Serbia: Alexander becomes King.
- Flight of General Boulanger: end of Boulangism in France.
- Franco-Russian entente.
- British South Africa Company formed.
- Pedro II deposed in Brazil: Brazil becomes a Republic.
- Carlos I King of Portugal.
- Treaty between Italy and Abyssinia.
  DEATHS
  Robert Browning, English poet.

1890

- Wilhelmina Queen of Holland.
- Fall of Bismarck.
- Britain cedes Heligoland to Germany.
- British protectorate over Zanzibar.
- French protectorate over Madagascar.
- First Japanese Parliament.
- Sherman Anti-Trust Act in US.

1891

- Trans-Siberian Railway begun.
- Agreement between Britain and Portugal regarding East Africa.
- Great famine in Russia.
  DEATHS
  Georges Seurat, French painter.

1892

- Abbas II becomes Khedive of Egypt.
- Panama scandals in France.
- France annexes the Ivory Coast.
- Indian Councils Act.

- Gladstone prime minister after a general election.
- Cleveland again elected US President.
  DEATHS
  Alfred, Lord Tennyson, English poet.

1893

- Matabele War in Rhodesia.
- Natal granted responsible government.
- Gladstone's second Home Rule Bill rejected by the Lords.
- New Zealand adopts women's suffrage.
- Behring Sea arbitration between Britain and the US.

1894

- Nicholas II becomes Tsar.
- Gladstone resigns: Rosebery becomes prime minister.
- Murder of President Carnot in France: Casimir-Périer elected successor.
- Trial and condemnation of Dreyfus in France.
- Armenian massacres.
- War between Japan and China: latter easily defeated.
- Return of King Milan in Serbia.
- British protectorate over Uganda.
- Motor vehicles becomes common.
  DEATHS
  Oliver Wendell Holmes, US author.
  Christina Rossetti, English poet.

1895

- Franco-Russian alliance.
- Salisbury again prime minister:

Conservative victory at general election.
- Jameson Raid.
- François Félix Faure President in France.
- Murder of Stambuloff in Bulgaria.
- British ultimatum to the Transvaal.
- Armenian massacres.
- X-rays discovered by Röntgen.

1896
- Franco-British treaty regarding Siam.
- France annexes Madagascar.
- Insurrection in Crete: international intervention.
- Battle of Adowa: Italians heavily defeated in Abyssinia.
- Outbreak of plague in India.
- William McKinley elected US President.
- Guglielmo Marconi perfected wireless telegraphy.
  DEATHS
  Edmund de Goncourt, French author.

1897
- Queen Victoria's Diamond Jubilee.
- Massacre in Crete: international occupation.
- War between Greece and Turkey: Turkey victorious.
- Autonomy proclaimed for Crete.
- Revolt of tribes on Indian northwest frontier.
- Germany seizes Kiao-chow in China.
- Philippine revolt against Spain.

1898
- US declares war against Spain.
- Egyptian army under Kitchener take Omdurman and reconquer the Sudan.
- The French under Marchand at Fashoda.
- Dargai stormed: Indian frontier rebellion ended.
- Treaty of Paris between Spain and US: Spain loses all her American pos sessions and also the Philippines.
- Russia obtains Port Arthur from China.
- Britain obtains Wei-hai-wei and new territories of Hong Kong on lease from China.
- US annexes Hawaii.
- Prince George of Greece High Commissioner in Crete.
- Irish Local Government Act.
- Radium discovered.
- Oscar Wilde *The Ballad of Reading Gaol.*
- Henry James *The Turn of the Screw.*
- H. G. Wells *The War of the Worlds.*
  DEATHS
  Lewis Carroll, English author.
  Aubrey Beardsley, English illustrator.

1899
- Loubet President in France.
- First Peace Conference at The Hague.
- End of Dreyfus affair in France.
- Outbreak of Boer War.
- Ladysmith, Mafeking and Kimberley besieged by Boers.

- Germany and the US annexe and share Samoa Islands.
- Venezuela boundary question settled.
- Gold discovered in Klondyke.
- The Khalifa defeated and killed in the Sudan.
- Battle of Modder River: Boers defeated by Lord Methuen.
- Battle of Stormberg: Boers defeat Gatacre.
- Battle of Magersfontein: Boers defeat Methuen.
- Battle of the Tugela: Boers defeat Buller.
- United Irish League formed.
- Wladyslaw Reymont *The Promised Land*.
- Edward Elgar *Enigma Variations*.

DEATHS
Robert Bunsen, German chemist.
Alfred Sisley, French painter.

1900
- Boer War: Boers attack Ladysmith (6 January); Field Marshal Lord Roberts takes command of British forces (10 January); relief of Kimberley (15 February); relief of Ladysmith (28 February) and Mafeking (17 May); British annexe Orange Free State (26 May) and Transvaal (25 October).
- Nigeria becomes British protectorate.
- Boxer Rebellion against Europeans in China begins.
- Victor Emmanuel III King of Italy after assassination of Humbert I.
- British archaeologist Sir Arthur Evans begins excavation of Knossos on Crete.

- Ramsay MacDonald named as secretary of newly organised Labour Representation Committee.
- World Exhibition opens in Paris.
- William McKinley re-elected as US President.
- Russia annexes Manchuria.
- Conservative Party returned to power with large majority in 'Khaki Election'.

DEATHS
Gottlieb Daimler, German motor car designer.
Sir Charles Grove, British musicologist.
Casey Jones, US railway engineer.
Friedrich Nietzsche, German philosopher.
Sir Arthur Sullivan, British composer.
Oscar Wilde, British author.

1901
- Commonwealth of Australia founded.
- Queen Victoria dies and is succeeded by Edward VII.
- Philippine revolt suppressed by US.
- Student rioters in St Petersburg dispersed by Cossacks.
- William McKinley assassinated. Theodore Roosevelt becomes US President.
- Peking Treaty ends Boxer Rebellion in China.
- Britain's first submarine launched.
- Trans-Siberian Railway opened.
- Marconi transmits telegraphic signal across the Atlantic from Cornwall to Newfoundland.

- Invention of the vacuum cleaner by Hubert Cecil Booth.
- First Nobel Prizes awarded in fields of literature, chemistry, physics, peace and medicine.

DEATHS

Henri de Toulouse-Lautrec, French painter.

1902

- Anglo-Japanese Alliance.
- Treaty between China and Russia over Manchuria.
- Treaty of Vereeniging ends Boer War.
- Arthur Balfour becomes prime minister.
- Aswan dam completed in Egypt.

DEATHS

Friedrich Krupp, German steel magnate.
Cecile Rhodes, British statesman.
Émile Zola, French writer.

1903

- Pius X becomes Pope.
- King Alexander I and Queen Draga of Serbia murdered: Peter I becomes king.
- Anti-Semitic pogroms in Russia.
- Mrs Emmeline Pankhurst forms Women's Social and Political Union to agitate for votes for women.
- US recognises Panama as independent republic and leases Canal Zone.
- Turkish troops massacre Bulgarians in Macedonia.
- Orville and Wilbur Wright fly heavier-than-air aircraft at Kitty Hawk.

- Commander Robert Scott and Lieutenant Ernest Shackleton travel further towards the South Pole than any previous expedition.

DEATHS

Dr Richard Gatling, US rapid-fire gun inventor.
Paul Gaugin, French painter.
Herbert Spencer, English philosopher.
James McNeill Whistler, US painter.
Camille Pissarro, French artist.

1904

- Russo-Japanese War begins.
- US occupation of Cuba ends.
- Rebellious tribesmen massacre German settlers in South West Africa.
- Anglo-French Entente signed aimed at solving all outstanding grievances.
- Theodore Roosevelt wins US presidential election.
- British military expedition to Tibet captures Lhasa (3 August); Anglo-Tibetan Treaty signed giving Britain exclusive trading rights (7 September).

DEATHS

Frederic Bartholdi, French sculptor.
Anton Chekhov, Russian writer.
Antonin Dvoràk, Czech composer.
Theodor Herzl, Hungarian-born Zionist.
Paul Kruger, Boer leader.
Henri Fantin-Latour, French painter.
Friedrich Siemens, German industrialist.
Sir Henry Morton Stanley, British explorer.

1905

- Russo-Japanese War: Japanese capture Port Arthur (5 January); Russians routed by Japanese at Battle of Mukden (10 March); Battle of Tsushima: Russian navy destroyed (28 May); Japanese capture Sakhalin (31 July); Treaty of Portsmouth ends conflict (5 September).
- Russian Grand Duke Sergei killed in bomb attack.
- Earthquake in India claims 10,000 victims.
- Norway separated from Sweden: Haakon VII becomes King of Norway.
- Riots in St Petersburg crushed by Tsarist police (22 January); first workers' soviet formed; sailors mutiny on battleship 'Potemkin' (27 June); revolt by students and workers in Moscow crushed by Tsarist troops (30 December).
- Sinn Fein founded in Dublin.
- Liberal leader Henry Campbell-Bannerman becomes prime minister.
- Automobile Association founded.
  DEATHS
  Thomas John Bernado, Irish-born doctor and philanthropist.
  Sir Henry Irving, British actor.
  Jules Verne, French writer.

1906

- First Duma (elected parliament with limited powers) convened in Russia.
- San Francisco destroyed by earthquake and fire.
- General election in Britain results in

Liberal landslide victory: first Labour MPs returned to parliament.
- Algeciras Conference on Franco-German crisis over Morocco: dispute settled in favour of France.
- Self-government granted to Transvaal in South Africa.
- Mount Vesuvius erupts leaving hundreds dead.
- Armand Fallières President in France.
- Frederick VIII King of Denmark.
- Simplon Tunnel opened for railway traffic.
- Campaign for women's suffrage gathers strength.
- Vitamins discovered by Frederick G. Hopkins.
  DEATHS
  Pierre Curie, French physicist.
  Henrik Ibsen, Norwegian playwright.
  Albert Sorel, French historian.

1907

- Earthquake devastates Kingston in Jamaica.
- Orange River Colony in South Africa becomes independent as Orange Free State.
- Lawyer Mahatma Gandhi leads civil disobedience movement ('Satyagraha') in South Africa.
- Second Hague Peace Conference.
- New Zealand gains Dominion status within the British Empire.
- Boy Scouts founded by Sir Robert Baden-Powell.
- Belgian parliament votes to annexe

the Congo and end absolute rule over the central African territory by King Leopold.

- Gustavus V succeeds Oscar II as King of Sweden.
- Cunard ship *Mauretania*, the world's largest liner, leaves Liverpool on her maiden voyage.

DEATHS

Edvard Grieg, Norwegian composer.
William Howard Russell, British journalist.
Dmitri Mendeleev, Russian chemist.
William Thomson, Lord Kelvin, British physicist.

1908

- Carlos I of Portugal and Crown Prince Luiz assassinated: Manuel II becomes king.
- Herbert Henry Asquith becomes prime minister after resignation of Sir Henry Campbell-Bannerman.
- Old Age Pensions introduced in Britain.
- King Edward VII is first British monarch to visit Russia.
- Mass demonstration of suffragettes in Hyde Park, London.
- Young Turks revolutionary movement forces Sultan Abdul Hamid II to restore the Turkish constitution.
- Bulgaria declares independence from Ottoman Empire.
- Austria annexes Bosnia-Herzegovina.
- Over 200,00 people killed in earthquake in southern Italy and Messina in Sicily, the most violent tremor ever recorded in Europe.

- William Howard Taft elected US President.
- Ford Motor Company produces first 'Model T' motor car.
- In Paris, Henri Farman makes the first aeroplane flight with a passenger.
- Franco-British Exhibition opens in London.

DEATHS

Henri Becquerel, French physicist.
Joel Chandler Harris, US author.
Nikolai Rimsky-Korsakov, Russian composer.
Rev. Benjamin Waugh, founder of the National Society for the Prevention of Cruelty to Children.

1909

- Chancellor of the Exchequer Lloyd-George introduces radical 'People's Budget' (April); vetoed by the House of Lords (November).
- Japanese statesman Prince Hirobumi Ito assassinated.
- Deposition of Abdul Hamid II: Mohammed V Sultan.
- North Pole reached by US explorer Commander Robert E. Peary.
- Louis Blériot crosses the English Channel for the first time in an aeroplane.
- Young Turks celebrate as Turkish parliament forces Sultan Abdul Hamid to abdicate in favour of reformist Mehemet V.
- Union of South Africa formed.
- US store Selfridge's opens branch in Oxford Street, London.

- The first bra is announced in American *Vogue*. It is patented in 1914 by Mary Phelps Jacob.

  DEATHS

  Geronimo, Apache chief.
  George Meredith, British writer.
  John Synge, Irish playwright.

1910

- Liberals cling on to power in general elections in January and December as crisis over the Budget and the power of the House of Lords escalates.
- Labour Exchanges established in Britain.
- Edward VII dies and is succeeded by George V.
- Japan annexes Korea.
- Montenegro declares itself a kingdom.
- King Manuel overthrown in Portugal: republic proclaimed.
- Captain Robert Scott sets out on expedition to South Pole.
- Girl Guides founded by Sir Robert Baden-Powell.

  DEATHS

  Henri Dunant, Swiss founder of the Red Cross.
  William Holman Hunt, British painter.
  Julia Ward Howe, US women's campaigner.
  Robert Koch, German bacteriologist.
  Samuel Langhorne Clemens (Mark Twain), US writer.
  Florence Nightingale, British nursing pioneer.

Henri Rousseau, French painter.
Count Leo Tolstoy, Russian writer.

1911

- Armed troops and police besiege Anarchist hideout in house in Sidney Street, London.
- James Ramsay MacDonald elected chairman of the Labour Party to succeed Keir Hardie.
- French move to suppress revolt in Morocco.
- Mexican dictator Porfirio Diaz deposed by rebels.
- Parliament Act reduces the power of the House of Lords.
- Payment of MPs begins in Britain.
- Coronation of George V.
- Assassination of Peter Stolypin, the Russian Premier.
- Italy declares war against Turkey over Italian claim on Tripoli: Tripoli annexed by Italy.
- Chinese revolution: Manchu dynasty overthrown (October); Dr Sun Yat Sen elected president of the new Chinese Republic (December).
- Andrew Bonar Law chosen to succeed Balfour as leader of the Conservative Party.
- Franco-German Treaty recognises French demand for protectorate in Morocco.
- Norwegian explorer Roald Amundsen beats Captain Robert Scott to the South Pole.

  DEATHS

  Sir William Gilbert, librettist.
  Gustav Mahler, Austrian composer.

1912

- Mass rallies in Ulster to protest at proposals for Home Rule for Ireland (January); Third Home Rule for Ireland Bill passed by Commons (May); 'Solemn Covenant' to oppose Home Rule signed at mass rally of Ulster loyalists led by Sir Edward Carson (September).
- Militant suffragettes riot in the West End of London.
- Coal Mines Act establishes principle of a minimum wage.
- The *Titanic* sinks in the Atlantic with the loss of 1,513 lives.
- Yoshihito becomes Emperor of Japan.
- Right of France to establish a protectorate over Morocco ceded in Fez Treaty.
- Peace of Ouchy between Italy and Turkey signed in Switzerland: Italy acquires Tripoli.
- War between Turkey and the Balkan States: Bulgarian and Serbian forces inflicts a series of defeats on Turkey.
- Democrat Woodrow Wilson elected US President.

DEATHS

General William Booth, founder of Salvation Army.

Joseph, Lord Lister, British pioneer of antiseptic.

August Strindberg, Swedish playwright.

Samuel Coleridge-Taylor, British composer.

Jules Massenet, French composer.

Wilbur Wright, US pioneer aviator.

1913

- Young Turks depose government of the Grand Vizier, Kiamil Pasha in Turkey.
- Bodies of explorers Captain Robert Falcon Scott and companions discovered in the Antarctic.
- Suffragette Emily Davison dies after throwing herself in front of the King's horse during the Derby.
- Raymond Poincaré elected President of French Republic.
- King George I of Greece murdered: Constantine I succeeds.
- Treaty of Bucharest settles Balkan wars: increases of territory to Serbia, Greece, Montenegro, Bulgaria and Romania; Turkey loses Macedonia, part of Thrace, Albania and most of the islands; Albanian kingdom founded.
- Panama Canal completed.

DEATHS

Alfred Austin, British poet.

Rudolf Diesel, German engineer.

FIRST WORLD WAR

1914

- Irish Home Rule Act creates separate parliament in Ireland with some MPs in Westminster.
- June: Murder of Archduke Franz Ferdinand, heir to Austrian throne, in Sarajevo, capital of Bosnia (28).
- July: Austria-Hungary declares war against Serbia (28);.
- August: Germany declares war against Russia (1); Germany de-

clares war against France (3); German invasion of Belgium (4); Britain declares war on Germany (4); British Expeditionary Force under Sir John French suffers heavy casualties in Battle of Mons (20-31); Japan declares war on Germany (23); Russians routed at Battle of Tannenberg on eastern front (31).

- September: Germans capture Rheims (5); Battle of the Marne (5-9); trench warfare begins in Aisne salient (16); three British cruisers sunk by a U-boat (22).
- October: First Battle of Ypres (12-Nov. 11).
- November: Britain declares war against Turkey (5).
- December: Royal Navy destroys German squadron off the Falkland Islands (8); British protectorate over Egypt proclaimed (17).

DEATHS

Henri Alain-Fournier, French writer.
August Macke, German painter.
Sir John Tenniel, British artist.

1915

- January: Turkish army surrenders to Russians in Central Asia (5); German Zeppelin raid on Norfolk towns (19); British sink German battleship *Blucher* in North Sea (24).
- February: German submarine blockade of Britain begins (2); Imperial troops repulse Turkish attack on Suez Canal (2); French begin offensive in Champagne on Western Front (12).
- March: Britain declares blockade of

German ports (1); Battle of Neuve Chapelle (10-13); Naval attack on Dardanelles aborted (22).

- April: Second Battle of Ypres (22-May 25); Germans use gas for first time on Western Front (22); British, ANZAC and French troops land at Gallipoli (25).
- May: Sinking of the Cunard liner *Lusitania* (7); Battle of Aubers Ridge (9-25); Italy declares war on Austria (22); British coalition government formed (26).
- June: British pilot Reginald Warneford awarded VC for destroying a Zeppelin (8); Austrians re-take Lemburg, capital of Galicia, from the Russians (23).
- July: Germans advance farther into Poland (3); General Botha accepts surrender of all German forces in South West Africa (9).
- August: Allied forces meet stubborn resistance at Gallipoli (13); Italy declares war on Turkey (20); Brest-Litovsk falls to the Germans (30).
- September: Allies breech German lines at Champagne and at Loos in Flanders (26); Turks defeated at Kut-el-Amara in Mesopotamia (28).
- October: Russia begins campaign against Bulgaria (8); British nurse Edith Cavell executed by Germans as a spy (12).
- November: Italians suffer heavy losses at Isonzo River (10); Serbia occupied by German-Austrian and Bulgarian forces (28).
- December: Sir Douglas Haig replac-

es Sir John French as British commander on Western Front (15); French and British troops occupy Salonika (13); Allied troops begin evacuation of Gallipoli (20).

DEATHS

Rupert Brooke, British poet.

Paul Ehrlich, German doctor and discoverer of diptheria antitoxin.

(James) Keir Hardie, British politician.

Alexander Skryabin, Russian composer.

1916

- January: Conscription introduced in Britain (6); Montenegro captured by Austrians (20).
- February: Allies complete occupation of German colony of Cameroons (18); Battle of Verdun begins (21).
- March: US troops defeat Mexican rebels led by Pancho Villa (31).
- April: Easter Rising by Sinn Fein in Dublin (24); British forces surrender to Turks after fall of Kut-el-Amara (29).
- May: Battle of Jutland, only major sea battle of the war, in which both sides claim victory (31).
- June: Lord Kitchener drowned as cruiser *Hampshire* struck by a mine off the Orkneys (5); Arab revolt against Turkish rule (21); Russians led by General Brusilov capture Galicia from the Austrians (23).
- July: Battle of the Somme (1-Nov. 13); Russians rout Turkish army at Erzinjan (27).

- August: Sir Roger Casement hanged in London for high treason (3); Italians capture Gorizia (10); Field Marshall Paul von Hindenburg appointed Chief of German General Staff (27); Romania declares war against Austria and Germany (27).
- September: Tanks first used by British on Western Front (15); Allies launch new offensive in Balkans (18).
- October: Allies occupy Athens (16); Captain T.E. Lawrence arrives in Jeddah to offer British support for Arab Revolt against Turkey (16); Second Battle of Verdun begins (24).
- November: Austro-Hungarian Emperor Franz Josef dies (21); Woodrow Wilson re-elected US President.
- December: General Joffre replaces General Robert Nivelle as head of French forces on the Somme (3); Lloyd George forms war cabinet as new prime minister (7); 'Mad Monk' Gregory Rasputin murdered by Russian nobles (30).

DEATHS

Sir Joseph Beecham, British pharmaceuticals manufacturer.

George Butterworth, British composer.

Henry James, US-born author.

Jack London, US author.

Henrik Sienkiewicz, Polish writer.

1917

- February: unrestricted submarine warfare begins (1).
- Russia: Tsar Nicholas II abdicates

and provisional government established (16); British defeat Turks near Gaza (27).

- April: US declares war on Germany (6); Battle of Arras (9-14); Vimy Ridge captured by Canadian troops (10); German government helps Bolshevik leader Vladimir Lenin return to Russia (16).

- June: Messines Ridge taken by British (7); German aircraft carry out first bombing raid on London (14); first US troops land in France (26); General Edmund Allenby assumes Palestine command (29).

- July: Russian provisional government crushes Bloshevik uprising (16); Alexander Kerensky appointed Russian prime minister (22); Third Battle of Ypres begins (31).

- August: French break German lines at Verdun on 11-mile front (20).

- September: Kerensky proclaims Russia a republic (15); Germans expel Russians from Riga (17); the ex-Tsar and his family are moved to Siberia (30).

- October: British victory on Passchendaele Ridge (4); French victory on the Aisne (23); Italians routed by Austrians at Battle of Caporetto (24).

- November: Passchendaele captured by British (6); Bolshevik Revolution: Kerensky overthrown (7); Balfour Declaration recognising Palestine as national home for the Jews (8); Hindenburg lines smashed on 10-mile front (20).

- December: British take Jerusalem

(9); Russo-German armistice (15); Bolsheviks open peace talks with Germans at Brest-Litovsk (22).

DEATHS

Colonel William F. Cody ("Buffalo Bill').

Edgar Degas, French painter.

Scott Joplin, US ragtime pianist and composer.

Auguste Rodin, French sculptor.

1918

- January: President Wilson outlines US war aims to Congress in his Fourteen Points (9); Lenin creates Red Army (28).

- February: Demoralised Russian army attacked by Germans in Estonia as Brest-Litovsk peace talks stall (20).

- March: Treaty of Brest-Litovsk (3); German offensive against British on the Somme opens (21); Battle of Arras (21-April 4);.

- April: Second German offensive against British (9-25); General Ferdinand Foch appointed commander of Allied armies (14); British naval raid on Belgian ports of Zeebrugge and Ostend (23).

- June: Conflict between Bloshevik Red Army and anti-Bolshevik White forces begins.

- July: Last German offensive against the French (15); ex-Tsar and his family shot by Bolsheviks in cellar in Ekaterinburg (16).

- August: Allied offensive near Amiens results in German collapse (8).

- September: Turkish army destroyed at Megiddo (19); Bulgarians sign armistice (29); Allies breakthrough along the whole Western Front (30).
- October: T.E. Lawrence leads Arabs into Damascus (1); Germany accepts President Wilson's Fourteen Points (23); Italian advance (24); surrender of Turkey (30).
- November: Austria accepts peace terms (4); Socialist republic declared in Bavaria (7); Kaiser abdicates and escapes to Holland (9); Armistice signed by Germany (11).
- December: British Women over 30 allowed to vote for first time.

  DEATHS
  Guillaume Apollinaire, French poet.
  Claude Debussy, French composer.
  Gustav Klimt, Austrian painter.
  Wilfred Owen, British poet.
  Egon Schiele, Austrian painter.

- Third International founded in Moscow.
- Benito Mussolini founds Fascist party in Italy, Fasci de Combattimento.
- Jan Christian Smuts Prime Minister of South Africa after death of Louis Botha.
- President Wilson suffers a stroke.
- Red Army close to victory over White forces in the civil war in Russia.
- Nancy Astor elected as first woman MP in Britain.
- Lloyd-George announces plan for the partition of Ireland.
- John Alcock and Arthur Brown fly nonstop across the Atlantic.

  DEATHS
  Andrew Carnegie, Scottish-born US philanthropist.
  Auguste Renoir, French artist.

1919

- Peace Conference in Paris; Germany signs Treaty of Versailles; Treaty of St Germain: dissolution of the Austro-Hungarian Empire. Kingdom of Serbs, Croats and Slovenes established consisting of Serbia, Montenegro and former regions of the Austrian-Hungarian empire (Croatia, Slovenia and Bosnia-Herzegovina).
- Interned German fleet scuttled at Scapa Flow.
- Communist 'Sparticist' uprising suppressed in Berlin, leaders Rosa Luxemburg and Karl Liebknecht arrested and then killed.

THE TWENTIES AND THIRTIES

1920

- Peace Treaty ratified in Paris.
- First meeting of League of Nations in Paris: Germany, Austria, Russia and Turkey excluded; US Senate votes against US membership of League.
- French troops occupy the Ruhr.
- 18th Ammendment to US constitution banning sale of alcohol goes into force: beginning of Prohibition.
- Treaty of Sévres concludes peace with Turkey and dissolves Ottoman Empire.

- Communist Party of Great Britain founded.
- Rebel leader Pancho Villa surrenders to Mexican government.
- Roscoe 'Fatty' Arbuckle charged with rape and murder of actress Virginia Rappe in Hollywood. Later acquitted
- 'Bloody Sunday': IRA kill 14 British soldiers in Ireland.
- Russian civil war ends with triumph of the Bolshevik Red Army.
- Warren G. Harding elected US President.
- King Constantine of Greece returns to Athens.

DEATHS

Amedeo Modigliani, Italian artist.

1921

- Spanish Prime Minister Eduardo Dato assassinated.
- First Indian parliament opens.
- Anti-Bolshevik mutiny of Russian sailors at Kronstadt naval base.
- Lenin's New Economic Policy introduces limited free enterprise in Soviet Union.
- Reparations Commission fixes Germany's liability at 200 billion gold marks (£10 billion).
- British troops sent to quell rioting in Egypt.
- Irish Free State established.
- Japanese Premier Takashi Hara assassinated.
- Crown Prince Hirohito named Regent of Japan.
- Treaty establishes Irish Free State.

- Eduard Benes Prime Minister of Czechoslovakia.
- British Broadcasting Company founded.

DEATHS

Enrico Caruso, Italian opera singer.

John Boyd Dunlop, British inventor of the pneumatic tyre.

Georges Feydeau, French playwright.

Engelbert Humperdinck, German composer.

1922

- Cardinal Achille Ratti, Archbishop of Milan, elected Pope Pius XI.
- Four Power Pacific Treaty ratified by US Senate.
- Treaty of Rapallo between Germany and USSR restoring full diplomatic relations.
- Walter Rathenau, German foreign minister, assassinated.
- King Constantine of Greece abdicates: succeeded by George II.
- Andrew Bonar Law prime minister after resignation of Lloyd-George.
- Friedrich Ebert re-elected German President.
- Mussolini's 'March on Rome': Fascist government formed.
- Tomb of Tutankhamun discovered.
- James Joyce *Ulysses*.

DEATHS

Alexander Graham Bell, inventor of the telephone.

Alfred Harmsworth, Lord Northcliffe, British newspaper proprietor.

Marcel Proust, French author.

Sir Ernest Shackleton, British Antarctic explorer.

1923

- Japanese earthquake: 300,000 dead in Tokyo and Yokohama.
- Miguel Primo de Rivera dictator in Spain after army coup.
- French troops occupy the Rhineland to secure reparations.
- King George II deposed by Greek army.
- Stanley Baldwin becomes prime minister.
- Calvin Coolidge President of US after death of Harding.
- Teapot Dome oil scandal in US.
- Turkish republic proclaimed with Mustapha Kemal as first president.
- Hitler's attempt to overthrow the Weimar Republic in Munich (the 'Beer Hall Putsch') fails.
- Catastrophic inflation in Germany: mark drops to 4 trillion to US dollar.

DEATHS

Sarah Bernhardt, French actress.
Gustav Eiffel, French engineer.
Jaroslav Hasek, Czech writer.
Katherine Mansfield, New Zealand-born writer.
Wilhelm Roentgen, pioneer of X-rays.

1924

- Vladimir Ilyich Lenin, founder of the USSR, dies.
- First Labour government elected in Britain with Ramsay MacDonald as prime minister (January).

- Britain recognises USSR.
- Dawes Plan for restructuring the payment of German reparations to the Allies agreed at the London Conference; French and Belgians agree to the evacuation of the Ruhr.
- Greece proclaimed a republic: King George II deposed by Greek parliament.
- Publication of the Zinoviev letter allegedly from the Communist International inciting British communists to start a revolution.
- Mussolini's Fascists gain convincing victory in Italian general election.
- Stanley Baldwin prime minister after Conservative victory in general election (October).
- J. Edgar Hoover appointed director of the Federal Bureau of Investigation.

DEATHS

Frances Hodgson Burnett, British author.
Joseph Conrad, Polish-born British author.
Gabriel Fauré, French composer.
Anatole France, French author.
Franz Kafka, German author.
Edith Nesbit, British children's author.
Giacomo Puccini, Italian composer.

1925

- Field Marshall Paul von Hindenburg elected President of Germany.
- Treaty of Locarno signed in London.
- Cyprus becomes a British colony.
- Rheza Khan King of Persia.
- Tennessee school teacher John T.

Scopes found guilty of teaching evolution in a state school and fined $100.

- Queen Alexandria, widow of King Edward VII dies.
- Adolph Hitler *Mein Kampf*.
- F. Scott Fitzgerald *Great Gatsby*.

DEATHS

William Jennings Bryan, US Democratic politician.
H. Rider Haggard, British author.
John Singer Sargent, US artist.

1926

- General Strike in Britain disrupts industry for nine days.
- Abdul Aziz ibn Saud proclaimed king of the Hejaz and names the province Saudi Arabia.
- British troops end occupation of the Rhineland.
- Hitler Youth founded in Germany.
- Ali Reza Khan crowned Shah of Persia with title King Pahlavi.
- Jósef Pilsudski stages coup and seizes power in Poland.
- Germany admitted to the League of Nations.
- Hirohito succeeds his father Yoshihito as Emperor of Japan.

DEATHS

Eugene Debs, US socialist leader.
Harry Houdini (Ernst Weiss), Hungarian-born US escapologist.
Claude Monet, French artist.
Annie Oakley, US sharpshooter.
Rainer Maria Rilke, Austrian poet.
Rudolph Valentino, Italian-born US film star.

1927

- Canberra inaugurated as new capital of the Australian Commonwealth.
- Allied military control of Germany ends.
- Tomas Masaryk re-elected president of Czechoslovakia.
- In Chinese civil war, Nationalist forces under Chiang Kai-Shek conquer Shanghai.
- Leon Trotsky and Grigori Zinoviev expelled from the Soviet Communist Party by Stalin.
- Italian-born anarchists Sacco and Vanzetti executed in US for armed robbery despite worldwide protests of their innocence.
- Captain Charles Lindbergh makes first solo nonstop flight across the Atlantic.
- Al Jolson stars in first talking film 'The Jazz Singer'.

DEATHS

Isadora Duncan, US dancer.
Jerome K. Jerome, British writer.

1928

- Earthquake destroys Corinth in Greece.
- Kellog-Briand pact renouncing war signed in Paris by 65 states.
- Chinese Nationalist forces led by Chian Kai-shek take Peking (July); Chiang Kai-shek becomes President of Republic of China (October).
- Women entitled to vote on same basis as men (age 21) in Britain.
- Herbert Hoover elected US President.

- First Five Year Plan begins in USSR.
- Hirohito crowned Emperor of Japan.
- Amelia Earhart is the first woman to fly the Atlantic.
- Professor Alexander Fleming of St Mary's Hospital, London discovers Penicillin.
- Otto Frederick Rohwedder of Battle Creek, Michigan, invents sliced bread.
- D. H. Lawrence's *Lady Chatterley's Lover.*

DEATHS

Thomas Hardy, English novelist and poet.

Leos Janacek, Czech composer.

Emmeline Pankhurst, Suffragette leader.

Sir George Trevelyan, British statesman and historian.

1929

- Kingdom of Serbs, Croats and Slovenes changes its name to Yugoslavia. King Alexander I declares himself dictator.
- St Valentine's Day Massacre in Chicago.
- Mussolini signs Lateran Treaty with Pope Pius XI establishing independent Vatican City.
- Trotsky expelled from the USSR.
- Ramsay MacDonald forms second Labour Government.
- Aristide Briand Premier of France.
- Wall Street Crash causes slump in US economy: Great Depression begins.
- Airship *Graf Zeppelin* flies around the world in 21 days.

- Ernest Hemingway's *A Farewell to Arms* is published.

DEATHS

Carl Benz, German engineer.

Sergei Diaghilev, Russian impresario.

Wyatt Earp, US marshal.

Lillie Langtry, British actress.

Gustav Stresemann, German statesman.

1930

- Stalin's collectivisation of agriculture in USSR accelerated at enormous human cost.
- Ras Tafari becomes Emperor Haile Salassie of Ethiopia.
- Treaty between Britain, US, France, Italy and Japan on naval disarmament.
- Last French troops withdraw from the Rhineland.
- Unemployment in UK reaches 2 million.
- Nazis come second in German general election.
- Mandate policy in government White Paper on Palestine suggests halting Jewish immigration.
- *R.101* disaster: world's biggest airship explodes in France on maiden flight to India killing 48 people.
- Uruguay wins first World Cup football competition.
- Planet Pluto discovered by C.W. Tombaugh.
- Nylon discovered in US by Wallace Carrothers of the Du Pont company.

DEATHS

Lon Chaney, US actor.

Sir Arthur Conan Doyle, British author.

D.H. Lawrence, British author.

1931

- Sir Oswald Mosley founds the New Party, along the lines of the Fascist movement, in Britain.
- King Alfonso abdicates and Spain is declared a republic.
- Mutiny over pay cuts at Invergordon naval base.
- Coalition government formed under Ramsay MacDonald.
- Britain abandons the gold standard and devalues the pound.
- US gangster Alphonse Capone jailed for income tax evasion.
- Empire State Building completed in New York.

DEATHS

Bix Beiderbecke, US jazz musician.
Arnold Bennett, British writer.
Thomas Alva Edison, US inventor.
Anna Pavlova, Russian ballerina.

1932

- Japanese capture Shanghai.
- Manchukuo, Japanese puppet regime, established in Manchuria.
- Kidnappers abduct Charles Lindbergh's baby son.
- Second Five Year Plan begins in USSR.
- Paul von Hindenburg narrowly defeats Hitler in German presidential contest; Nazis win majority of seats in Reichstag (July); Hitler fails to become Chancellor (August).

- Assassination of French President Paul Donner; replaced by Albert Lebrun.
- Eamon de Valera elected President of Ireland.
- Olivier Salazar elected Premier of Portugal.
- Franklin D. Roosevelt elected US President in landslide victory.
- Sydney Harbour Bridge opened in Australia.
- Aldous Huxley *Brave New World*.

DEATHS

George Eastman, US industrialist.
John Philip Sousa, US musician.
Edgar Wallace, British crime writer.

1933

- Adolf Hitler appointed Chancellor of Germany (January); Reichstag building in Berlin destroyed by fire (February); commercial boycott of Jews begins and violence against Jews and their property escalates (April); Germany becomes one-party state as Hitler bans all political opposition (June); use of concentration camps for Jews and opponents of the regime confirmed (August); Germany withdraws from the League of Nations (October) and walks out of the Geneva Disarmament conference (November).
- Communist uprising in Spain.
- Japan withdraws from the League of Nations.
- Economic legislation in US to combat the Great Depression.
- End of Prohibition in US.

DEATHS
Adolf Loos, Austrian architect.

1934

- Leopold III becomes king of the Belgians after death of Albert I.
- Hitler eliminates rivals in the SA (Storm Troopers' Association) in the 'Night of the Long Knives'.
- Austrian Chancellor Englebert Dollfuss is assassinated by Nazis.
- Death of President Hindenburg: Hitler announces the end of the republic and beginning of the Third Reich with himself as Führer and Reich Chancellor.
- King Alexander of Yugoslavia and Louis Barthou, French foreign minister, assassinated in Marseilles.
- Assassination of Sergei Kirov and purge of the Communist Party in USSR.
- Robert Graves *I Claudius*.

DEATHS
Marie Curie, Polish-born French physicist.
Frederick Delius, British composer.
Sir Edward Elgar, British composer.
Roger Fry, British painter and art critic.
Gustav Holst, British composer.

1935

- Saar plebiscite for return to Germany.
- Bruno Hauptmann sentenced to death for kidnapping and murder of US aviator Charles Lindbergh's baby son.

- Germany repudiates Versailles Treaty and accelerates rearmament programme.
- Jews banned from public office in Germany.
- Stanley Baldwin succeeds MacDonald as prime minister and forms new National Government.
- Mussolini invades Abyssinia: League of Nations imposes ineffectual economic sanctions against Italy.
- US Senator Huey Long assassinated.
- Long March of Communists from Nationalist-held areas in southern China ends: Mao Tse-tung establishes Soviet state in northern China.

DEATHS
Colonel T. E. Lawrence 'Lawrence of Arabia', British soldier and author.

1936

- Death of George V and accession of Edward VIII (January); Edward VIII abdicates to marry US divorcee Wallace Simpson and is succeeded by his brother the Duke of York as George VI (December).
- German remilitarisation of the Rhineland.
- Italy annexes Abyssinia.
- Spanish army led by General Franco revolts against the Republican government: Spanish Civil War begins.
- Mussolini and Hitler announce the Rome-Berlin Axis.
- Stalin initiates the great purges that are to last for two years and cost up to 10 million lives.

- F. D. Roosevelt re-elected US President by landslide.
- March of unemployed workers from Jarrow to London begins.
- The first suntan lotion is launched by L'Oreal.

DEATHS

Alexander Glazunov, Russian composer.

Rudyard Kipling, British poet and author.

Ivan Pavlov, Russian physiologist.

1937

- Guernica bombed by German air force in Spanish Civil War.
- Neville Chamberlain becomes prime minister after the resignation of Stanley Baldwin.
- German airship Hindenburg explodes on landing in New Jersey.
- Japanese begin attempted conquest of China; Shanghai bombed (August); forces of Chiang-Kai-shek unite with Mao's Communists to combat Japanese threat (September).
- Stalin stages show trials of ex-colleagues in Moscow and purges army generals.
- The shopping trolley is introduced by Sylvan Goldman, manager of a supermarket in Oklahoma.

DEATHS

Sir James Barrie, British author.

George Gershwin, US composer.

Jean Harlow, US actress.

Guglielmo Marconi, Italian engineer.

Maurice Ravel, French composer.

John D. Rockefeller, US oil tycoon.

Lord Ernest Rutherford, British scientist.

Bessie Smith, US blues singer.

1938

- Austria annexed by Germany.
- Singapore naval base opened.
- Japanese bomb Canton.
- Munich Agreement between Chamberlain, French Premier Daladier, Hitler and Mussolini appeases Hitler over Czechoslovakia.
- Germans march into Czechoslovakia.
- Kristallnacht: Jewish homes and businesses are attacked and looted throughout Germany (November); all Jewish property is confiscated (December).
- John Logie Baird demonstrates the colour television.

DEATHS

Gabriele d'Annunzio, Italian soldier and poet.

Karel Capek, Czech writer.

Constantin Stanislavsky, Russian stage director.

SECOND WORLD WAR

1939

- Madrid falls to Nationalist forces led by General Franco (March): end of the Spanish Civil War.
- Bohemia and Moravia annexed by Hitler.
- Britain signs treaty of mutual assistance with Poland.

- Conscription introduced in Britain.
- Mussolini invades Albania.
- Italy and Germany sign alliance.
- Germany and USSR sign Non-Aggression Pact.
- Hitler invades Poland: World War II begins.
- September: War declared between Britain and Germany (1); first enemy air raid on Britain (6); British Expeditionary Force lands in France (11); Warsaw capitulates and Nazi-Soviet pact signed in Moscow for partitioning of Poland (29).
- October: *Royal Oak* sunk in Scapa Flow with the loss of 810 lives (14).
- November: Finland attacked by Russia.
- December: Battle of the River Plate, Graf Spee scuttled by Germans after being trapped in Montevideo harbour by British warships.
- John Steinbeck *The Grapes of Wrath.*
- James Joyce *Finnegan's Wake.*
- Henry Miller *Tropic of Cancer.*

DEATHS

Douglas Fairbanks, US actor.

Sigmund Freud, Austrian psychoanalyst.

W. B. Yeats, Irish poet and playwright.

1940

- January: Food rationing begins in Britain; Finnish Winter War.
- March: Finns defeated by Red Army.
- April: Hitler invades Denmark and Norway; British troops join fighting in Norway.

- May: Holland, Belgium and Luxembourg suffer German blitzkrieg: National Government formed under Winston Churchill; British troops encircled on French coast around Dunkirk (31).
- June: evacuation of British army from Dunkirk completed (4); Italy declares war on Britain and France (10); Paris captured by the Germans (14); France accepts terms for an Armistice (22).
- July: Channel Islands occupied by Germany (1); Battle of Britain begins (10).
- August: British Somaliland attacked by Italy (7); Britain begins night bombing of Germany.
- September: Blitz on London begins; Battle of Britain ends in victory for the Allies (15); Japanese invade Indochina.
- October: Bucharest occupied by Axis troops.
- November: Greek troops repel Italian attacks; Coventry bombed in worst air raid of the war, 1,000 killed.
- December: Sidi Barani captured by British troops in North Africa, General Archibald Wavell begins destruction of Italian forces in the Western Desert; Germans drop incendiary bombs on London.

DEATHS

John Buchan, British author.

F. Scott Fitzgerald, US novelist.

Harold Harmsworth, Lord Rothermere, British newspaper baron.

Paul Klee, German artist.
Leon Trotsky, revolutionary socialist.

1941

- January: Tobruk captured by Commonwealth troops.
- February: Benghazi captured (7); Mogadishu in Somaliland captured by Imperial troops (26); General Erwin Rommel's Afrika Korps lands in Tripoli.
- March: President Roosevelt signs Lease-Lend agreement with Britain (11); British raid on Lofoten Islands off Norway (4); Italian fleet virtually destroyed by British in Battle of Cape Matapan, off Crete (28); Rommel begins campaign in North Africa (30).
- April: Addis Ababa captured by Imperial troops (4); Germans occupy Yugoslavia (17); Athens captured by Germans (27).
- May: Rudolf Hess parachutes into Scotland (10); heavy German bombing raid on London (11); Germans invade Crete and British forces withdraw (20); German battleship *Bismark* sunk (27).
- June: Clothes rationing begins; Germany attacks Russia (20);.
- July: US troops take over Iceland (7): Smolensk falls to German advance in Russia (16); Syrian capital Damascus surrenders to Allied forces (21); Japanese troops move into Thailand and Cambodia, and occupy Saigon (27).

- August: British and Russian troops attack Iran (25); the Dnepropetrovsk dam blown up by the Russians to halt German advance (27).
- September: Intense fighting around Leningrad (12); Kiev falls to the Germans (19); in London, General de Gaulle announces the formation of a French Provisional government in exile (25).
- October: Germans attack Moscow (6); Soviet government leaves Moscow (20); Germans take Kharkov in the Ukraine (25).
- November: *Ark Royal* sunk by Italian torpedo (13); Eighth Army begins first offensive in Libya (18); Russians re-take Rostov (30).
- December: German attack on Moscow stalls (4); Japanese attack Pearl Harbour (7); Britain declares war on Finland, Romania and Hungary (8); Japanese forces land in Malaya (8); Philippines invaded by Japanese (10); Hong Kong surrenders to Japanese (25).

DEATHS

Lord Robert Baden-Powell, British founder of the Scouting movement.
Henri Bergson, French philosopher.
Amy Johnson, British airwoman.
James Joyce, Irish author.
Rabindranath Tagore, Indian author.
Virginia Woolf, British author.

1942

- January: Manila captured by Japanese (2); Japanese forces land in New Guinea and Solomon Islands

(23); German and Italian troops take Benghazi (29).
- February: Singapore falls to the Japanese (15); Battle of Java Seas (28).
- March: Java surrenders to Japan (9); German U-boat base at St Nazaire attacked by British commandoes (27); RAF begins intensive bombing campaign against Germany (28).
- April: George Cross awarded to the people of Malta (16); US B-52s bomb Tokyo (18).
- May: Battle of the Coral Sea (4-8); Britain allied with Russia (26); Rommel launches offensive in Libya (27); 1000 RAF bombers raid Cologne (31).
- June: US routs Japanese navy in Battle of Midway Island (3–7); Czech village of Lidice destroyed by Germans in reprisal for assassination of Reinhard Heydrich (10); Tobruk captured by Germans (20).
- July: Sevastopol falls to the Germans (1); RAF makes first daylight raid on the Ruhr (16).
- August: General Bernard Montgomery assumes command of the Eighth Army (6); Germans advance on Stalingrad (6); US forces attack Solomon Islands (7); Allied raid on Dieppe (19).
- September: Germans clear Warsaw Jewish ghetto (2); Germans halted at Stalingrad (8); Madagascar falls to Britain (18); Eighth Army seizes key German positions at El Alamein (30).
- October: Battle of El Alamein, Rommel in full retreat (30).

- November: Allies invade North Africa (7); Germans defeated near Stalingrad (26); French fleet scuttled in Toulon harbour (27).
- December: Physicists led by Enrico Fermi at Chicago University achieve first controlled nuclear chain reaction (2); Admiral Darlan, Vichy leader in North Africa, assassinated (24).

DEATHS
John Barrymore, US actor.
Carole Lombard, US actress.
Stefan Zweig, Austrian author.

1943
- January: Tripoli taken by the Eighth Army (23); conference of Allied powers at Casablanca (24); US bombers make their first attack on Germany (27); Germans surrender at Stalingrad (31).
- February: Japanese cleared from Guadalcanal in the Solomon Islands (9); Kharkow retaken by the Russians (16).
- March: Battle of Bismarck Sea (1-3); Rommel almost surrounded by US and British forces in North Africa (26).
- April: Mass grave of Polish officers discovered by Germans in Katyn forest near Smolensk.
- May: remaining German and Italian forces surrender to Allies in North Africa (12); RAF Dambuster raid on the Ruhr dams (17).
- June: French Committee for National Liberation formed in Algiers.
- July: Allied invasion of Sicily (10);

Germans routed in Battle of Kursk (13); Mussolini overthrown (25).

- August: Sicily falls to the Allies (17).
- September: Allies invade Italian mainland (3); Italy surrenders (8); US forces land at Salerno, near Naples (10); Germans occupy Rome (10); Smolensk taken by the Russians (25).
- October: Naples falls to Allies (1); Russians cross the River Dneiper and capture Zaporozhie and Dnepropetrovsk (29).
- November: Kiev taken by the Russians (6); Churchill, Roosevelt and Stalin meet at Allied conference in Tehran (28).
- December: General Dwight D. Eisenhower chosen as supreme commander of Allied invasion of Europe (24); German battleship *Scharnhorst* sunk (26).

DEATHS

Leslie Howard, British actor and director.

Sergei Rachmaninov, Russian composer.

Thomas 'Fats' Waller, US jazz pianist.

Beatrix Potter, British writer.

Beatrice Webb, British Socialist and writer.

1944

- January: Allied landings at Anzio (22); Russians raise German siege of Leningrad (19);.
- February: US forces land on the Marshall Islands (1); Russians destroy ten German divisions on the Ukrainian front (17).
- March: Monte Cassino destroyed by Allied bombing (15); Allied force lands in Burma (19); General Orde Wingate killed in air crash.
- April: General de Gaulle appointed head of the Free French Forces (9); Russians drive Germans from the Crimea (16).
- May: Sevastopol captured by the Russians (9); Monte Cassino falls to the Allies (18); 47 Allied airmen shot after mass escape from Stalag Luft III prison camp in Silesia.
- June: Rome liberated by Allies (4); D-Day invasion of Europe (6); first V-1 rocket falls on England (18).
- July: Minsk captured by Russians (3); Caen falls to Allies (9); Bomb Plot fails to kill Hitler (20); Guam captured by Americans (21).
- August: Warsaw uprising (1); Allies land in southern France (15); Paris liberated (23); Romania declares war on Germany (25).
- September: Antwerp and Brussels taken by Allies (4); Boulogne taken by Allies (7); Bulgaria declares war on Germany (7); V-2 rockets begin to fall on England (8); Allies enter German soil (11); Allied landings near Arnhem (17); US forces attack Japanese near Manila (21).
- October: Warsaw rising crushed by Germans (3); British troops land on mainland Greece (5); Rommel commits suicide (14); Athens occupied by Allies (14); Aachen taken by Al-

lies (20); Red Army liberates Belgrade (20); Battle of Leyte Gulf, Japanese sea power destroyed (25).

• November: British troops capture Salonika (1); German battleship *Tirpitz* is sunk by RAF bombs (12).

• December: Civil war begins in Athens (6); German counter-offensive in the Ardennes (16); Budapest surrounded by Red Army (26).

DEATHS

Sir Edwin Lutyens, British Architect.

Glen Miller, US band leader.

Piet Mondrian, Dutch artist.

Edvard Munch, Norwegian artist.

Heath Robinson, British humorist.

Sir Henry Wood, British conductor.

1945

• January: US troops land Luzon in Philippines (11); Warsaw captured by Russians (17); Hungary declares war on Germany (21); Red Army liberates Auschwitz (27); Ledo road from Burma to China reopened (28).

• February: Allied conference at Yalta (4); Bombing of Dresden (14); US forces land on Iwo Jima (19).

• March: Cologne captured by Allies (6); Marshall Tito takes power in Yugoslavia (6); Allies cross the Rhine (25).

• April: US invades Okinawa (1); Red Army enters Vienna (11); death of President Roosevelt (12); US troops and Red Army link up in Germany (27); Mussolini and his mistress shot by Italian partisans (28); Allies penetrate Berlin (30); Hitler and his mistress commit suicide (30).

• May: Germans surrender in Italy (2); Berlin captured by Red Army (2); Rangoon falls to the British (3); war against Germany ends officially (8); naval air attacks on Japan (28).

• June: United Nations Charter signed in San Francisco (26).

• July: Polish government in Warsaw recognised by Allies (5); Labour party wins landslide in general election: Clement Attlee becomes prime minister (26).

• August: Atomic bombs dropped on Hiroshima (6) and Nagasaki (9); Russia declares war against Japan and advances into Manchuria (8); unconditional surrender of Japan (14).

• September: Second World War ends (2).

• November: de Gaulle elected President of France (13); Nuremburg Trials begin (20).

DEATHS

Bela Bartok, Hungarian composer.

David Lloyd George, British Liberal statesman.

General George S. Patton, US commander.

Anton von Webern, Austrian composer.

COLD WAR AND AFRO-ASIAN NATIONALISM

1946

• General Assembly of the United Nations meets in New York for the first time.

- Winston Churchill warns of 'Iron Curtain' descending across Europe in speech at Fulton, Missouri.
- Leon Blum forms Socialist government in France.
- Juan Péron elected President of Argentina.
- Abdication of Victor Emmanuel III as King of Italy; his son Umberto II reigns briefly then leaves the country after referendum in favour of a republic under Premier de Gasperi.
- King David Hotel, British military HQ in Jerusalem, bombed by Jewish terrorists.
- Leading Nazis executed at Nuremburg.
- Civil war between Nationalists and Communists resumes in China.
- Biro pen, invented by Hungarian journalist Ladislao Biro, goes on sale.

DEATHS

John Maynard Keynes, British economist.

John Logie Baird, British scientist and pioneer of television.

1947

- Coal mines nationalised in Britain.
- Burma proclaimed independent republic.
- India becomes independent and partitioned into India and Pakistan.
- US Secretary of State George Marshall inaugurates US funding for European reconstruction (Marshall Plan).

- Cominform, a new international Communist organisation, established in Belgrade.
- Edinburgh International Festival of Music and Drama launched.
- UN determines the partition of Palestine.
- Tennessee Williams *A Streetcar Named Desire.*

DEATHS

Pierre Bonnard, French artist.
Henry Ford, US car manufacturer.
Max Planck, German physicist.
Sidney Webb, British Socialist and author.

1948

- Railways and the electricity industry nationalised in Britain.
- Burma becomes independent.
- Mahatma Gandhi assassinated.
- Communists seize power in Czechoslovakia.
- Marshall Plan for $17 billion in economic aid to Europe passed by US Senate.
- State of Israel established with Chaim Weizmann as president.
- Russian blockade of Berlin: Western airlift of supplies begins.
- National Health Service begins in Britain.
- North Korea becomes a republic: Korea now divided between Communist North led by Kim Il Sung and Republic of Korea in the south led by Syngman Rhee.
- Harry S. Truman elected US President.

Sergei Eisenstein, Soviet film director.

Mohammed Ali Jinnah, Pakistani statesman.

Franz Lehar, Austrian composer.

1949
• People's Republic of China founded with Mao Tse-tung as leader (October); Chinese Nationalist government establishes headquarters on Formosa (December).
• North Atlantic Treaty signed in Washington by twelve Western nations, establishing Nato.
• Republic of Eire proclaimed in Dublin.
• Berlin blockade lifted (12 May); German Federal Republic created with Bonn as capital (23 May); Konrad Adenauer elected first Chancellor of the FDR (August); Soviet sector becomes German Democratic Republic (October).
• Pandit Nehru elected Prime Minister of India.
• George Orwell *1984*.
• Simone de Beauvoir *The Second Sex*.
• Arthur Miller *Death of a Salesman*.

DEATHS
Tommy Handley, British comedian.

Margaret Mitchell, US author.

Richard Strauss, German composer.

1950
• Britain recognises Communist China.
• Sino-Soviet Alliance signed.

• Labour wins general election.
• Senator Joseph McCarthy begins Communist witchhunt in US.
• US starts building hydrogen bomb.
• Klaus Fuchs found guilty of betraying secrets of atomic bomb construction to Russia.
• North Korea invades South Korea (25 June): US military forces dominate UN forces, led by General MacArthur, sent to repel Communist advance (June-July); Britain sends troops (August); UN landings at Inchon (September); UN forces capture Communist capital Pyongyang (October); massive Chinese offensive in North Korea (November); Chinese take Pyongyang (December).
• Vietnam partitioned between Communist North and regime in the south under Emperor Bao Dai.
• China invades Tibet.

DEATHS
Edgar Rice Burroughs, US author.

Al Jolson, US entertainer.

Sir Harry Lauder, British comedian.

Heinrich Mann, German author.

Vaslav Nijinsky, Russian ballet dancer.

George Orwell (Eric Blair), British author.

Cesare Pavese, Italian author.

George Bernard Shaw, Irish author and playwright.

Kurt Weill, German composer.

1951
• Korean War: Seoul captured by

Communist forces (4 January); General MacArthur sacked by Truman after threatening invasion of China (April); cease-fire talks begin (July); truce-line established along the 38th parallel (November).

- Vietminh guerillas suffer heavy losses in offensive against the French in Tonkin.
- Treaty of Paris creates European Coal and Steel Community.
- British diplomats Guy Burgess and Donald Maclean escape to Russia.
- British troops seize Suez Canal Zone.
- Winston Churchill prime minister after Conservative victory in general election.
- 22nd Amendment to the US Constitution limits presidents to two terms, a maximum of eight years in office.
- Julius and Ethel Rosenberg sentenced to death for passing wartime atomic secrets to Russia.
- Libya gains independence.
- Festival of Britain opens.

DEATHS

Ernest Bevin, British statesman.

André Gide, French author.

William Randolph Hearst, American newspaper magnate.

Sinclair Lewis, US author.

Ivor Novello, British actor and composer.

Arnold Schoenberg, Austrian-born US composer.

Ludwig Wittgenstein, Austrian philosopher.

1952

- Death of George VI (6 February) and succession of Queen Elizabeth II.
- Japan regains sovereign status.
- US launches air strikes against North Korea as peace talks stall.
- State of Emergency declared in Kenya after series of Mau Mau terrorist killings.
- General Neguib leads coup and seizes power in Egypt; King Farouk abdicates in favour of his infant son.
- Riots in South Africa against apartheid laws.
- US tests first hydrogen bomb on Eniwetok atoll in the Pacific.
- Britain tests its first atomic bomb.
- Dwight D. Eisenhower elected US President.
- Anne Frank's *Diary*.
- Ernest Hemingway *The Old Man and the Sea*.

DEATHS

Paul Eluard, French poet.

Eva ('Evita') Peron, Argentine political activist.

George Santayana, Spanish philosopher.

1953

- Marshall Tito elected President of Yugoslavia.
- General Naguib declares republic in Egypt.
- Stalin dies: Nikita Krushchev emerges as Soviet leader after power struggle.
- Coronation of Queen Elizabeth II in Britain.

- Atom spies Julius and Ethel Rosenberg executed in US.
- Korean War ends: armistice signed at Panmunjom.
- Russia tests hydrogen bomb.
- Mau Mau leader Jomo Kenyatta jailed in Kenya.
- French Legionnaires capture Dien Bien Phu.
- Cambodia gains independence.
- Agreement signed for laying of the first transatlantic telephone cable.
- E. P. Hillary and Sherpa Tensing reach summit of Everest.

DEATHS
Hilaire Belloc, British author.
Eugene O'Neill, US playwright.
Sergei Prokofiev, Soviet composer.
Django Reinhardt, jazz guitarist.
Dylan Thomas, Welsh poet.
Hank Williams, US country singer.

1954

- Colonel Gamel Abdul Nasser seizes power in Egypt.
- St Lawrence Seaway approved by Eisenhower.
- French defeated by Vietminh forces at Dien Bien Phu (May); Geneva Agreement divides Vietnam into North and South along 17th Parallel.
- US Supreme Court rules against racial segregation in state schools.
- South East Asia Treaty Organisation (SEATO) established.
- Senator McCarthy's anti-Communist Senate hearings televised in US: McCarthy eventually censured and condemned by Congress (December).

- Food rationing ends in Britain.
- Anti-British rioting in Cyprus by EOKA supporters demanding union with Greece.
- Anti-polio vaccine developed by Dr Jonas E. Salk begins intensive trials.
- Roger Bannister is the first person to run a mile in under four minutes.
- Bill Haley and the Comets 'We're Gonna Rock Around the Clock'.
- Kingsley Amis *Lucky Jim.*
- William Golding *Lord of the Flies.*

DEATHS
Lionel Barrymore, British actor.
Enrico Fermi, Italian physicist.
Wilhelm Furtwangler, German conductor.
Auguste Lumiere, French cinema pioneer.
Henri Mattisse, French artist.

1955

- Anthony Eden becomes prime minister after resignation of Churchill.
- Civil war between rival factions in Saigon, South Vietnam.
- Italy, West Germany and France establish European Union.
- East-West Geneva Conference.
- Warsaw Pact signed by USSR and Eastern Bloc nations.
- Germany becomes member of Nato.
- State of emergency declared in Cyprus after violent demonstrations against British rule.
- Eighty spectators die in crash disaster at Le Mans.
- Commercial TV begins broadcasting in Britain.

1956

- Civil Rights campaign emerges in US South; Blacks begin bus boycott in Alabama.
- Clement Atlee resigns as Labour Party leader; replaced by Hugh Gaitskill.
- Vladimir Nabokov *Lolita*.

DEATHS

James Dean, US actor.

Albert Einstein, German-born US physicist.

Arthur Honegger, Swiss composer.

Fernand Leger, French artist.

Thomas Mann, German novelist.

Charlie Parker, US jazz musician.

Maurice Utrillo, French painter.

1957

- Fidel Castro lands in Cuba to lead rebellion against President Batista.
- US film star Grace Kelly marries Prince Rainier III of Monaco.
- Premium bonds launched in Britain.

DEATHS

Sir Max Beerbohm, British author and cartoonist.

Bertold Brecht, German playwright.

Alfred Kinsey, US sociologist.

Sir Alexander Korda, British film director.

Alan Alexander Milne, British author.

Jackson Pollock, US artist.

1956

- Sudan becomes independent republic.
- Nikita Khruschev denounces Stalin at 20th Communist Party Congress.
- Race riots in Alabama.
- British deport Archbishop Makarios, leader of the Greek-Cypriot community, to the Seychelles.
- Pakistan becomes Islamic republic.
- Suez Crisis: Colonel Nasser, President of Egypt seizes the Suez Canal Zone (July); Israel attacks Egypt (29 October); Anglo-French forces bomb Egyptian military targets (October 30); Allied forces retake Canal Zone (6 November); UN-imposed cease-fire (8 November); Canal blocked (16 November); British withdraw forces after financial pressure from the US (23 November).
- Uprising in Hungary against Soviet control crushed by Soviet tanks.

1957

- Harold Macmillan becomes prime minister after resignation of Sir Anthony Eden.
- Ghana gains independence.
- Treaty of Rome, signed by France, Germany, Italy and the Benelux nations, inaugurates the European Community.
- Malaya gains independence.
- Suez Canal reopened.
- Tunisia becomes republic after Bey is deposed by Premier Bourguiba.
- President Eisenhower send National Guard into Little Rock, Arkansas to enforce school desegregation.
- Russia launches first man-made space satellites, Sputnik-I and Sputnik II.
- Jack Kerouac *On the Road*.

DEATHS

Humphrey Bogart, US actor.

Constantin Brancusi, Romanian sculptor.

Christian Dior, French fashion designer.

Jimmy Dorsey, US band leader.

Oliver Hardy, US comedian.

Diego Rivera, Mexican painter.

Jean Sibelius, Finnish composer.

Erich von Stroheim, Austrian actor and film director.

Arturo Toscanini, Italian conductor.

1958

- Anti-British riots in Cyprus.
- Seven members of Manchester United football team killed in plane crash at Munich airport.
- Egypt and Syria proclaim union as United Arab Republic.
- Alaska becomes 49th US State.
- Dr Vivian Fuchs completes first overland crossing of Antarctica.
- Campaign for Nuclear disarmament (CND) founded (February): organises first march from London to Aldermaston (April).
- French Nationalist settlers rebel in Algeria.
- King Faisal of Iraq assassinated.
- Cardinal Giuseppe Roncalli becomes Pope John XXIII.
- EOKA terrorists step up campaign against British in Cyprus.
- First heart pacemaker inserted.
- Fifth Republic established in France with General Charles de Gaulle as first president.
- US nuclear submarine 'Nautilus' sails under the icecap at the North Pole.
- Thalidomide drug implicated in birth defects.

DEATHS

Sir William Burrell, Scottish shipping magnate and art collector.

Ronald Coleman, British actor.

Robert Donat, British actor.

Tyrone Power, US actor.

Marie Stopes, British pioneer of family planning.

Ralph Vaughan Williams, British composer.

1959

- Fidel Castro overthrows Batista regime and takes power in Cuba.
- Indira Gandhi becomes president of Congress Party in India.
- Hawaii becomes 50th US State.
- China suppresses uprising in Lhasa: Dalai Lama flees.
- Conservatives re-elected under Harold Macmillan win general election.
- European Free Trade Association inaugurated as rival trading bloc to European Community.
- Archbishop Makarios elected as the first president of the new Republic of Cyprus.
- British Motor Corporation launches the Mini.

DEATHS

Raymond Chandler, US author.

Lou Costello, US comedian.

John Foster Dulles, US statesman.

Sir Jacob Epstein, British sculptor.

George Grosz, German-born US artist.

Errol Flynn, US actor.

Billie Holliday, US singer.

Buddy Holly, US singer.

Cecil B. de Mille, US film director.
Sir Stanley Spencer, British artist.
Frank Lloyd Wright, US architect.

1960

- Harold Macmillan delivers 'Wind of Change' in speech to South African Parliament in Capetown.
- Sharpeville Massacre in South Africa, 56 Africans killed by police.
- American U-2 spy plane shot down over Soviet territory.
- Adolf Eichmann captured by Israeli secret service Mossad in Argentina.
- Belgian Congo granted independence as Congo Republic under president Patrice Lumumba (1 June); Congolese army mutiny (6 June); Katanga province declares itself independent from Congo and civil war begins (July); Congolese army takes power under Colonel Mobutu (September); Congolese army in conflict with UN troops (November); ex-premier Lumumba arrested (December).
- British rule ends and Cyprus becomes independent republic.
- Nigeria gains independence.
- US nuclear submarine 'Triton' completes first underwater circumnavigation of the globe.
- Charles van Doren and 12 other contestants arrested for perjury in testifying that they were not given the answers in advance to questions on top US TV quiz '21'.
- 'Lady Chatterley' trial in London:

Penguin Books found not guilty of publishing obscene material.
- John Fitzgerald Kennedy elected US President.
- Harper Lee *To Kill a Mockingbird*.

DEATHS
Aneurin Bevan, British statesman.
Albert Camus, French author.
Clark Gable, US actor.
Sylvia Pankhurst, British suffragette.
Boris Pasternak, Soviet author.
Mack Sennett, US film director.
Nevil Shute, Australian author.

1961

- In referendum French and Algerian voters support De Gaulle's policy of home rule for Algeria.
- British police arrest members of Portland spy ring.
- US severs diplomatic relations with Cuba.
- Contraceptive pill goes on sale in Britain.
- President Kennedy establishes US Peace Corps.
- Soviet cosmonaut Major Yuri Alexeyevitch Gagarin becomes first man in space.
- US-armed Cuban exiles stage unsuccessful invasion of Cuba at Bay of Pigs.
- Berlin Wall constructed.
- UN Secretary-General Dag Hammarskjöld killed in plane crash.
- Adolf Eichmann sentenced to death for war crimes at trial in Jerusalem.
- Britain begins negotiations to join the European Community.

- Joseph Heller *Catch 22*.
  DEATHS
  Sir Thomas Beecham, British conductor.
  Gary Cooper, US actor.
  (Samuel) Dashiell Hammett, US author.
  George Formby, British comedian.
  Ernest Hemmingway, US author.
  Augustus John, British painter.
  Carl Jung, Swiss psychoanalyst.
  James Thurber, US author.

1962

- US steps up military aid to South Vietnam.
- Adolf Eichmann hanged for Nazi war crimes.
- France recognises independence of Algeria.
- Riots in Deep South as University of Mississippi enrols black student James Meredith.
- Uganda and Tanganyika gain independence.
- Cuban Missile crisis.
- Trans-Canada Highway opened.
- Telstar communications satellite launched: brings first live trans-Atlantic television pictures.
- World's first passenger Hovercraft entered service.
  DEATHS
  Niels Bohr, Danish nuclear physicist.
  William Faulkner, US author.
  Herman Hesse, German-born Swiss author.
  Charles Laughton, British actor.
  Marilyn Monroe, US actress.

Richard Tawney, British socialist historian.
George Trevelyan, British historian.
Victoria Sackville-West, British writer.

1963

- Harold Wilson elected leader of the Labour Party after the death of Hugh Gaitskill.
- Beeching Report recommends extensive cuts in British railway branch lines.
- Britain agrees to buy Polaris missiles from the US.
- President de Gaulle of France vetoes British entry into the European Community.
- Profumo Affair in Britain: Secretary of State for War John Profumo resigns after lying to parliament about affair with prostitute.
- Civil Rights demonstrations in Birmingham, Alabama: Martin Luther King arrested.
- Cardinal Giovanni Battista Monitine elected Pope John XXIII.
- Great Train Robbery: £2.5 million stolen.
- 200,000 join civil rights 'Freedom March' on Washington DC.
- Buddhist riots in Saigon.
- Russia put first woman in space, Lieutenant Valentina Tereshkova.
- Sir Alec Douglas Home succeeds Harold Macmillan as prime minister.
- Test Ban Treaty signed by Britain, US and Russia.
- President John F. Kennedy assassi-

nated by Lee Harvey Oswald in Dallas, Texas: succeeded by Vice President Lyndon Baines Johnson.

- Lee Harvey Oswald shot by nightclub owner Jack Ruby at Dallas police headquarters.
- Military coup overthrows regime of President Ngo Dinh Diem in South Vietnam.
- Kenya gains independence.

DEATHS

Georges Braque, French Cubist painter.

Jean Cocteau, French artist and writer.

Robert Frost, US poet.

Paul Hindemith, German composer.

Aldous Huxley, British writer.

Max Miller, British comedian.

Edith Piaf, French singer.

Francis Poulenc, French composer.

Dinah Washington, US blues singer.

William Carlos Williams, US poet.

1964

- Zanzibar becomes a republic and unites with Tanganyika to form Tanzania.
- Northern Rhodesia becomes independent republic of Zambia.
- Constantine II King of Greece on death of King Paul I.
- Ian Smith premier of Southern Rhodesia.
- Violent clashes between Turkish and Greek Cypriots in Cyprus: UN peace forces intervene.
- Gulf of Tonkin Incident: US destroyers allegedly attacked by North Viet-

namese torpedo boats; President Johnson orders air strikes against the North.

- Warren Commission finds Lee Harvey Oswald acted alone in assassination of President Kennedy.
- Harold Wilson leads Labour Party to victory in general election.
- Jawaharl Nehru, Indian Prime Minister since independence dies after heart attack.
- Black Nationalist leader Nelson Mandela sentenced to life imprisonment in South Africa.
- President Johnson signs Civil Rights Act.
- Soviet leader Nikita Khrushchev deposed; replaced by Leonid Brezhnev as Communist party leader and Alexei Kosygin as prime minister.
- Martin Luther King awarded Nobel Peace Prize.
- Lyndon Johnson wins landslide victory in US presidential election.
- Kenya becomes independent with Jomo Kenyatta as president.

DEATHS

Lord Beaverbrook, Canadian-born British newspaper tycoon.

Brendan Behan, Irish playwright.

Ian Fleming, British novelist.

Alan Ladd, US actor.

Peter Lorre, US actor.

Harpo Marx, US comedian.

General Douglas MacArthur, US soldier.

Sean O'Casey, Irish writer.

Flannery O'Connor, US novelist.

Cole Porter, US composer.

1965

- Gambia becomes independent.
- Militant Black leader Malcolm X assassinated in New York.
- President Johnson sends marines into Vietnam.
- Edward Heath elected leader of the Conservative Party.
- Race riots in Watts, Los Angeles.
- India and Pakistan at war over disputed territory of Kashmir.
- Singapore separates from Malaysia.
- Ian Smith announces Universal Declaration of Independence of Rhodesia; Britain imposes oil embargo.
- General de Gaulle wins French presidential election.
- Death penalty for murder abolished in Britain.

DEATHS

Sir Winston Leonard Churchill, British statesman.
Nat King Cole, US singer.
Thomas Stearns Eliot, US poet.
Stan Laurel, British-born US comedian.
Le Corbusier (Charles Edouard Jeanneret), Swiss-born French architect.
Albert Schweitzer, German-born French doctor and missionary.

1966

- Indira Gandhi becomes prime minister of India.
- British Guiana becomes independent as Guyana.
- Barbados becomes and independent state within the British Commonwealth.

- Moors murderers Myra Hindley and Ian Brady sentenced to life imprisonment.
- Mao Tse-tung proclaims 'Cultural Revolution' in China.
- Prime Minister Dr Hendrik Verwoerd assassinated in South Africa and is succeeded by B. J. Vorster.
- President de Gaulle announces that France is to withdraw her troops from Nato.
- Aberfan disaster in Wales: 116 children and 28 adults killed by collapsing slag heap.
- English football team win the World Cup.
- Truman Capote *In Cold Blood*.

DEATHS

André Breton, French poet and author.
Lenny Bruce, US comedian.
Montgomery Clift, US actor.
Walt Disney, US animator.
Alberto Giacometti, Italian sculptor.
Buster Keaton, US actor and director.
Evelyn Waugh, British novelist.

1967

- Jeremy Thorpe elected leader of the Liberal Party.
- Six Day War between Israel and Arab nations: Israel takes territory from Egypt, Jordan and Syria.
- 50,000 demonstrators against the Vietnam War gather at the Lincoln Memorial in Washington DC.
- Ernesto ('Che') Guevara shot dead in the Bolivian jungle.

- Britain re-applies to join the European Community.
- Oil tanker *Torrey Canyon* goes aground off Land's End causing major pollution of coastline.
- Eastern region of Nigeria breaks away as independent state of Biafra.
- Brian Epstein, manager of the Beatles, commits suicide.
- US airforce intensifies bombing of North Vietnam.
- Christian N. Barnard performs first heart transplant in Groote Schuur Hospital, Cape Town.
- Cunard liner *Queen Elizabeth II* launched.
- Donald Campbell killed in jet-powered boat Bluebird while attempting to break the world water-speed record.
- Fire kills three US astronauts in Apollo spacecraft on launch pad.
- Expo 67 opens in Montreal.

  DEATHS

  Konrad Adenauer, German statesman.

  John Coltrane, US jazz musician.

  Sir Victor Gollancz, British publisher.

  J. Vivian Leigh, British actress.

  René Magritte, Belgian artist.

  John Masefield, British poet.

  J. Robert Oppenheimer, US nuclear physicist.

  Joe Orton, British playwright.

  Dorothy Parker, US author and critic.

  Claude Rains, US actor.

  Arthur Ransome, British author.

Carl Sandburg, US poet.

Siegfried Sassoon, British poet.

Spencer Tracy, US actor.

1968

- Tet (New Year) Offensive in Vietnam: Vietcong launch widespread attacks against southern cities.
- Alexander Dubcek named First Secretary of Czechoslovak Communist Party; begins reform of socialist system.
- US President Johnson announces he will not seek re-election.
- Violent anti-Vietnam war demonstrations in London.
- Martin Luther King assassinated in Memphis hotel.
- Robert Fitzgerald Kennedy assassinated in Los Angeles hotel.
- Student riots and street-fighting in Paris.
- Soviet tanks move into Prague to suppress 'Prague Spring' reform programme.
- Violent anti-Vietnam war demonstrations disrupt Democratic Party Convention in Chicago.
- Richard M. Nixon elected US President.

  DEATHS

  Enid Blyton, British author.

  Jim Clark, British racing driver.

  Anthony John Hancock, British comedian.

  Mervyn Peake, British author and artist.

  Upton Sinclair, US author.

1969

- British troops sent to suppress conflict between Protestants and Roman Catholics in Northern Ireland.
- Jan Palach, Czech student, burns himself to death in protest against.

Soviet occupation of Prague.

- Golda Meir President of Israel.
- General de Gaulle resigns as French president: George Pompidou elected to replace him.
- Yassar Arafat appointed leader of the Palestine Liberation Organisation.
- Neil Armstrong, commander of US spacecraft Apollo 11, becomes the first man on the moon.
- Chappaquiddick Incident: Senator Edward Kennedy fails to report car accident in which his passenger, Mary Jo Kopechne, is killed.
- Sharon Tate, pregnant wife of film director Roman Polanski, is brutally murdered in Beverly Hills mansion by Charles Manson gang.
- Colonel Muammar Gaddafi seizes power in Libya.
- 'Vietnam Moratorium': largest ever anti-Vietnam war demonstrations in the US.
- Oil discovered in the British and Norwegian sectors of the North Sea.
- Nigeria bans Red Cross aid for starving Biafrans.
- British-built supersonic airliner Concorde makes maiden flight.
- Kurt Vonnegut *Slaughterhouse Five*.
- Philip Roth *Portnoy's Complaint*.

DEATHS

Richmal Crompton, British author.
Otto Dix, German artist.
Judy Garland, US actress and singer.
Walter Gropius, German architect.
Brian Jones, British rock musician.
Jack Kerouac, US author.
John Wyndham, British author.

1970

- Conservatives win general election and Edward Heath becomes prime minister.
- Britain makes third application to join the European Community.
- Biafran Civil War ends with Biafran capitulation to Nigerian Federal forces.
- Gambia gains independence.
- President Nixon sends US troops into Cambodia.
- Four students killed by National Guard during anti-Vietnam war demonstration at Kent State University, Ohio.
- Salvador Allende elected President of Chile.
- Palestinian commandos hijack and blow up three airliners at Dawson's Field, Jordan.
- Anwar Sadat succeeds Gamel Abdul Nassser as President of Egypt.
- Civil war beings in Cambodia.
- Typhoon and tidal wave kill 150,000 in East Pakistan.
- Germaine Greer *The Female Eunuch*.

DEATHS

Sir John Barbirolli, British conductor.

General Charles de Gaulle, French statesman.

Edward Morgan Foster, British novelist.

John Dos Passos, US author.

Eva Hesse, German-born US sculptor.

Jimi Hendrix, US guitarist.

Yukio Mishima, Japanese author.

Erich Maria Remarque, German author.

Mark Rothko, US artist.

Bertrand Arthur William Russell, British philosopher.

1971

- Fighting in Vietnam spreads to Laos and Cambodia.
- General Idi Amin seizes power from President Milton Obote in Uganda.
- Sixty-six football fans crushed by collapsed barrier at Ibrox Park stadium, Glasgow.
- Lieutenant William L. Calley Jr found guilty of massacre in My Lai village, Vietnam in 1968.
- 'Pentagon Papers' exposing secret history of US involvement in Vietnam begin to appear in the *New York Times*.
- Britain introduces internment (imprisonment without trial) to combat IRA terrorism in Northern Ireland.
- Civil war in Pakistan after East Pakistan declares itself independent as the new state of Bangladesh.
- Jean-Claude Duvalier succeeds his father Francois 'Papa Doc' Duvalier as president of Haiti.

- China is admitted to the United Nations.
- Agreement signed to prepare Rhodesia's legal independence from Britain and settle issue of transition to African majority rule.
- Attica prison revolt: 10 warders and 32 prisoners die in five days of mayhem.
- India defeats Pakistan in two-week war.
- Decimal currency introduced in Britain.
- Open University inaugurated.
- Earthquake in Los Angeles kills 51 people.

DEATHS

Louis Armstrong, US jazz trumpeter.

Gabrielle 'Coco' Chanel, French fashion designer.

Harold Lloyd, US film actor and comedian.

Ogden Nash, US poet.

Igor Stravinsky, Russian composer.

1972

- Bangladesh (East Pakistan) established as independent state.
- President Nixon visits Russia and China.
- Five burglars arrested in Democratic National Headquarters in the Watergate Building in Washington DC: beginning of Watergate Affair.
- George Wallace, Governor of Alabama, paralysed after assassination attempt.
- Lon Nol takes power in Cambodia.
- Bloody Sunday in Ulster: British

paratroopers fire on civil rights demonstrators killing thirteen.

- Heath government imposes direct rule on Northern Ireland.
- Ireland, Britain and Denmark become full members of the European Community.
- Japanese terrorists massacre 25 people at Lod International airport, Tel Aviv.
- Last US combat troops withdraw from South Vietnam: US bombing of North Vietnam and Viet Cong supply routes in the south intensified.
- 'Black September' Arab terrorists kill two Israeli athletes at Munich Olympics.
- Idi Amin expels 50,000 Ugandan Asians with British passports.
- Earthquake in Managua, Nicaragua kills 10,000.
- Philippine President Marcos declares martial law to combat so-called 'Communist rebellion'.

DEATHS

Maurice Chevalier, French actor and singer.

J. Edgar Hoover, FBI director since 1924

Dr Louis Leakey, British anthropologist.

Cecil Day Lewis, British poet and novelist.

Ezra Pound, US poet.

1973

- Cease-fire in Vietnam agreed at Paris peace conference.
- Yom Kippur War: Egyptian forces

launch surprise attack on Israeli positions along Suez Canal.

- Top Nixon aids including H.R. Haldemann and John D. Ehrlichman resign as Watergate scandal penetrates the Oval Office (April); Senate Watergate hearings begin (May).
- President Salvador Allende killed during military coup in Chile.
- Greek army seizes power in Athens overthrowing President George Papadopoulos.
- Arab oil countries increase prices and cut production in protest at US support of Israel in Yom Kippur War.
- Miners' strike brings government announcement of three-day week to conserve fuel stocks.
- Value Added Tax (VAT) introduced in Britain.
- Aleksandr Solzhenitsyn *Gulag Archipelago*.

DEATHS

Wystan Hugh Auden, British poet.

Elizabeth Bowen, Irish writer.

Sir Noel Coward, British playwright.

John Ford, US film director.

Bruce Lee, Kung Fu film star.

Pablo Picasso, Spanish artist.

Edward G. Robinson, US actor.

John Ronald Reuel Tolkein, British author.

1974

- Edward Heath resigns and Harold Wilson leads minority government after snap election (March); Labour win second election with tiny majority (October).

- IRA bombs kill 21 and injure 120 in two Birmingham pubs.
- Bloodless coup in Portugal: dictatorship ended by military intervention and democratic reforms inaugurated.
- Syria and Israel agree to cease fire on the Golan Heights.
- Turkish invasion of Cyprus.
- President Nixon resigns as White House tape recordings implicate him in Watergate cover-up and Senate moves to impeach him; Gerald Ford sworn in as new president.
- Greek military junta collapses and ex-Premier Constantine Karamanlis returns from exile to head new government.
- President Haile Salassie overthrown by coup in Ethiopia.
- Civil war ends in victory for the communist Khmer Rouge under Pol Pot. The country is renamed Kampuchea.

DEATHS

Duke Ellington, US jazz musician.
Samuel Goldwyn, US film producer.
Virttorio de Sica, Italian film director.
Eric Linklater, British novelist.
Walter Lippman, US journalist.

1975

- Angola achieves independence from Portugal (January); civil war breaks out (November).
- Margaret Thatcher elected leader of the Conservative Party.
- Saigon surrenders to North Vietnamese troops.

- Communist Khmer Rouge seize control of Cambodia: Pol Pot regime inaugurates 'Year Zero'.
- Beirut erupts in civil war between Christians and Moslems.
- Spain reverts to monarchy after the death of General Franco: Prince Juan Carlos crowned as King Juan Carlos I.
- Suez Canal reopened for first time since 1967 Arab-Israeli War.
- First live broadcast of House of Commons debate.
- Internment (detention without trial) ends in Northern Ireland.
- Terrorists led by Carlos the Jackal raid Vienna headquarters of the Organisation of Petroleum Exporting Countries (OPEC).

DEATHS

Sir Pelham Grenville Woodhouse, British-born US author.
Sir John Frederick Neville Cardus, British music critic and cricket writer.
Sam Giancana, Chicago Mafia boss.
Susan Hayward, US actress.
Graham Hill, British racing driver.
Sir Julian Huxley, British scientist and philosopher.
Aristotle Onassis, Greek shipping magnate.
Dimitri Shostakovich, Russian composer.
Thornton Wilder, US writer.

1976

- Harold Wilson resigns: James Callaghan becomes prime minister.
- Jeremy Thorpe resigns as leader of

the Liberal Party: David Steel elected to replace him.

- Ian Smith accepts British proposals for majority rule in Rhodesia, ending 11 years of illegal independence.
- President Isabel Peron overthrown by Argentine military in bloodless coup.
- US celebrates its bicentennial.
- Dr Mario Soares elected Prime Minister of Portugal.
- North and South Vietnam reunified as Socialist Republic of Vietnam with Hanoi as capital: Saigon renamed Ho Chi Minh City.
- Death of Chairman Mao Tse-tung.
- Jimmy Carter elected US President.
- World's first scheduled supersonic passenger service inaugurated: two Concorde airliners take off simultaneously from London and Paris.
- Israeli commandos rescue 103 hostages held at Entebbe airport, Uganda by pro-Palestinian hijackers.
- Widespread anti-apartheid riots in black townships of South Africa.

DEATHS

Dame Agatha Christie, British crime writer.

Benjamin Britten, British composer.

Max Ernst, German-born French artist.

John Paul Getty, US oil tycoon.

Howard Hughes, US tycoon.

Chou En-lai, Chinese Premier.

Fritz Lang, German film director.

Man Ray, US artist and photographer.

André Malraux, French writer and politician.

Field Marshal Bernard Law Montgomery, first Viscount Montgomery of El Alamein, British commander.

Paul Robeson, US singer and Black activist.

Laurence Stephen Lowry, British artist.

1977

- Liberal and Labour parties form Lib-Lab Pact.
- Moraji R. Desai prime minister of India after resignation of Indira Gandhi.
- Menahem Begin prime minister of Israel after resignation of Yitzhak Rabin.
- Convicted murderer Gary Gilmore executed by firing squad in Utah State prison: first convict to be executed in the US in ten years.
- Egyptian President Anwar Sadat visits Israel, the first visit by an Arab leader since the Jewish state was founded in 1948.
- Two Jumbo jets collide at Tenerife airport: 574 passengers killed in world's worst aviation disaster.
- Prime minister of Pakistan Zulfikar Ali Bhutto overthrown by General Zia ul-Huq.
- Rock singer Elvis Presley dies of drug overdose at age of 42.
- South African black leader Steve Biko beaten to death in prison cell at Port Elizabeth.
- US Space Shuttle makes maiden flight on top of a Boeing 747.

DEATHS

Maria Callas, Greek soprano.

Sir Charles Chaplin, British actor and director.

Joan Crawford, US actress.

Bing Crosby, US singer and actor.

Peter Finch, Australian actor.

Julius 'Groucho' Marx, US actor and comedian.

Vladimir Nabokov, Russian-born US author.

Anais Nin, US author.

1978

- Former Italian prime minister Aldo Moro is kidnapped and murdered by Red Brigade terrorists.
- Military junta seizes power in Afghanistan.
- US establishes full diplomatic relations with People's Republic of China.
- Pieter Willem Botha Prime Minister of South Africa after resignation of John Vorster.
- Military coup in Bolivia.
- Prime Minister of Israel Menaham Begin and Egyptian President Anwar Sadat agree on framework for Middle East peace treaty at Camp David summit organised by President Carter.
- Shah of Iran imposes martial law to suppress anti-government demonstrations.
- Cardinal Luciani elected Pope John Paul I; he dies after 33 days in office and is succeeded by Polish Cardinal Karol Wojtyla as Pope John Paul II.

- Members of the People's Temple, a US religious cult led by Rev. Jim Jones, commit mass suicide in Guyana.
- Louise Brown, the world's first test-tube baby, born in Britain.

DEATHS

Charles Boyer, French actor.

Jacques Brel, Belgian singer.

Jomo Kenyatta, Kenyan statesman.

Margaret Mead, US anthropologist.

1979

- Shah of Iran is driven into exile by supporters of Moslem leader Ayatollah Khomeini who returns to Tehran after 14 years in exile.
- Vietnam invades Cambodia and crushes Khmer Rouge regime: evidence of mass killings under leader Pol Pot emerge.
- Regime of Idi Amin collapses in Uganda.
- Egypt and Israel sign peace treaty sponsored by President Carter.
- Nationalist hopes for devolution are killed by referendum results: a majority vote against a Welsh Assembly, and only 33% for a Scottish Assembly, short of the 40% required.
- Conservatives win general election: Margaret Thatcher becomes first woman prime minister.
- Leonid Brezhnev and President Carter sign SALT-2 arms limitation treaty.
- Accident at Three Mile Island nuclear plant in Pennsylvania.
- Sandinista rebels overthrow dictator

General Anastasio Samosa in Nicaragua.
- Earl Mountbatten of Burma murdered by IRA bomb.
- Supporters of Ayatollah Khomenei attack US embassy in Tehran and seize Marines and staff as hostages.
- Sir Anthony Blunt, the Queen's art adviser, revealed as a Russian spy, the 'Fourth Man' in the Burgess, MacLean and Philby affair.
- Soviet troops invade Afghanistan.
- Lancaster House agreement arranges cease-fire in the guerilla war in Rhodesia and elections to effect transfer to Black majority rule in a new state to be called Zimbabwe.

DEATHS

Dame Gracie Fields, British actress and singer.
Herbert Marcuse, German-born US philosopher.
Mary Pickford, US actress.
Jean Renoir, French film director.
Nelson Rockefeller, US politician.
Jean Seberg, US actress.
John Wayne, US actor.

1980

- Robert Mugabe elected prime minister of Zimbabwe.
- US military bid to rescue hostages held by Iranians in Tehran embassy aborted due to mechanical failures.
- SAS storm Iranian embassy in London to release hostages held by terrorists.
- Archbishop Romero shot in San Salvador, El Salvador.

- Sanjay Gandhi, the 33-year-old youngest son of Indira Gandhi, killed in plane crash.
- Polish strikers led by Lech Walesa win concessions from Communist government on trade union rights; Solidarity, central workers' organisation, formed with Lech Walesa as leader.
- Iraq attacks Iranian oil installations at Abadan: Iraq-Iran War begins.
- Ronald Reagan elected US President.
- Michael Foot succeeds James Callaghan as Labour Party leader.
- Jeremy Thorpe, former leader of the Liberal Party, acquitted in conspiracy trial.
- John Lennon murdered in New York by Mark David Chapman.
- William Golding *Rites of Passage*.

DEATHS

Joy Adamson, naturalist.
Sir Cecil Beaton, British photographer and designer.
Jimmy Durante, US comedian.
Sir Alfred Hitchcock, British film director.
Oscar Kokoschka, Austrian artist.
Steve McQueen, US actor.
Henry Miller, US writer.
Jean-Paul Sartre, French philosopher.
Peter Sellers, British actor and comedian.
Mae West, US actress.

1981

- Iran releases US embassy hostages after 444 days in captivity.

- General Jarulzelski appointed prime minister in Poland as strikes and demonstrations led by Solidarity intensify (February); martial law declared (December).
- President Reagan wounded in assassination attempt outside Hilton Hotel, Washington.
- Gang of Four (Roy Jenkins, David Owen, Bill Rodgers and Shirley Williams) break with Labour and announce the formation of a new party - the Social Democrats.
- Rioting in Brixton, Liverpool and Manchester in response to allegedly heavy policing.
- Hunger strike by IRA prisoners at the Maze Prison in Northern Ireland: 10 die.
- Peter Sutcliffe convicted of Yorkshire Ripper murders.
- Pope John Paul II survives assassination attempt by Turkish gunman in St Peter's Square, Rome.
- French elect François Mitterrand as new president.
- Prince Charles marries Lady Diana Spencer in St Paul's Cathedral: 700 million watch on television worldwide.
- Egyptian President Anwar Sadat assassinated at military parade in Cairo.
- Kampuchea is renamed Cambodia.

DEATHS

Samuel Barber, US composer.
Karl Bohm, Austrian conductor.
Bill Haley, US rock singer.
William Holden, US actor.

Bob Marley, Jamaican reggae star.
Jessie Matthews, British actress and singer.
Albert Speer, German architect.
Natalie Wood, US actress.

1982

- Unemployment in Britain reaches over three million.
- Barbican Centre arts complex opens in London.
- Argentina invades the Falkland Islands in the South Atlantic (2 April); Thatcher sends Task Force (5 April); Argentine cruiser *General Belgrano* sunk by torpedoes (2 May); HMS *Sheffield* hit by Exocet missile (4 May); first land battles between Argentinian and British troops (21 May); Argentine attack on two British supply ships off Bluff Cove (7 June); Argentinians surrender (14 June).
- Israel invades Lebanon in reprisal for Palestinian guerilla activities (June); Israeli forces drives the PLO out of Beirut (August); Lebanese Christian militia massacre hundreds in Palestinian refugee camps of Sabra and Chatila in West Beirut.
- Leonid Brezhnev dies; Yuri Andropov becomes Soviet leader.
- Women's Peace Camp established at Greenham Common in Berkshire to protest against planned siting of US Cruise missiles at nearby US military base.
- Britain's fourth TV channel, Channel Four, goes on the air.

- Princess Grace of Monaco (Grace Kelly) killed in car crash.
- Thames flood barrier raised for the first time.

DEATHS

Ingrid Bergman, Swedish actress.
Rainer Werner Fassbinder, German film director.
Henry Fonda, US actor.
Glenn Gould, Canadian pianist.
Theolonis Monk, US jazz pianist.
Carl Orff, German composer.
Romy Scheider, Austrian actress.
Jacques Tati, French film director and actor.

1983

- 'Star Wars' defence system proposed by President Reagan.
- 'Hitler Diaries' exposed as fake after extracts are published in the German news magazine *Stern* and the *The Sunday Times*.
- Margaret Thatcher re-elected in landslide general election.
- Benigno Aquino, leading opponent of President Marcos, assassinated at Manila airport.
- Soviet Union shoots down Korean Airlines' Boeing 747 flight 007 with the loss of 269 lives over Sakhalin Island off Siberia: Soviets claim the aircraft was on spying mission.
- Shia Muslim suicide bombers kill 241 Marines and 58 French paratroopers in Beirut by driving trucks filled with explosives into their compounds.
- Neil Kinnock elected leader of the Labour Party.

- US troops invade Grenada to remove Cuban presence from the island.
- Civilian rule restored in Argentina with the inauguration of Raul Alfonsin as president.

DEATHS

Luis Buñuel, Spanish film director.
George Cukor, US film director,.
Arthur Koestler, Hungarian-born British writer.
Joán Miró, Spanish artist.
David Niven, British actor.
Ralph Richardson, British actor.
Gloria Swanson, US actress.
Sir William Walton, British composer.
Dame Rebecca West, British author.

1984

- Konstantin Chernenko succeeds Andropov as Soviet Communist Party leader.
- Pierre Trudeau resigns as Canadian prime minister.
- Diplomatic ties with Libya are severed after the shooting of WPC Yvonne Fletcher outside the Libyan embassy in London.
- Discovery of the AIDS virus announced in Washington.
- Miners' national strike against pit closures begins.
- IRA bomb at Conservative Party conference in Brighton kills five.
- Prime Minister of India Indira Gandhi assassinated by Sikh bodyguards: she is succeeded by her son Rajiv.
- BBC television report on Ethiopian famine prompts massive aid effort.
- Gas leak from a chemical processing

plant in Bhopal, India kills over 2,000 people.

DEATHS

William 'Count' Basie, US jazz band leader.

Sir John Betjeman, British poet.

Richard Burton, British actor.

Truman Capote, US author.

Diana Dors, British actress.

Marvin Gaye, US singer.

Lillian Hellman, US author and playwright.

Joseph Losey, US film director.

James Mason, British actor.

Eric Morecambe, British comedian.

Sam Peckinpah, US film director.

J.B. Priestley, British author and playwright.

Sir Arthur Travis 'Bomber' Harris, British commander of RAF during World War II.

Francois Truffaut, French film director.

Johnny Weismuller, US actor and athlete.

THE EMERGENCE OF A NEW WORLD ORDER

1985

- Miners vote to end year-long national strike.
- Mikhail Gorbachev appointed new leader of the Soviet Union: begins to initiate wide-ranging liberal reforms (Glasnost) and economic restructuring (Perestroika).
- House of Lords proceedings televised for the first time.

- British football teams banned indefinitely from European competition after 38 people die as Liverpool fans riot at Heysel Stadium, Brussels.
- Live Aid Concert raises £40 million for famine victims in Ethiopia.
- President Reagan and Soviet leader Mikhail Gorbachev establish rapport at Geneva summit.

DEATHS

Laura Ashley, British fashion designer.

Yul Brynner, US actor.

James Cameron, British journalist and author.

Marc Chagall, Russian-born French painter.

Robert Graves, British poet.

Rock Hudson, US actor.

Philip Larkin, British poet.

Sir Michael Redgrave, British actor.

Orson Welles, US actor and director.

1986

- US space shuttle *Challenger* explodes on takeoff killing crew of seven.
- Construction of the Channel Tunnel begins.
- Cabinet ministers Michael Heseltine and Leon Brittain resign over the Westland Affair.
- Swedish Prime Minister Olof Palme assassinated in Stockholm.
- Ferdinand Marcos overthrown and replaced by Mrs Corazon Aquino as President of the Philippines.
- Jeffrey Archer resigns as chairman of the Conservative Party after alle-

gations of payments to a prostitute.

- US launches air strikes against terrorist targets in Libya.
- Russian nuclear reactor at Chernobyl is seriously damaged by fire and contaminates a wide area.
- President Reagan denies any knowledge of 'Irangate' scandal whereby profits from US weapons sales to Iran were used covertly to fund the Contra rebels fighting the left-wing Sandinista government in Nicaragua.

DEATHS

Simone de Beauvoir, French author.
Jorge Luis Borges, Argentine author.
James Cagney, US actor.
Benny Goodman, US jazz clarinettist.
Cary Grant, British-born US actor.
Henry Moore, British sculptor.
Otto Preminger, US film director.

1987

- Terry Waite, special envoy of the Archbishop of Canterbury, is kidnapped in Beirut by members of the militant Islamic group Hezbollah.
- The car ferry *Herald of Free Enterprise* capsizes off Zeebrugge with the loss of 188 lives.
- Margaret Thatcher re-elected for third term as prime minister.
- Government announces plans to introduce a Poll Tax to replace the rates system for funding local services.
- Former SS officer Klaus Barbie, the 'Butcher of Lyons', is sentenced in a court in Lyons to life imprisonment for war crimes.

- Rudolph Hess found dead in Spandau prison after apparently hanging himself.
- David Owen resigns as leader of the SDP in opposition to talks about merging with the Liberals.
- 'Black Monday' in the City of London: over £100 billion wiped off the value of shares on the stock market.
- IRA bomb kills eleven people at Remembrance Day service in Enniskillen, Northern Ireland.
- President Reagan and Mikhail Gorbachev sign treaty to arrange for the dismantling of Soviet and US medium-and shorter-range missiles.

DEATHS

Fred Astaire, US dancer and actor.
Rita Hayworth, US actress.
John Huston, US film director.
Danny Kaye, US actor and comedian.
Lee Marvin, US actor.
Jacqueline Du Pré, British cellist.
Andy Warhol, US artist.

1988

- Intifada uprising by West Bank and Gaza Arabs against Israeli occupation begins.
- Piper Alpha disaster: 167 workers killed North Sea oil rig explosion.
- Iran and Iraq agree a cease-fire to end eight years of conflict.
- Floods in Bangladesh kill 300 and leave over 20 million people homeless.
- Social and Liberal Democratic Party formed by the merger of the Liberals and SDP.

- Canadian sprinter Ben Johnson is found guilty of using drugs and is stripped of his gold medal for the 100 metres at the Seoul Olympics.
- George Bush elected US President.
- President Gorbachev announces dramatic reduction in Red Army strength in speech to the United Nations.
- Earthquake in Armenia kills over 100,000 people.
- Pan American jumbo jet blown up by terrorist bomb over Lockerbie in Scotland, killing all 259 passengers on board and 11 people from the town (December).

DEATHS

Sir Frederick Ashton, British ballet choreographer.

Enzio Ferrari, Italian racing car magnate.

Richard Feynman, US physicist.

Trevor Howard, British actor.

Roy Orbison, US singer.

Kenneth Williams, British comedy actor.

1989

- Emperor Hirohito dies and is succeeded by his son Crown Prince Akihito.
- Author Salman Rushdie goes into hiding after the Ayatollah Khomenei orders his execution for blaspheming Islam in his book *The Satanic Verses*. Diplomatic relations between Britain and Iran are broken off.
- Soviet troops leave Afghanistan after ten-year occupation.

- Supertanker *Exxon Valdez* spills cargo of oil in Price William Sound, Alaska, the worst oil spillage in US history.
- Ninety-four football fans crushed to death at Hillsborough stadium in Sheffield.
- People's Liberation Army crush student pro-democracy demonstration in Tiananmen Square in Peking.
- Poland elects Tadeusz Mazowiecki first non-Communist Prime Minister.
- Vietnamese troops leave Cambodia after eleven years of occupation.
- Nigel Lawson, Chancellor of the Exchequer, resigns from the government over differences on economic policy.
- Hungary announces changes to its constitution to allow free elections.
- Guildford Four (Gerard Conlon, Carole Richardson, Patrick Armstrong and Paul Hill), convicted of IRA pub bombings in 1974 based on confessions fabricated by the police, are released.
- The Berlin Wall is dismantled as political reform in East Germany allows free movement of East German citizens to the west.
- Communist leadership in Czechoslovakia resigns; playwright Vaclav Havel is elected as president to prepare for free elections.
- Romanian dictator Nicolai Ceausescu and his wife Elena are executed by firing squad as Communist rule collapses.
- National Assembly in Bulgaria ap-

proves liberal political reforms in response to mass demonstrations.

- US troops invade Panama to oust dictator Manuel Noriega.
- House of Commons proceedings begin to be televised.

DEATHS

A. J. Ayer, British philosopher.
Lucille Ball, US comedienne.
Samuel Beckett, Irish writer.
Irving Berlin, US songwriter.
Salvador Dali, Spanish artist.
Bette Davis, US actress.
R.D. Laing, British psychiatrist.
Herbert von Karajan, Austrian conductor.
Daphne du Maurier, British novelist.
Lord Olivier, British actor.
Georges Simenon, Belgian novelist.

1990

- Ban on African National Congress (ANC) lifted in South Africa; Black nationalist leader Nelson Mandela freed from prison in Cape Town after 27 years; Mandela and ANC enter talks with President F. W. de Klerk about political future of the country.
- Sandinista government in Nicaragua defeated in democratic elections by National Opposition Union led by Senora Violeta Chamorro.
- Anti-poll tax march in London turns into a riot.
- Boris Yeltsin elected President of the Republic of Russia.
- David Owen disbands Social Democratic Party because of lack of support.

- Brian Keenan, one of several Western hostages held by militant Islamic groups in Beirut, is freed after 1,597 days in captivity.
- Iraq invades Kuwait (August): UN imposes economic sanctions to persuade Saddam Hussein to withdraw his forces: UN resolution imposes ultimatum on Iraq to withdraw from Kuwait by 15 January 1991 (November).
- West and East Germany are reunited (October); Helmut Kohl elected Chancellor of reunited Germany (December).
- Britain rejects timetable for a single European currency by the year 2000 at EC summit in Rome.
- Margaret Thatcher withdraws from Conservative Party leadership contest and is replaced by John Major.
- Channel Tunnel excavation teams from English and French side meet in the middle.

DEATHS

Leonard Bernstein, US composer and conductor.
Aaron Copland, US composer.
Sammy Davis Jr, US entertainer.
Greta Garbo, Swedish-born actress.
Ava Gardner, US actress.
Rex Harrison, British actor.
Barbara Stanwyck, US actress.
A. J. P. Taylor, British historian.
Paul Tortellier, French cellist.
Irvine Wallace, US writer.

1991

- Gulf War begins with operation

'Desert Storm', a massive air assault with bombs and missiles on Iraq by British, US and Saudi forces (17 January); land war begins (24 February) and Iraq capitulates after 100-hour conflict.

- Soviet troops crack down on Baltic states as demands for independence intensify.
- Last of the apartheid laws in South Africa are abolished.
- The British government replaces the poll tax with a new 'council tax' based on property values.
- Saddam Hussein suppresses Kurd revolt in northern Iraq.
- Prime Minister of India Rajiv Gandhi assassinated.
- Black motorist Glen King, known as Rodney King in police reports, viciously assaulted by four white policemen: caught on videotape (March 3).
- Boris Yeltsin elected President of Russia.
- Violence escalates in Yugoslavia as the Serbian-dominated federal army attempts to suppress demands for independence by Slovenia and Croatia (June); Dubrovnik besieged by army (October).
- The Soviet Union comes to an end: President Gorbachev is temporarily ousted by hardline Communists opposed to his reform program and then reinstated after Boris Yeltsin leads popular resistance to coup leaders (August); Russia, Byelorussia, Ukraine and eight other former

Soviet republics form the Commonwealth of Independent States (8 December); Gorbachev resigns (25 December).

- British hostages in Beirut released by Islamic fundamentalist group Hezbollah: John McCarthy (August), Terry Waite (November) and Jackie Mann.
- Tycoon Robert Maxwell drowns at sea and his publishing empire collapses with massive debts.

DEATHS

Dame Peggy Ashcroft, British actress.

Miles Davis, US jazz musician.

Dame Margot Fonteyn, British dancer.

Graham Greene, British novelist.

Sir David Lean, British film director.

Freddie Mercury, British rock star.

1992

- European Commission recognises independence of breakaway republics Croatia and Slovenia, legitimising the disintegration of the former Yugoslavia (January); Bosnia-Herzegovina votes for independence (March); fighting between the Serb-dominated Yugoslav army and the secessionist republics intensifies; revelation of emaciated Moslem prisoners in Serbian camps in Bosnia confirms Serbian policy of 'ethnic cleansing' from Serb-dominated areas (August); Macedonia declares independence. Yugoslavia now consists of Serbia and Montenegro.

- The four police officers who were caught on video beating Rodney King, 3 March 1991, are acquitted. Race riots break out in Los Angeles in response (April 29).
- Judge Giovanni Falcone, Italy's chief anti-Mafia investigator, murdered by the Mafia in Palermo.
- John Smith elected leader of the Labour Party.
- Windsor Castle badly damaged by fire.
- US Marines land in Somalia to curb Somali warlords and allow humanitarian aid for famine victims to be distributed.
- Prince Charles and Diana the Princess of Wales announce their separation.
- Bill Clinton is elected US President.

Deaths

Isaac Asimov, US science-fiction writer.

Francis Bacon, British artist.

Richard Brooks, US film director.

Marlene Dietrich, German-born US actress.

Denholm Elliot, British actor.

Alex Haley, US author.

Benny Hill, British comedian.

Frankie Howerd, British comedian.

Robert Morley, British actor.

Anthony Perkins, US actor.

Sanjit Ray, Indian film director.

1993

- Oil tanker *Braer* runs aground off the Shetland Isles. Oil spillage causes environmental damage.

- Czechoslovakia is split into Slovakia and the Czech Republic.
- Inauguration of the Single European Market.
- President Bush and President Yeltsin sign START-2 treaty cutting nuclear arsenals by two thirds.
- Queen Elizabeth II agrees to pay tax on private income.
- Two Los Angeles police officers found guilty of beating black motorist Rodney King.
- FBI siege of Branch Davidian cult headquarters at Waco, Texas, ends in mass suicide as building is deliberately set on fire.
- Lord Owen and Cyrus Vance peace plan for division of Bosnia abandoned.
- Violence in South African black townships escalates as 1994 date for democratic elections is announced: President de Klerk and ANC leader Nelson Mandela ratify new democratic constitution (November).
- Flooding in US mid-West causes $5 billion damage.
- Buckingham Palace opened to the public.
- Sarajevo placed under UN rule.
- PLO-Israeli peace deal agreed after secret negotiations: Palestinians given control in Gaza and Jericho; Yasser Arafat signs mutual recognition agreement with Israel.
- Jordan and Israel sign peace accord for dealing with disputes.
- State of Emergency declared in Moscow: President Boris Yeltsin uses

military force to oust opponents from the Russian parliament building.

• There are elections in Cambodia and a democratic monarchist constitution is adopted, restoring Sihanouk to the throne.

• Two 11-year-old boys are found guilty of the murder of the two-year-old James Bulger.

• European Union inaugurated as Maastricht Treaty comes into force.

• Government admits to clandestine meetings with the IRA (November); Downing Street Declaration on Northern Ireland by John Major and Taoiseach Albert Reynolds opens the way to all-party talks (December).

DEATHS

John Birks (Dizzy) Gillespie, US jazz musician.

Anthony Burgess, British author, composer and critic.

Sir William Golding, British author.

William Randolph Hearst, US newspaper magnate.

Audrey Hepburn, US actress.

Rudolf Nureyev, Russian-born ballet dancer.

Albert Sabin, US virologist.

1994

• Serb forces withdraw from around Sarajevo as Nato threatens air strikes against their artillery positions.

• Italian media tycoon Silvio Berlusconi becomes prime minster of Italy (March); resigns (December).

• Massacres of Tutsis by Hutus in

Rwanda leaves estimated 500,000 dead and 1.5 million homeless.

• Nelson Mandela leads African National Congress to victory in South African elections (April); Mandela inaugurated as first black president (May).

• Israel and PLO sign pact ending Israeli occupation of Gaza Strip and Jericho.

• Labour Party leader John Smith dies. Tony Blair is elected leader.

• President Kim Il Sung dies and is succeeded by his son Kim Jong Il as North Korean leader.

• Jordan and Israel sign peace treaty.

• US forces invade Haiti to oust military government.

• IRA announces cease-fire in Northern Ireland, opening way for political settlement (August); Loyalists announce cease-fire (October); peace talks begin between government and Sinn Fein (December).

• Roll-on roll-off car ferry *Estonia* sinks in Baltic with loss of 900 lives.

• Queen Elizabeth II visits Russia.

• Russia invades breakaway Caucasian state of Chechnya.

• Channel Tunnel opens.

• Sunday shopping introduced.

DEATHS

Sir Harold Acton, British author and historian.

Lindsay Anderson, British film director.

Cab Calloway, US band leader.

John Candy, Canadian actor.

Elias Canetti, British author.

Joseph Cotton, US actor.

Peter Cushing, British actor.

Robert Doisneau, French photographer.

Derek Jarman, British filmmaker.

Burt Lancaster, US actor.

Harry Nilsson, US singer-songwriter.

Richard M. Nixon, US statesman.

Henri Mancini, US composer.

Jacqueline Kennedy Onassis, former US First Lady.

John Osborne, British actor and playwright.

Sir Karl Popper, British philosopher.

Dennis Potter, British television dramatist.

Madeleine Renaud, French actress.

Fernando Rey, Spanish actor.

Cesar Romero, US actor.

Telly Savalas, Greek-born US actor.

Mai Zetterling, Swedish actress.

1995

• Bosnian conflict: cease-fire begins (9 January); violated (11 February) as fighting breaks out in Bihac. Croatia and Bosnia establish a military front against Serbs (6 March). Bosnian government forces attack Serbs near Tuzla (4 April). Croatian capital Zagreb is shelled by Serbs (2 May). Serb attacks on Sarajevo begin; Nato responds with air srikes. Serbs take UN troops hostage (26 May) – released June. Srebrenica, a Muslim 'safe area', falls to Serbs (July). Croatian and Bosnian Serb troops mobilise (5 August). Croatian and Bosnian Muslim allies defeat Serbs to take Knin, capital of Krajina. Nato air strikes suspended for 24 hours for peace talks (1 September). Nato ceases bombing the Serbs (18 September). Slobodan Milosevich, President of Serbia, Croatian leader Franjo Tudjman and Bosnian President, Alija Izetbegivic, agree to plan for unified Bosnia-Herzegovina at Dayton, Ohio (21 November). Accord is signed in Paris (14 December).

• Republic of Ireland votes for legalisation of divorce.

• Peru and Ecuador end border fighting (14 February).

• Winnie Mandela dismissed from government of her estranged husband Nelson Mandela.

• Gerry Adams of Sinn Fein meets President Clinton at the White House (16 March). President Clinton visits Northern Ireland (November) – the first US president to do so.

• Frederick West, alleged serial killer, hangs himself in prison (1 January) while awaiting trial. His widow, Rosemary (3 October–22 November) is found guilty of the murder of ten young women and jailed for life.

• Trial of actor and former football star O. J. Simpson starts in Los Angeles (24 January) for the murder of his estranged wife and her friend (in 1994). Verdict is not guilty (October).

• Japanese city of Kobe hit by earthquake with loss of over 5000 lives (17 January).

- Oklahoma: Alfred P. Murrah building (offices of federal government) bombed with loss of 158 lives.
- Merchant bank, Barings, collapses after rogue trader, Nick Leeson, loses an estimated £17 billion on Japanese futures market. Leeson found guilty of fraud, sentenced to six and a half years' imprisonment (December 2).
- Israeli Prime Minister Yitzakh Rabin assassinated by right wing extremist Yigal Amir (November 4): succeeded by Shimon Peres (November 15).
- Space stations *Mir* (Russian) and *Discovery* (American) rendezvous in space.
- Water is found on Mars.
- Gas explosion beneath a road in Korea kills 100 (28 April).
- Ebola outbreak in Zaire, killing 108 by 24 May.
- Nerve gas released in Tokyo subway kills ten people and injures over 5000 (March); second attack in April in Yokahama. Leader of religious cult arrested and admits to attacks (May).
- Nigerian writer and political activist Ken Saro-Wiwa sentenced to death (31 October) following deaths of four leaders of Ogoni people at rally. Despite worldwide outrage, he and eight other environmental campaigners hanged.
- South Africa wins Rugby Union World Cup.

DEATHS

Kingsley Amis, British novelist.

Mohammed Siad Barre, President of Somalia from 1969, overthrown 1991

Robert Bolt, British playwright.

Peter Cook, British comedian.

Robertson Davies, Canadian journalist.

Gerald Durrell, British author and conservationist.

J. William Fulbright, US Democrat and campaigner against the Vietnam war.

Sir Michael Hordern, British actor.

Ronnie Kray, British gangster.

Brian Lenihan, Irish politician and Deputy Prime Minister 1987–90

Louis Malle, French film director.

Jackie Mann, Battle of Britain fighter pilot, Beirut hostage from 1989–91

Dean Martin, US actor and singer.

Prof. Benjamin Mazar, Israeli archaeologist.

Fred Perry, British tennis player.

Donald Pleasance, British actor.

Yitzakh Rabin, Prime Minister of Israel.

James Reston, US journalist.

Ginger Rogers, US actress.

Joe Slovo, South African Communist leader.

Sir Robert Stephens, British Actor.

Harold Wilson, British Prime Minister 1964–76

1996

- President Clinton meets Gerry Adams, Sinn Fein leader, at White House (February 1).

- IRA bomb explodes at South Quay in London's Docklands killing two people, injuring 200 and causing extensive damage (9 February).
- Concern grows over risk from exposure to meat infected with BSE. More European countries ban import of British beef (March).
- At a Dunblane primary school, 13 children and a teacher shot dead by gunman Thomas Hamilton, who then shot himself. 12 other children and two teachers also injured (13 March).
- Robert Mugabe is re-elected president of Zimbabwe (17 March).
- Fighting breaks out in Liberia following dismissal of Roosevelt Johnson from government (6 April) A cease-fire follows (10 April). Fighting resumes 1 May.
- Benyamin Netanyahu, Likud leader, elected as Prime Minister of Israel.
- Mary Robinson, president of Republic of Ireland, makes official visit to Britain; first Irish president to do so since foundation of Republic of Ireland (June).
- President of South Africa, Nelson Mandela, makes four-day visit to Britain (July).
- Liberia's warring factions agree to a cease-fire (31 July).
- Prince and Princess of Wales are divorced (28 August).
- British forces begin withdrawing from Hong Kong (29 August).
- Somalia's warring factions agree to a cease-fire (15 October).

- Colonel Yayah Jammeh wins first presidential election in Gambia since disbanding of its ruling military council.
- Euthanasia legalised in Australia's Northern Territory.
- France carries out sixth nuclear test at Fangataufa.
- In Australia, Labor Party defeated by Liberal-National coalition.
- Bill Clinton re-elected as president of USA (5 November).
- 700 people are killed when a cyclone hits southern India (6 November).
- When two aircraft collide mid-air near New Delhi, India all 351 passengers are killed (12 November).
- Fossils of bacteria discovered in meteorite provide first evidence of life on Mars.
- Hutu-Tutsi crisis: 51 Tutsi refugees killed by Hutu rebels in Burundi (28 May); Rwandan government starts issuing new passports, invalidating those held by Hutu refugees in exile (20 June); 300 Tutsis massacred by Hutus at Bugendana Burundi (20 July); President Ntibantaganya of Burundi overthrown by army and Major Pierre Buyoya, a moderate Tutsi, installed as head of state (31 July). Armies of Rwanda and Zaire exchange fire across their border. In Zaire, fighting breaks out between army and Tutsis. 200,000 Rwandan Hutu refugees flee from camps in eastern Zaire (2 November). Thousands of

Hutu refugees forcibly repatriated to Rwanda from refugee camps in Tanzania.

- Bosnian crisis: Serb soldiers and officers brought before International War Crimes Tribunal. Exhumation of bodies of Muslims massacred following capture of Srebrenica by Bosnian Serbs in July 1995.

DEATHS

Spiro Agnew, vice president of the USA 1969–73.

Dorothy Lamour, American actress.

Hang Ngor, Vienamese actor.

Cubby Broccoli. American-born film producer.

George Burns, American comedian.

Simon Cadell, British actor.

Ossie Clark, fashion designer, is murdered.

Joseph Brodsky, Russian poet.

Max Factor Junior, make-up artist.

Greer Garson, Irish-born actress.

Norman McCaig, British poet.

Timothy Leary, American psychologist.

Francois Mitterand, President of France 1981–95.

Muhammad Najibullah, president of Afghanistan 1986–92.

Stavros Niarchos, Greek financier.

Andreas Papandreou, Prime Minister of Greece 1981–9.

Sultan Rahi, Pakistani film actor.

Willie Rushton, British satirist, cartoonist and comedian.

Jean Sinclair, founder of the Black Sash Anti-apartheid movement.

Jerry Siegel, creator of Superman.

1997

- Ordination of first women priests in Anglican Church takes place in Wales (11 January).
- President Bill Clinton sworn in for his second term as President of USA (20 January).
- Civil trial in Santa Monica finds O.J. Simpson to be responsible for the deaths of his ex-wife and her friend: ordered to pay £15.2 million in damages to the relatives of the victims (February).
- Inquest of the death of south London black teenager, Stephen Lawrence, finds that he was murdered by five youths in an unprovoked racist attack (13 February).
- Louise Woodward, a British nanny working in the USA, charged with the murder of Matthew Eappen, the baby in her care (13 February).
- 39 members of Heaven's Gate sect in California, USA, commit suicide (27 March).
- Labour Party, with Tony Blair as leader, wins general election with majority of 179 seats in House of Commons (1 May).
- Dr Mo Mowlam appointed Secretary of State for Northern Ireland and visits Belfast (2 May). Tony Blair makes his first visit to Northern Ireland, stating that he is prepared to have discussions with Sinn Fein (16 May). Detailed talks to be held leading to an agreement that will be put to a referendum of Northern Irish electorate. Sinn Fein will be invited

to take part in talks after declaration of an IRA cease-fire (25 June). IRA cease-fire announced to be in effect from 12 noon 20 July. Sinn Fein invited to join the peace talks process (29 August).

- President Clinton is alleged to have sexually harassed Paula Jones when he was Governor of Arkansas. Supreme Court rules that he cannot claim constitutional immunity to escape a lawsuit (27 May).
- 29 people killed by tornadoes in Texas (28 May).
- In Canada the Liberal party is returned to power (2 June).
- Hong Kong is no longer a British colony: China assumes sovereignty (1 July).
- Islamic fundamentalists continue their terrorist activities in Algeria: many people are murdered.
- Mary McAleese becomes president of Ireland (31 October).
- Diana, Princess of Wales and her companion, Dodi Fayed, killed in car crash in Paris; her bodyguard is also seriously injured. Driver, who also dies in crash, reported to have more than three times legal limit of alcohol in his blood (31 August). Her funeral held in London 6 September.
- Referenda held in Scotland and Wales. Scottish electorate vote on setting up of devolved Scottish Parliament (11 September). Turnout 62 per cent, of which 74.3 per cent vote in favour of parliament and 63.5 per cent vote in favour of it having tax-raising powers. Welsh electorate vote in favour of an assembly with a turnout of 50 per cent of the electorate, of which 50.3 per cent vote in favour of the assembly (17 September).
- Janet Jagan becomes President of Guyana (15 December).
- Socialist party leader, Milan Milutinovic elected president of Serbia (22 December).

DEATHS

Deng Xiaoping, leader of China since 1978.

William S. Burroughs, American writer.

Jeanne Calment, the world's oldest person, aged 122.

Melvin Calvin, American chemist and Nobel laureate 1961.

Denis Compton, British cricketer.

Jacques Cousteau, French underwater explorer.

Allan Ginsberg, American poet.

Pamela Harriman, US Ambassador to France since 1993.

Chaim Herzog, President of Israel, 1983–93.

Ben Hogan, American golfer.

Cheddi Jagan, President of Guyana since 1992.

Laurie Lee, British poet and author.

Edward Purcell, American physicist.

Sir George Solti, conductor.

James Stewart, American actor.

Nikolai Tikhonov, Prime Minister of the USSR 1980–85.

Gianni Versace, fashion designer

1998

- Britain assumes presidency of the European Union for six months (1 January).
- Northern Ireland: Tony Blair addresses Irish parliament, first British politician to do so since 1922 (26 November). Sinn Fein expelled from Northern Ireland peace talks (20 February) but readmitted. Northern Ireland accord, 'Good Friday Agreement', reached (10 April). Irish Parliament backs peace agreement (22 April). In two referenda Irish voters approve peace accord: 71% in favour in Northern Ireland and 94% in favour in the Republic of Ireland (22 May). New assembly elected in Northern Ireland (26 June). Unionist leader David Trimble is elected First Minister (July). Three Catholic brothers are killed by a bomb while they are asleep (July). John Hume of the SDLP and David Trimble are awarded the Nobel Peace Prize (October). Orange Order parades through Catholic neighbourhood of Portadown despite ban by Parades Commission (5 July). Orange Order given permission to march through Lower Ormeau in Belfast (13 July).
- Sexual harassment case brought by Paula Jones against President Clinton dismissed (April).
- Investigation begins into alleged affair between President Clinton and White House intern Monica S Lewinsky. Clinton is accused of per-

suading her to lie under oath (January 21). He continues to deny they had a sexual relationship. Lewinsky gives evidence to Grand Jury stating that she and President Clinton did have sexual contact (26 July). President Clinton gives evidence from the White House via a closed-circuit camera, admitting to an extramarital affair with Miss Lewinsky (17 August). Kenneth Starr's report on Clinton delivered to Congress and published on Internet (11 September). The House of Representatives votes to impeach President Clinton on four articles (19 December).

- Iranian government withdraws its support of fatwa on Salman Rushdie, author of the *Satanic Verses* (24 September). Britain resumes diplomatic relations with Iran.
- Italian prime minister, Romano Prodi, sacked in vote of no confidence (9 October).
- Former Chilean dictator General Augusto Pinochet arrested in London by police acting for Spanish judges who seek his extradition (16 October); claim of immunity rejected; ordered to remain in custody (25 November).
- China signs agreement to improve human rights (5 October).
- German Chancellor of 16 years, Helmut Kohl, defeated by Gerhard Shröder of Social Democrats (27 September).
- Former Palestinian guerilla fighters vote to drop clause calling for Is-

raels's destruction from their charter (14 December).

- Saddam Hussein expels a UN weapons inspection team from Iraq (January). UN Secretary General Kofi Annan persuades Saddam Hussein to allow inspection team access to suspected chemical weapon sites (February). United Nations Human Rights Commission reports that Iraq has executed at least 1,500 during the past year (13 April). Iraqis fire on British and US planes in no-fly zones (30 December).
- Pope John Paul II begins his first visit to Cuba (21 January) and makes visit to Poland (31 May).
- Jack Kevorkian, 'Dr Death', charged with murder after a film of him administering a fatal injection to a terminally ill man is aired on national television in USA (22 November). Found guilty (9 December).
- The USA with British backing bomb a factory in Sudan.
- Two boys, aged 13 and 11, kill four girls and a teacher and wound 11 others at Jonesboro Middle School, Arkansas, USA.
- Male impotence pill Viagra approved in USA.
- Pol Pot, founder and leader of Cambodian Khmer Rouge, dies of a heart attack aged 73 (15 April).
- Canada's Supreme Court rules that Quebec does not have right to separate from rest of country.
- Daniel arap Moi is re-elected President of Kenya for a fifth term.

- Ezer Weizman is re-elected President of Israel (4 March).
- Islamic fundamentalist suicide bombers kill 43 people in Coimbatore, India.
- US President Bill Clinton meets Benyamin Netanyahu to propose phased pull-out of Israel from West Bank. Netanyahu insists on compliance with Israeli demands (20 January). Clinton meets Palestinian leader Yasser Arafat who rejects Israeli offer of phased withdrawal from the West Bank as insufficient (22 January).
- The soccer World Cup held in France (10 June); France wins (12 July).
- Burundi Peace talks resume in Tanzania (20 July).
- Massachusetts State Supreme Judicial Court hears appeal for Louise Woodward, accused of killing baby Matthew Eappen (6 March). Civil trial begins to determine damages she must pay (4 January 1999).
- Europe agrees on single currency at the Brussels conference (3 May).
- Indonesian students protest to demand resignation of President Suharto: police kill 6 (13 May). President Suharto resigns because of economic crisis, after 32 years in power. Succeeded by Vice President B. J. Habibie (21 May).
- India stages underground nuclear testing (11, 13 May). Pakistan stages nuclear tests in response (29 May).
- Space shuttle *Discovery* launched on a 10-day mission (2 June).
- Astronaut, John Glenn, aged 77, re-

turns to space in *Discovery* to perform experiments on ageing (29 October).

- Russian President Boris Yeltsin sacks his entire cabinet (23 March); travels to Japan (11 April).
- Operation Desert Fox: USA fires air missiles at Iraqi military sites (December).
- Conflict in Kosovo: UN imposes arms embargo on Federal Republic of Yugoslavia to force negotiations between government and Kosovan nationalists (31 March); Serb tanks enter Kosovo (27 April); villages burned; rebel ethnic Albanians attacked by Serb military forces; refugees flee; UN condemns massacre of ethnic Albanians (2 October); Nato countries support possible military action against Yugoslavia (12 October); forces from Organisation for Security and Co-operation in Europe (OSCE) act to ensure Yugoslavia complies with Belgrade cease-fire agreement (13 October); Serbs break cease-fire in response to killing of a Serb by ethnic Albanian guerillas (24 December).

DEATHS

Sonny Bono, American actor, singer, US Representative.

Phil Hartman, American actor

Alan J. Pakula, film director and producer.

Yeffim Geller, chess player.

Professor Susan Strange, international relations expert.

Frank Sinatra, American singer.

John Derek, American film director.

Joe Di Maggio, American baseball player.

Lew Grade, British impresario.

Florence Griffith Joyner, American athlete.

Giant Haystacks, British wrestler.

Robin Ray, actor, writer and broadcaster.

'Tiny' Walter Rowland, businessman.

Albert Gore Senior, Democratic Senator of Tennesee.

Sir Alan Hodgkin, Nobel prize-winning scientist.

1999

- The Euro, a single European currency, launched (1 January).
- Civil trial of Louise Woodward begins (4 January). Civil action brought by the Eappens against Woodward settled out of court (February).
- UN troops pull out of Angola after ten years of peacekeeping in civil war (January).
- Earthquake in Colombia kills more than 2,000 people (January).
- Labour Party in Barbados wins power, leading way for former British colony to become republic (January).
- King Hussein of Jordan names his eldest son, Prince Abdullah, as heir instead of his brother, Prince Hassan (January). King Hussein dies from cancer (8 February).
- The border between Gibraltar and Spain blockaded by Spanish fishermen seeking access to Gibraltarian waters (February)

- Details emerge of a famine in North Korea (February).
- Kurdish leader Abdullah Ocalan arrested in Greece and returned to Turkey, prompting a series of demonstrations around Europe and kidnapping of Greek ambassadors in Zurich, Vienna and the Hague (February).
- Jury members in trial of Anthony Sawoniuk, for his part in murder of 3,000 Jews in 1942, travel to Belarus to site of murder (February).
- Amadou Diallo, an unarmed immigrant from Guinea, shot dead in New York by four white policemen who fired 41 shots, hitting him with 19 bullets (February).
- A series of avalanches in the French, Italian, Austrian and Swiss Alps claim the lives of nearly 30 people (February).
- On a visit to the USA Pope John Paul II condemns capital punishment (February).
- USA fires air missiles at Iraqi military sites (March).
- Rwandan rebels based in Congo abduct 14 tourists from three camps in Bwindi National Park in Uganda. A game warden, three rangers and eight tourists murdered before survivors released (March).
- Death of Sheikh Isa bin Sulman al-Khalifa, ruler of Bahrain. Succeeded by his eldest son, Prince Hamad. (March).
- Number of Nato countries is now 19: admission of Poland, Hungary and Czech Republic (March).
- Bushmen of Kalahari allowed to return to part of their ancestral hunting grounds in Kalahari Bemsbock National Park from which they were evicted in 1973 (March).
- Fire in Mont Blanc tunnel under Alps kills at least 40 people (March).
- Following report on corruption, President of European Commission and all 20 of his Commissioners resign (March).
- Libya agrees that men suspected of placing a bomb in Pan Am Flight 103 can stand trial under Scots law in Holland in front of a panel of three judges (March).
- President Raul Cubas of Paraguay resigns and seeks asylum in Brazil following the assassination of Vice-President Luis Maria Argana, his political rival (March).
- The self-governing region of Nunavut in the Northwest Territories province of Canada comes into existence with a population of 85 per cent Inuit (April).
- Ukrainian serial killer Anatoly Onoprienko is sentenced to death for the murder of at least 52 people (April).
- India and Pakistan both launch ballistic missiles (April).
- Two expelled pupils of a Colorado high school kill 12 pupils, a teacher and then themselves in worst school massacre in US history (20 April).
- President Yeltsin escapes impeachment following his role in starting the war against Chechnya (April).
- Elections for the devolved Scottish

Parliament (6 May). Labour and Liberal Democrats form coalition; Donald Dewar is First Minister and Jim Wallace is deputy. Labour come top in election of Welsh assembly but with no overall majority. Official opening of Scottish Parliament on 1 July.

- Worst tornadoes in living memory devastate Oklahoma City: 45 killed, 2000 homes destroyed (May).

- Allied jets attack missile site in Northern Iraq, bringing Allied aircraft responses to Iraqi 'provocation' to 150 since December 1998 (May).

- President Mohammed Khatami is the first Iranian leader to visit Saudi Arabia in a bid to improve relations between the countries (May). President also attempts to mend relations with Israel (June).

- Johannes Rau of Social Democrat party is elected president of Germany (May).

- Indonesia holds its first democratic elections for 44 years The Indonesian Democratic Party for Struggle, lead by Megawati Sukarnoputri, win the most votes (7 June).

- India agrees to Pakistan's proposals for peace talks over the disputed state of Kashmir (June).

- Evidence of worst serial killings in Australia's history uncovered in Snowtown, Adelaide. Eight bodies found; three men charged with murder (June).

- Lost Mayan city is found at border of Mexico and Guatemala (June).

- President Nelson Mandela of South Africa stands down from politics (2 June). ANC lead by Thabo Mbeki win 66 per cent of vote in country's second democratic election since abolition of apartheid.

- Japan agrees to allow sale of birth control pill, ending 40-year ban. Health ministry took 9 years to make its decision (June).

- EU ends duty-free (20 June).

- Manjit Kaur Basuta, UK nanny working in California, found guilty of shaking baby to death;. faces life imprisonment; appeal begins.

- 10,000 mummies found in a tomb in Bawiti in Egypt's Western Desert (June)

- Ehud Barak becomes new Prime Minister of Israel (May).

- Jill Dando, British TV presenter, shot dead outside her home in Fulham, London (26 April).

- Nick Leeson is released from prison in Singapore (3 July).

- German parliament returns to Berlin.

- The Conflict in Kosovo: Nato authorises military action if latest peace deal fails (30 January); Kosovo peace conference begins at Rambouillet, France (7 February); partial agreement reached for autonomy for Kosovo (23 February); Yugoslav army moves troops to Kosovo border (26 February); thousands of ethnic Albanians flee; second round of peace talks begins in Paris (15 March); Slobodan Milosevic rejects plan for Kosovan autonomy secured by presence of Nato (23 March); Nato begins substantial air strikes against Serb targets (24 March until 10 June) — first time it has attacked a sovereign European country; Russia condemns Nato strikes (27 March) and prepares to send warships to region; UN warns that refugee crisis is out of control (2 April); Nato mistakenly make several hits on Serb civilians, and ethnic Albanian refugee convoys and forces; Russia and the main industrial countries agree to a provisional peace plan for Kosovo (6 May); Nato bombs Chinese embassy in Belgrade by mistake, causing a diplomatic crisis (8 May); Nato begins plans for sending in ground troops (17 May); Milosevic indicted for war crimes by International War Crimes Tribunal (26 May); Russian and European envoys agree a peace proposal (2 June) that Milosevic accepts – Nato will stop bombing when Serbia cooperates with demands; Nato and Yugoslav generals hold talks in Macedonia (5 June); draft UN resolution for peacekeeping in Kosovo is agreed by Russia and leading industrialised nations (8 June); Serbs agree to full military withdrawal (9 June); Nato ends bombing of Yugoslavia (10 June); evidence of over 100 massacres of ethnic Albanians in Kosovo and over 10,000 deaths (17 June). 40,000 Serb civilians flee Kosovo, dashing hopes for a united multi-ethnic province.

DEATHS

Sir Dirk Bogarde, British actor.

Lionel Bart, British songwriter.

Betty Box, British film producer.

Boxcar Willie, American singer and songwriter.

Robert Douglas, British actor.

John Erlichman, White House aide to President Nixon.

Ann Haddy, Australian actress.

Rod Hull, British children's entertainer.

Cardinal Basil Hume, British Roman Catholic Archbishop of Westminster 1976–99.

Stanley Kubrick, US film director.

Derek Nimmo, British comic actor.

Joshua Nkomo, Zimbabwean politician

Kenny MacIntyre, British broadcaster and journalist.

Yehudi Menuhin, US-born British musician.

Naomi Mitchison, British author.

Brian Moore, Irish author.

Johnny Morris, British children's broadcaster.

Dame Iris Murdoch, British novelist and philosopher.

Bob Peck, British actor.

Oliver Reed, British actor.

Dusty Springfield, British singer.

Lord William Whitelaw, British Conservative cabinet minister.

Ernie Wise, British comedian.

Sir Alf Ramsay, British footballer and manager.

'Screaming Lord' David Sutch, British singer and political activist.